POETS AND PUNDITS

By the same Author

Criticism and Biography

WALT WHITMAN
THE LOST LEADER
THE PROVING OF PSYCHE
WILLIAM COWPER
TOLSTOY
SAMUEL TAYLOR COLERIDGE
JOHN DONNE
TENNYSON
ETC.

Autobiography

A MODERN PRELUDE

Fiction

THE LAST DAYS
BETWEEN THE TIDES

POETS AND PUNDITS

Essays and Addresses

by

HUGH I'ANSON FAUSSET

JONATHAN CAPE
THIRTY BEDFORD SQUARE
LONDON

FIRST PUBLISHED 1947

PRINTED IN GREAT BRITAIN IN THE CITY OF OXFORD
AT THE ALDEN PRESS
BOUND BY A. W. BAIN & CO. LTD., LONDON

CONTENTS

PART ONE

THREE ADDRESSES

PART TWO

POETS AND POETRY

CONTENTS

PART THREE

THE REALM OF SPIRIT

ACKNOWLEDGMENTS

Grateful acknowledgment is made to the editors of *The Times Literary Supplement*, *The Aryan Path*, *The Adelphi*, *The Poetry Review*, *The Yorkshire Post*, in whose columns many of these essays first appeared, and also to Messrs. Allen & Unwin for allowing me to include the essay, 'Science and the Self', which originally appeared in a volume published by them entitled *Science in the Changing World*; to J. M. Dent & Sons for the essay on Donne written as an introduction to a limited edition of his 'Holy Sonnets'; and to Dennis Dobson Ltd., for the address on Tolstoy which first appeared in a volume entitled *The New Spirit*.

PREFACE

THE substance of the essays and reviews, but not of the addresses, contained in this volume, has appeared in periodicals, much of it in the *Times Literary Supplement*, during the last ten or twelve years. They have all been revised, some considerably re-written and extended. Reviewing is notoriously a thankless task and doubtless often deserves the opprobrium heaped on it by touchy authors. But it can be a spiritual adventure, and one who began to review books while he was still at the university and has continued doing so week by week for twenty-seven years has perhaps earned the right to retrieve a little of his work from the waste of journalistic oblivion.

The ordinary review is, of course, ephemeral and even when the reviewer is allowed space, as he seldom is to-day, to build up an essay round an author or a book, his first and foremost task is a practical one. In this he differs from the independent critic who is free to express much more of himself, often it may be at his subject's expense. The reviewer's first duty is to act as a reliable mediator between an author and the public and to serve both as sensitively as he can. This calls for a considerable degree of perceptive self-effacement. The temptation to exploit an author for one's own destructive or constructive ends is one to which the independent (though not the pure) critic may yield. Books for him can be an opportunity for starting hares and pursuing them, pegs on which to hang philosophies, or pretexts for elaborate analysis or self-display.

But this temptation the honest reviewer must firmly resist. For him the author and his book must always take precedence over any impulse of self-expression in himself. Like every true craftsman he must subdue himself to the medium in which he is called to work. At its simplest this means for the reviewer presenting to the reader a fair account of another person's work and this is the more necessary if it be a work which has to be severely criticized.

Indeed, all critical analysis, if it is not to be intellectually arid, must be rooted in a primary sympathy, a desire not to destroy but, even when the vices of bad writing have to be frankly exposed, to appreciate the impulse and the toil of the writer who has failed to achieve effectively what he set out to do.

The reviewer who strives to be true to this aim will find that sympathy can lead to imaginative co-operation, that with certain authors he can enter into a closer relation than that of reviewer and reviewed, into a communion of spirit and even a combined labour of expression.

I have chosen those of the essays in this volume, which were originally written as reviews, because I believe them to embody something of this creative relation. The creation belongs primarily to the poets and philosophers whose works provide both the fuel and the fire by which the critic's spirit is kindled. But in the kindling the appraiser becomes himself, in a small way, a co-creator or at least a co-perceiver, and both in his assent and dissent can affirm the values which he is struggling to vindicate himself.

It is because they are all fundamentally concerned with such values that I have brought these particular essays and addresses together. They have a common underlying theme, that 'destruction of the Negation and redemption of the Contraries' which I believe to be the task which humanity is called now, as never before, to undertake, if it is not to destroy itself. This theme gives, I hope, a unity to the book's diversity and a significance to it beyond that of a mere collection of literary essays.

H. I'A. F.

Widdington, Essex

PART ONE

THREE ADDRESSES

I

THE TESTIMONY OF TOLSTOY

DURING the War a writer in a Sunday paper declared that 'we're all Tolstoyans now'. He was referring, of course, to the carefully expurgated Tolstoy whose novel *War and Peace* had been broadcast, and not to the Tolstoy who denounced the barbarity of war and preached the way of peace. But the real Tolstoy can no more be contained in the pocket of the doctrinaire pacifist than in the clever hands of the propagandist exploiting the historical parallels between Napoleon's and Hitler's invasion of Russia.

The title which he gave to his great novel, he might have given to his own life. It was a life in which peace had to be incessantly won from war, which is to say that he was deeply rooted in human existence. So, to understand his views on anything, those views which he strove to define in his later didactic works, we need to know what he was, the forces and ideas which possessed him and which he struggled to reconcile in himself, and something even less definable than this, something which we can only experience in the astonishing sweep and simplicity and naturalness of his writing, when we do not try to explain it.

For great as was Tolstoy's reasoning power, and it became more dominating as he grew older, he could never be a detached thinker. To that we owe the exceptional compulsion of everything he wrote. He may be at times extremely partial in his view of social problems or institutions. He refuses compromise, he over-simplifies. But never is he anything but a man searching with every faculty he possesses for the truth, convinced that truth must be lived as well as thought, and that for each one of us, as for him, it is a matter of life and death.

There are two early incidents in Tolstoy's life which symbolize what his primitive attachment to nature was to cost him. The first is his earliest and most vivid impression of lying bound, as a tightly swaddled baby, and screaming because he wanted to free his arms. The second was the occasion of his removal from his childhood nursery to the lower storey where his older brothers and their tutor lived. Never again, he wrote, did he feel so strongly the cross of duty, of moral and ethical obligation, which every one of us is called to carry. 'It was hard for me to part from all I had known since I was born. I was sad less because I had to part from human beings, my nurse, my sisters, my aunt, than because I was leaving my little bed with its curtains and pillows. Moreover, I was apprehensive of the new life I was entering.'

Thomas Mann, who quotes this passage in his essay, *Goethe and Tolstoy*, remarks that the process of loosing oneself from nature was always to be felt by Tolstoy as painful and ethical, that to be humanized meant for him to be denaturalized and that, from this moment on, the struggle of his existence consisted in this sort of humanizing process, regarded as a divorce from everything that was natural and to him peculiarly so. There is truth in this, but he distorts it when he adds that 'Tolstoy's critical and moral faculty, in short his bias toward spirit, was but a secondary impulse, and a feeble one at that'. If it had been, the struggle would not have been so intense or so prolonged.

In few men has that struggle, common to us all, between that part of our nature which is bound to earth by its physical instincts, and the spirit which knows itself in essence to be free, been so implacable. For no man was committed more deeply to the life both of the senses and the spirit than he. Hence his ecstatic and organic response to the world of nature and his immense love and understanding of people, a love devoid utterly of either sentimentality or cynicism. For elemental and nihilistic, primeval and pagan, as one part of his being was, and that the most deeply rooted, there was a humanity in him too, a peasant simplicity, an integral goodness which made him, as Gorky testified, 'a man of the whole of mankind'. Such a man may not be humanistic, but he can be the more profoundly human for that.

As a child Tolstoy knew the harmony of being possessed by life without the anguish. But as the child changed into the youth and the man, the unity of the spirit and the senses was broken, never again to be wholly healed. Consequently his greatness lies as much in the immense force of his moral seriousness as in the unique richness of his physical awareness. If he had merely been a great artist turned into a moral preacher, which is the trite explanation of his development, he would not have been nearly so significant or so human. But he was at one and the same time a supreme imaginative writer and the most formidable moralist of the last hundred years. The two sides of his nature could and did function separately, but they were never really dissociated. He was that rare thing, an imaginative moralist, a moralist who felt with all the physical, mental and human immediacy of the artist and to whom therefore the quest of perfection in life was the supreme art.

It was his insistent striving to approach perfection as a man which so exasperated Turgenev who was content to achieve a limited perfection in his art. That there was egoism, at times intolerant, in Tolstoy's pursuit of moral perfection and that he never wholly outgrew this, hard as he strove to, is undeniable. But there was an imaginative depth in it, too, and a relentless sincerity which dictated the whole painful course of his later life and his intrepid exposure of the corruption of Church and State and of the sickly civilization which they so selfishly maintained.

From boyhood Tolstoy kept a diary of every little sin he committed. He kept it even when he was serving in the Caucasus as a soldier, and this is a characteristic entry.

'How strong I seem to myself to be against all that can happen; how firm in the conviction that one must expect nothing here but death; yet a moment later I am thinking with pleasure of a saddle I have ordered, on which I shall ride dressed in a Cossack cloak, and of how I shall carry on with the Cossack girls; and I fall into despair because my left moustache is higher than my right and for two hours I straighten it out before the looking glass.'

Tolstoy was only in his twenties when he wrote this. But already he had begun to see the struggle for a meaning in things which nothing could assail as one in which death confronted life. And his horror of death, moral and physical, was the measure of his instinctive love of life. In childhood life had intoxicated him.

As a young man he was so physically alive that he felt death for the most part only as a kind of loss of instinctive virtue. In the finest of his early stories, *The Cossacks*, he drew from his own experience an unforgettable picture of a people that 'lives as nature lives: they die, are born, unite, and more are born — they fight, eat and drink, rejoice and die, without any restrictions, but those that nature imposes on the sun and grass, on animal and tree. They have no other laws.'

Olenin, the hero of the tale, who is essentially Tolstoy himself, loves these people. Compared to himself they appear to him beautiful, strong and free, and the sight of them makes him feel ashamed and sorry for himself, particularly when a Cossack girl, Maryanka, whom he hopes to marry, spurns him with abhorrence.

In this experience, which was his own in the Caucasus, was contained what one might describe as the first phase of the conflict that was to be fought out in Tolstoy's soul — the primitive in him confronting the self-conscious and spurning it, and the self-conscious knowing it can never return to the primitive, yet ever longing for an Eden regained. And so again and again in his great novels we find the characters in whom there is the most of himself struggling to throw off the cramp of the self and to be caught up into that spring of being which he so often associated with the coming of the Russian spring and the resurrection of natural life from the icy grip of winter.

How closely the physical sensation of life could be associated with a moral sensation of goodness is shown in passage after passage of his writings, in this one from *Youth*, for example, in which, after evoking an April morning through natural detail that quivers with life as he describes it, he went on: 'Something new to me, something extraordinarily potent and unfamiliar, had suddenly invaded my soul . . . Everything spoke to me of beauty, happiness, and virtue as three things which were both easy and possible for me, and said that not one of them could exist without the other two, since beauty, happiness and virtue were one. "How did I never come to understand that before?" I cried to myself. "How did I ever manage to be so wicked? Oh, but how good, how happy, I could be — nay, I *will* be — in the future! At once, at once — yes, this very minute — I will become another being, and begin to live differently." '

That was in his youth. To the end of his days he could resolve to become another being almost as ardently and impulsively. But the years taught him how far from 'easy and possible' it was. In such characters as Prince Andrew and Pierre Bezúkhov in *War and Peace* or Levin in *Anna Karenina* we see the second phase of the struggle. They, too, on occasions can be seized with an unreasoning spring-time feeling of joy and rejuvenation, as Prince Andrew was when, after falling in love with Natasha, he rode past the old oak and found it spreading out a canopy of sappy, dark-green foliage.

But such moments are infrequent and all too soon found to be delusive. It is when Prince Andrew lies wounded on the field of Austerlitz and sees the distant sky, not clear, yet immeasurably lofty with grey clouds gliding slowly across it, that for the first time he really knows release from the intolerable burden, the insoluble dilemma, of himself. 'How is it I did not see that lofty sky before?' he asks. 'How happy I am to have recognized it at last! Yes, all is vanity, all is falsehood, except that infinite heaven. There is nothing, nothing but that.' But the sense of release, of being part of an immense, harmonious whole, is only momentary. It fades as death ceases to cast its shadow upon him.

In such characters as these, as I have said, we may see reflected the second phase of the struggle in Tolstoy's soul. 'Spring, love, happiness', thinks Prince Andrew as he first rides past the leafing oak-tree, 'how is it you are not weary of this eternal, stupid and meaningless fraud?' It was the fraud of nature, the feud she provoked between the temporal and the eternal, the instinctive impulse and the moral imperative, which Tolstoy, because he was profoundly divided in himself, came increasingly to see and to be tortured by in the years immediately after these great novels were written.

As his physical energies began to decline, his intellectual questioning grew. It proved a knife which cut at the roots of all that was merely instinctive in his faith. It cut no less searchingly through all that was conventional in contemporary religious faith and evasive in worldly philosophy. And it left him standing in horror on the edge of an abyss in which life was as meaningless as death, in which his past activities seemed a self-indulgent lie and the future contained no reasonable incentive for continuing to live.

And so at the age of fifty he turned with a relentless sincerity which alarmed and shocked the worldly-wise to answer the three fundamental questions which he could not silence, 'What am I?' 'Why do I live?' 'What must I do?'

In answering those questions he was led on inevitably to ask the whole European world, which lay under the same condemnation as he felt himself to lie, the same question. The only difference was that the Churches and States of Europe seemed unconscious of the infamous life they countenanced. And no scientific adjustment, no rationalized reform on the surface, Tolstoy was convinced, could save them from the abyss of destruction to which they were surely moving. 'The more fully men believe', he wrote, 'that humanity can be led, in spite of itself, by some external, self-acting force (whether religion or science) to a beneficial change in its existence — and that they need only work in the established order of things — the more difficult will it be to accomplish any beneficial change.' There must be an inward change, a real revolution. 'All the great revolutions in men's lives', he declared, 'are made in thought.' The rationalist in him tended to undervalue the heart's share in such revolutions. But he knew that the thought that men ordinarily think must be transformed and renewed by something more integral than itself, by a redirection of the will. 'Repent,' cried John the Baptist, 'for the kingdom of heaven is at hand.' 'Repent,' pleaded Tolstoy, 'or hell will overtake you. Change your view of life and your way of living or you will all perish.'

Merely to change the system of Government by violence could only, he believed, result in the eventual re-establishment, under a new form, of the old combination of autocracies and servitudes, in an even more frenzied arming of the nations, in terrible massacres and in the ruin and degeneration of all the peoples.

In this, as in all else, Tolstoy spoke out of his own experience.

He had erred in his own life, he concluded, not primarily because he thought incorrectly, but because he lived badly. And all his searching logic led to this conclusion as the foundation of any life that should be reasonable and fruitful.

'I quite returned', he wrote, 'to what belonged to my earliest childhood and youth. I returned to the belief in that Will which produced me, and desires something of me. I returned to the belief that the chief and only aim of my life is to be better, i.e. to live in accord with that Will . . . There was only this difference, that then all this was accepted unconsciously, while now I know that without it I could not live.'

That was the gulf which had to be crossed — the gulf between an unconscious and a conscious acceptance of a mysterious creative will. The acid of self-consciousness had poisoned the springs of unconscious living. Somehow this crippled, wary ego had to die, if health was to be renewed. It was this death which Tolstoy for the rest of his life strove so hard and patiently to die. None knew better than he the subtle power and pride of the ego. All the circumstances of his birth and upbringing as a Count, an officer and a landowner had nourished pride. And behind all this there was the overruling force of his genius.

Of the arrogance with which he had to struggle we catch a glimpse in Turgenev's remark: 'Personally I never encountered anything more disconcerting than that inquisitorial look, which, accompanied by two or three biting words, was enough to drive to fury any man who lacked self-control.'

The humility of such a man was as challenging as pride itself, his life-instinct as tenacious as his need of death. Yet through all the failures for which he never ceased to reproach himself, he held firmly to his quest. Excommunicated, harried and abused in his own home, tortured by the contradiction he felt between what he preached and the way he lived, he strove to achieve what the old Mason in *War and Peace* named the chief virtue, the love of death, a love from which the spring his heart hungered for, the spring he had known so beatifically as a child, might break in his heart into second leaf.

2

In Tolstoy, then, because he lived and thought and suffered so fundamentally, the tragic drama of the modern world was enacted with this difference, that he had the strength and imagination to create in himself at least a part of a saving third act. He offered his experience of this third act to the world, crying, 'I cannot keep silent', as he wrung his hands over the inhumanity of its rulers and the credulity of their victims, 'the everlastingly deceived, foolish working people,' as he called them, 'who with their blistered hands have built all those ships and fortresses, and arsenals, and barracks, and cannons and steamers, and harbours and bridges, and all those palaces, halls, and platforms and triumphal arches, and have printed all the newspapers and pamphlets ... It is always the same good-natured foolish people who, showing their healthy white teeth as they smile, gaze like children, naïvely delighted at the dressed-up admirals and presidents, at the flags waving above them, and at the fireworks, and the playing bands; though before they have time to look about them, there will be neither admirals, nor presidents, nor flags, nor bands, but only the desolate wet plain, cold, hunger, misery – in front of them the slaughtering enemy, behind them the relentless government, blood, wounds, agonies, rotting corpses, and a senseless, useless death.'

No wonder that the Tsarist Government did its best to suppress such words; no wonder that M. Maisky, the Russian Ambassador, in his preface to the B.B.C. pamphlet introducing the broadcast of *War and Peace* flatly disowned that Tolstoy. Had he been living in the Russia of the last twenty years his voice would doubtless have been forcibly silenced. For what Totalitarian government could tolerate a man, however prophetic, however devoted to the common man, who declared unceasingly, that the truth in men's souls, if they would but be faithful to it, was irresistible. 'Governments', he wrote, 'know this and tremble before that force, and with all the means at their disposal try to resist it or gain possession of it. They fear the expression of independent thought more than an army.'

Tolstoy lived before the wireless and expertly organized propaganda had still further reduced the capacity for independent thought. His standard of true manhood was the peasant and the saint. And passionate as his indictment was of the slums of Moscow, he hardly visualized a society in which misdirected mechanism and profit-seeking industrialism might sap even the peasant's integrity and create a rootless spiritually-starved proletariat.

But such a development was implicit in the diseased condition which he diagnosed so powerfully because he had lived through certain crucial phases of the disease so intensely himself. He was convinced that civilization had reached that inner point of cleavage between an old and a new order of being which had brought him to the edge of an abyss where the choice lay between suicide and a revolutionary integration. The war within man was reflected not only in social sickness but in the increasing destructiveness and futility of war between nations, its degeneration from what was still a life-struggle, in which the combatants were bound together, into a death-orgy of mutual extermination.

Tolstoy had fought in wars himself. He had seen how degenerate was the national war in the Crimea compared with the tribal warfare of the Caucasus, and his descriptions of national warfare in *War and Peace* reveal how strongly the imagination of the moralist in him repudiated what the artist so graphically described. But war then still retained certain conventions which linked it with a traditional human code.

In his own history Tolstoy lived through such a phase of diminishing equilibrium between his conscience and his instincts during the first fifteen years of his married life. But it became harder and harder for him to maintain this balance. And when it broke down, when the pure human values which a truly self-conscious being must live or be in eternal contradiction with himself, had become irresistibly real to him, he saw with a terrible urgency that European civilization had reached the same point of extreme peril as himself, that, above all, its science, the instrument and portent of its partial self-consciousness, would destroy it unless it struck roots in a new humanity, a greater and truer selfhood.

He had no 'atomic bomb' to shock him into this realization, but there had been times, he knew, when at the height of his own inner conflict, he had nearly gone mad. The same fate, he could not doubt, awaited mankind, if it could not resolve the same conflict. Significantly the last unfinished essay he wrote in 1910, the year of his death, was entitled 'On Insanity' and to the question in it why kind reasonable people learn how to kill and set out killing people they do not know he answered that 'those who order others to accomplish such deeds, as well as those who will accomplish them, are in a state of insanity. Not in any figurative or exaggerated sense, but literally, in the most direct sense of the word . . . We live an insane life contrary to the first and simplest demands of common sense. Because we all, or the great majority of us, lead this kind of life, we no longer see the difference between insane life and rational life, and regard our insane life as sound and rational.'

Gerald Heard has come to much the same conclusion when he writes in *Man the Master* that 'short of union with the eternal and infinite life we are all of us in some degree insane, "idiotic", and sooner or later we must break down'. But Tolstoy knew that there was no short cut to the sanity of such union, that a merely emotional faith in the eternal was only a drug against the pains of growing up. He insisted that the supreme criterion for distinguishing real life from what was merely its resemblance 'has been and always will be self-consciousness, the highest property of the soul'. Yet mere ego-consciousness brought division and conflict. It was, as Dostoevsky wrote and so terribly portrayed, 'a great torment'.

Tolstoy writhed under this torment. All that may well seem too absolute in his repudiation of an industrial civilization and of the intelligence that served it, as also his sweeping denunciation of dogmas or of forms of art, the inner meaning of which he did not understand, was related to this unresolved war in himself. His refusal, too, to compromise in any way with the machinery of modern government, his inveterate distrust of officialdom and his belief that all efforts to organize the external conditions of men's lives diverts attention from their inner needs, may well seem too extreme. Yet it was consistent with his view of the revolution required of the individual. Governments based on and practising violence were the exact equivalent of the predatory ego which it was essential to disown in oneself. To support a modern state was, in his view, as much a sin as to support the selfish, unsocial and atavistic part of oneself, the part which had served a necessary purpose, maybe, in the adolescent struggles of the past, but which now had to be outgrown. The Christian anarchy he visualized was not, of course, social chaos, but a new organic order, a substitution of real self-government through the brotherly co-operation of free men working together in federated groups for the forceful government imposed by a self-interested or class-interested or power-seeking minority on a deluded and subservient majority. The clean cut with the predatory State which he preached is perhaps at present as unattainable, except by spiritual devotees or small groups dedicated to living in community, as the clean cut with the predatory ego which it necessitates. But in view of the increasing servitude which the modern State has imposed, the ultimate rightness of his outlook has become much more convincing, nor did he have any difficulty in answering the usual objection that without a government based on violence we should be at the mercy of worse violence than we are already.

Tolstoy was equally absolute in his interpretation of the injunction not to resist evil. This was shown particularly in the correspondence which he had with a Mr. Ballou, an enlightened American expounder of 'Non-Resistance'. Tolstoy enthusiastically approved of Ballou's writings, but rejected the concessions which Ballou made for employing what he called 'uninjurious benevolent physical force' against drunkards and insane people. 'A true Christian', Tolstoy wrote, 'will always prefer to be killed by a madman, than to deprive him of his liberty.' To this Ballou replied that, if so, a true Christian watching over a delirious sick man, would prefer to see him kill his wife, children and best friends, rather than restrain or help restrain him. Christ, he argued, could never have meant that.

Most of us would agree with Mr. Ballou, even if he did assume too easily the adequacy for all insane situations of 'uninjurious physical force'. But Tolstoy was not to be reasoned out of his absoluteness. In theory at least he was an unrepentant dogmatist. Such theorizing may well seem academic to-day when men in cold and calculated delirium kill fifty thousand wives and children and justify it as not only strategical but moral expediency. But the underlying problem remains, the old question as to how such precepts as those in the Sermon on the Mount should be lived.

Tolstoy took them literally and tried to live them literally. He failed to do so, at least until that last bitter hour of despairing renunciation when he went out from his home into the night and the snow, never to return. Yet he never ceased to believe that he ought to live them literally and this belief embittered his life and the lives of others to whom he was closely tied.

This, of course, is no proof that he was wrong. And seeing to-day how slippery is the slope down which those who compromise with the injunctions of faith and love slide into acceptance of the utmost infamy, we may be more ready to think that he was right. It may be, too, that he who would commit himself to a life of creative love must be an offence to all who lack the courage and maturity to do so.

But it is well to be clear just what such a literal interpretation of 'resist not evil' does socially involve. Tolstoy was quite clear about it. In theory and as much as he could in practice he repudiated the State and all it existed to uphold, because government, as it existed, was at bottom regulated violence. That being so, he had no legal standing in the society to which he belonged.

If you refuse military service on the grounds of absolute obedience to the Sermon on the Mount, you must also refuse police protection, refuse to support or help administer the existing law, to pay taxes or to seek any redress if a criminal steals everything you have and leaves you to starve. You must be prepared to do and to suffer all this. And worse — you must be prepared to find yourself in the situation in which Tolstoy found himself, faced by an intolerable alternative, either to preach what you don't practise or to inflict suffering on someone dear to you who sees your renunciation, not as humble selflessness, but as insane egotism. Of course you may not be called to suffer all this. In the degree that your faith is pure of egotism, of all pride of self-seeking, your suffering is likely to be the more inwardly redemptive, the more hidden and fruitful. For as Eckhart wrote, 'to him who suffers not for love, to suffer is suffering and is hard to bear. But he who suffers for love does not suffer, and this suffering is fruitful in God's sight'.

It is, perhaps, only in this deeply inward sense that such injunctions as 'Resist not evil' should be read and lived. This does not mean that they should be less fully accepted, but more integrally, more creatively, and less logically or as legal and moral ordinances. The instinct against moral absolutes is a sound one. Human life is only fruitful when the absolute is humbled to the relative. To impose a moral dictate upon life is as much an error as to live without a sense of inner direction. And such dictates are imposed because the moralist in some degree cannot yield himself to life. He clings to something absolutely fixed for fear his impulses should get the better of him. It may be a doctrine of absolute non-resistance he clings to. But in doing so he is really still fighting evil, in himself and in the world, with the bayonet of a moral dictate. That at a certain stage of growth into full and free self-awareness such absolute prohibitions may be necessary, as discipline to predatory impulses not yet inwardly redeemed, is undeniable. But they involve an inevitable and unhappy division between absolute doctrine held in theory and compromise, grudgingly and dangerously consented to, in practice.

So it was with Tolstoy. He was too great an artist and too profoundly human to be a rigid moralist in practice. No man strove harder in the continual testings of his relationship with others to quell the pride of a supremely powerful mind or the compulsive force of his convictions. No man learnt more hardly to be patient or reproached himself more bitterly for his failures. Yet he does at times seem to have been too much preoccupied with personal salvation, though a new self *be* the first condition of real service to and understanding of others.

As a Russian writer said: 'He listened so intently to the noise in his own ears, that he hardly heard what other people were saying.' This overstates his self-absorption. But in seeing the world so exclusively in the mirror of his own intense moral struggle, he did tend to deny all virtue to those who, if working on the surface, were trying disinterestedly to better the world by applying humane intelligence to it.

When Tchekhov, who as a doctor knew what sick men were, said, 'You live badly, my friends', there was forgiveness in his words. Tolstoy found it hard to forgive the world for being what it was, because he found it hard to forgive himself. He knew all too well his own sickness, his own incapacity to be the truth which his mind so cogently defined.

A visitor to 'Yasnaya Polyana', his home, has left on record that after one of the all too frequent stormy scenes when the Countess denounced her husband's ideas and projects, he and Tolstoy talked all the evening on the theme that 'a man's enemies are those of his own household', and how Tolstoy said that opposition from relatives gave an indication of the measure of a man's readiness to serve the truth. 'It means', he said, 'that there is in us something that renders it impossible for others to suspect us of being insincere people playing at simplification . . . It is only on that subtle instinct which discerns with wonderful exactitude the weak spot in another's soul, that the world's whole attack on those who seek the truth, rests. Also that attack will continue till we believe in the truth as sincerely as they believe in falsehoods. It all depends on that. That is the only conquering strength'.

We have only to think of the world's martyrs to know that this is but partially true, that the world more often hates than loves the highest, because it fears the little that it can see. Fear of the good, as Kierkegaard has shown, is as potent and demonic a force as fear of the evil. But as a reflection upon a weakness in himself Tolstoy spoke truly enough. His moral over-emphasis was a sign that his imagination was still at war with his will, that his ego was insufficiently subdued to a truth greater than itself.

This feud between the natural man in him and the spiritual is most clearly shown in his attitude to women. No novelist has entered into the instinctive soul of a woman or evoked her physical charm more compellingly than the creator of Anna Karenina. Yet even when he wrote that great novel something in him feared and hated what sense and imagination found so irresistible. It was not only because the plot dictated it that he had to kill Anna. And the feud was never resolved. Indeed it was intensified, as the *Kreutzer Sonata* and other stories of his middle and later years show, or that anecdote of Gorki's which has in it an element of terrible comedy. With Tchekhov, Gorki and one or two others, Tolstoy, then an old man, had been sitting in the park. They had been talking about women, but for a long time Tolstoy listened in silence. Then he suddenly said: 'And I will tell you the truth about women, when I have one foot in the grave — I shall tell it, jump into my coffin, pull the lid over me, and say, "Do what you like now".' The look he gave us, Gorki adds, 'was so wild, so terrifying, that we all fell silent for a while'.

In such a story Gorki makes us see what passion was embodied in the man, how deep and tenacious his roots in the physical, how intense the counter force of his spirit which found bondage to the physical intolerable. Perhaps only in the wonderful tales and parables he wrote for the people was the moral man in him perfectly reconciled with the imaginative. There the moral injunction ceased to be a doctrine and became what he always longed for it to be, as natural and necessary, as simple and spontaneous an expression of inherent human goodness as it was in the little peasant of *War and Peace*, the loving, suffering, smiling Platon Karataev.

Such imaginative simplicity which no subtle reasoning can contravert is perhaps Tolstoy's greatest gift as a teacher. It enshrines the real ideal which never seems fantastic and which no practical arguments can discredit. All didactic truth is in some degree partial and reflects a certain assumption of moral superiority in its enunciator. Tolstoy himself acknowledged this when he wrote: 'When people consider me as one who cannot make a mistake, every error seems like a lie or a piece of hypocrisy. But if I am understood to be a weak man, the discord between my words and acts appears as a sign of weakness, but not as a lie or an hypocrisy. And then I appear to be what I am: a sorry but sincere man now and always wishing with his soul to be quite good.'

Tolstoy's moral crisis is so significant because he endured and so memorably expressed the tension of self-consciousness which, on a vast surface if seldom at his depth, has become the anguish of our age. No one has experienced more intensely than he the tragic power to understand that life cannot be understood or the breaking point which sooner or later is reached by the man who tries to be an end in himself or who, in despair, offers himself as a means to false ends.

If he did not actually see the full horror of a world in which individualism, dying at its roots for want of sustenance, had begotten industrialized man and mechanized societies, and then collapsed into warring masses, he saw enough to declare how inevitable such an issue was. He saw that man, shut off from the mysteries of his being in a prison of materialistic assumptions, must find his soul again or perish, that he must regain consciously those unconscious depths which were a constant peril, if denied. He must live in faith, if he was not to die of fear. This was what religion meant to Tolstoy. He defined its fundamental principles very simply as amounting to this: 'that while conscious of the Divine within ourselves and acknowledging its presence in everybody else, we should love everybody and refrain from doing to others what we do not wish to be done to ourselves'.

We may think that here as elsewhere he put it all too simply, that he over-estimated the natural man's powers of resistance to secular authority which denied his status as a son of God and cajoled or compelled him to be a cog in a machine; that he equally under-estimated the aberrations in man's soul and will, those demonisms of the underworld which Dostoevsky so unforgettably portrayed.

But even if Tolstoy overlooked the psychological and technical complexities, of which we are so conscious, or reduced economic issues to too simple terms, he saw the fundamental issues clearly enough. He knew that there was no retreat possible from self-consciousness, that a conscious being was the goal of evolution and that men had reached a crisis in human development when they must pass from one conception and order of life to a new one. And he knew that this birth into a new life of co-operation meant and cost a death to the old life of predatory and combative egotism, that life which the primitive in him understood so well and relished. It was not merely a common-sense recognition that by co-operation instead of conflict the share of personal happiness gained by each man would be greater, and human life in general would be reasonable and happy instead of a succession of contradictions and sufferings.

Most of us know that, but our knowledge does not compel us to live it except partially and spasmodically. For such knowledge to become act, said Tolstoy, like all the great teachers before him, we must die to what is false in us, to the delusions of pride and separateness, and be reborn in the unity of a greater selfhood. But it was not a blind death. Faith in a power and a Being greater than himself was, he affirmed, as necessary to the soul of man as air and food to his body. Without it he became sick with fear and impotent to create. But he must not cease to think because conceit of thought had weakened his power of action. He must recover the true power of action on a new creative level by living and so thinking better. Only thus can modern man extricate himself from the mechanism which his mind has contrived to stultify his heart and dehumanize his life; only by surrendering to what is eternal within and beyond himself can he find strength not to be caught up into the flood of mass insanity or enslaved by material powers. Only by this surrender, consciously made and sustained, can he become a fully responsible and adult human being. The one alternative to the standardized man is the newly integrated man. That in essence is what Tolstoy taught us and what in a life of compulsive sincerity he strove to be.

II

WHITMAN'S MYSTICISM

MYSTICISM is a misty word and is too often supposed to denote a misty experience. But the true mystics are not responsible for this. Whether in the East or the West they have defined what is definable in the experience with great precision and much that cannot be defined they have expressed in images and symbols which communicate, to those who can enter into them, a reality that can transform the meaning and the conduct of life.

But it is true of all experience that we can only receive that of which we are already at least half-possessed. And this is particularly true of mystical experience because it breaks through the habitual bounds of the practical consciousness and reveals what seems to be a new dimension. The same may be said of a certain kind of poetic experience with which the mystical is closely akin. Those whose vision is not yet ready to open or extend itself into this new realm inevitably find it as mystifying as a human face is to the week-old infant, or as talk about sight and things seen was to the inhabitants of Wells's *Country of the Blind*.

Yet there are, of course, different kinds of mysticism, as there are different degrees of it, and some of them are confused or false. The mystic has to cross a gulf from the habitual world known to his ordinary senses to a world revealed in the light of a supersensual vision, a world in which the reality of existence is infinitely deepened and extended. Truly to cross this gulf, as all the great mystics have testified, is a costly adventure. Some who have crossed have been blinded by the light which broke into their darkness before their eyes were ready to receive it. Others have abandoned the normal ways of thought and feeling without fully attaining to the new consciousness to which they aspired. So, to borrow the language of the *Bhagavad-Gita*, they have fallen from both paths, and even perished 'like a riven cloud'.

For the mystic has to enter a cloud of unknowing to become the organ of a new knowing. He has to surrender himself in faith to a Power, to a Being, whom he regards as ineffable and incomprehensible that he may eventually know even as he is known. That is the leap, the plunge which he has to take. It is no simple leap. All his natural instincts, fortified by self-consciousness, are ranged against it or seem to be. It is hard for him to believe that on the far side, if he can reach it, they will be found approving his leap and delighting in the grace that has transformed them. And so it may take him a lifetime of enlightening 'heart-work', as Rilke called it, before the gulf is really crossed.

But meanwhile he may again and again imagine that he has crossed and is delightfully at his ease on the other side, when in fact he has not. Nor is he necessarily altogether deluded. Reality unfolds by degrees in us and if only gradually we become at home in it, we may be grateful to those whom it possesses, however partially, in a new and impressive way.

Whitman was surely one of these. Even those who feel the mechanical monotony of much that he wrote, find themselves strangely moved and magnetized by the spirit that chants its assurance of universal identity, if it be with an exuberant disregard of finer shades and issues. Whether in the elemental solitude of the sea-shore or in the crowds of Broadway his whole tendency was to escape from the intimately personal and from every sort of dualism into the vast and multitudinous. And this, perhaps, is why his affirmations of comradeship have failed to bite into the hearts and minds of men as deeply as he hoped and believed they would.

Curiously enough the average man for whom he wrote has always been singularly unresponsive. It was intellectuals, craving to lose themselves in a larger life than that of the mind, who first hailed him as a master. And it is foiled intellectuals to-day who have been saying that he was a vociferous fraud or at least more of a poseur than a prophet.

His habit of writing anonymous laudatory notices of himself, his unfounded claim to be the father of several illegitimate children and other evidence that has come to light suggesting that he enjoyed playing a part, have certainly shaken confidence in his integrity. But it is possible to be a divided personality and even to be guilty of some duplicity without being a posturing windbag.

Whitman may, as Miss Esther Shephard, for example, argues, have modelled his appearance on the vagabond poet of George Sand's novel, *Consuelo*. He may even have conceived his mission as the voice of Universal Man through the reading of that book. But not through that only. Goethe, Frances Wright, Margaret Fuller and Emerson, all contributed something to the scheme and substance of *Leaves of Grass*. A poet inevitably owes much to other minds and can only be condemned as a plagiarist if he fails to give much of himself in return.

Whitman's writings certainly contain much that he failed to make wholly his own, but much also that bears the indubitable stamp of his own imaginative experience and aspiration. That there was an element of charlatanry in the man is probably true. But to admit this is very far from saying that he was a grandiloquent trickster, always pretending to be what he was not. He had, in fact, a genius for not-being, for reflecting the world about him, for slipping out of himself. It is this elusiveness, despite the bulk and apparent candour of his writings, which his severe critics have unfairly denounced as fraudulence. They have tried to grasp and hold him and he has got away, as he boasted that he always would.

Certainly D. H. Lawrence had a good deal of excuse for crying: 'Oh, Walter, Walter, what have you done with it? What have you done with yourself? With your own individual self? For it sounds as if it had all leaked out of you, leaked into the universe.'

Whitman would not have liked that suggestion at all. For with all his elusiveness — and he said once he was as furtive as an old hen — few men have prided themselves more on being 'a body' in the literal as well as the colloquial sense. His body, as he boasted more than once in print, was 'a perfect body, free from taint from top to toe'. This genial, lumbering giant who put folk at their ease because he took life easily and who radiated a sort of sympathetic virtue out of his whole large childlike being, was real enough, though he was not half as simple as he looked. Indeed it is likely that he would not have blown his own trumpet so loud if he had been as self-confident as he professed.

D. H. Lawrence called him a ghost, but a very great poet of the transitions of the soul as it loses its integrity and, as such, a great changer of the blood in the veins of men. Certainly the men and women who knew Walt and loved him, above all the wounded to whom he ministered for two years in those lazar-houses, the military hospitals, during the Civil War, were quite sure he was no fraud. The voices that called after him as he left the wards late at night, 'Walt! Walt! Walt! Come again! Come again!' were sure. So were the eyes of the dying whom he had convinced by simply sitting by them that although all was over, love was not over. They were sure of him when they could be sure of nothing else.

But when we turn to that 'new offspring' out of literature, of which he claimed to be the begetter, and the famous challenge rings in our ears,

> Camerado, this is no book,
> Who touches this touches a man,

we are not quite so sure.

It is worth asking for a moment how one does touch the man in a poet's work. Doubtless after reading a man's poetry we usually get a feeling of the kind of man he is or was, even if we know nothing else about him. And there are some poems, like Wordsworth's *Prelude*, which are specially designed to tell us much about that.

But even the *Prelude* is not the portrait of a man, stepping out to display himself, but a record of the growth of a poet's mind. In all the truest poetry the manhood of the poet is incarnated in the poem itself. It shapes and holds the poem together, gives it its particular form and tone, its inner logic, its imaginative and sensuous texture. The poet, in short, is more than a man. Or rather he is the completed man, the creative and creating man, who is woman too, and has found, if only for a moment, his whole being, and of that wholeness made something. In such moments he is far from thrusting his manhood or his personality at us. Yet he is never more truly and appreciably himself. Anyone who has practised making anything, whether as artist or craftsman or both, will bear this out. And it has a direct bearing on Whitman's characteristics as a poet and through them on the gospel he preached.

From the first line of his challenging *Song of Myself*,

> I celebrate myself and sing myself,
> And what I assume you shall assume . . .

he advanced personally upon any reader — and there were few enough for a long time — who would give him his shocked attention. He wished less to lose and find himself in his poem than to inject himself through his poem into his reader.

Of course, in *himself*, he claimed to be announcing, to be impersonating the new American man, the New World man, and, more than that, the cosmic principle itself. It is this super-self assuming, as its own, all selves, all nature, all materials, all mysteries, every human hope and despair, that speaks in such lines as these:

> In all people I see myself, none more and not one a barley-corn less,
> And the good or bad I say of myself I say of them . . .
> I exist as I am, that is enough,
> If no other in the world be aware I sit content,
> And if each and all be aware I sit content. . . .
>
> I am he that walks with the tender and growing night.
> I call to the earth and sea half-held by the night.
> Press close bare-bosom'd night — press close magnetic nourishing night!
> Night of South winds — night of the large few stars!
> Still nodding night — mad naked summer night. . . .
>
> I am not the poet of goodness only, I do not decline to be the poet of wickedness also,

THREE ADDRESSES

What blurt is this about virtue and vice? . . .
My gait is no fault-finder's or rejecter's gait,
I moisten the roots of all that has grown. . . .

I speak the pass-word primeval, I give the sign of democracy.
By God! I will accept nothing which all cannot have their counterpart of on the same terms . . .

I am afoot with my vision.
By the city's quadrangular houses — in log huts, camping with lumbermen,
Along the ruts of the turnpike, along the dry gulch and rivulet bed,
Weeding my onion-patch or hoeing rows of carrots and parsnips,
Crossing savannas, trailing in forests,
Prospecting, gold-digging, girdling the trees of a new purchase,
Scorch'd ankle-deep by the hot sand, hauling my boat down the shallow river,
Where the panther walks to and fro on a limb overhead,
Where the buck turns furiously at the hunter,
Where the rattlesnake suns his flabby length on a rock, where the otter is feeding on fish. . . .

I do not ask who you are, that is not important to me,
You can do nothing and be nothing but what I will infold you. . .

I seize the descending man and raise him with resistless will,
O despairer, here is my neck,
By God, you shall not go down! hang your whole weight upon me. . . .

The spotted hawk swoops by and accuses me, he complains of my gab and my loitering.
I too am not a bit tamed, I too am untranslatable,
I sound my barbaric yawp over the roofs of the world.
The last scud of day holds back for me,
It flings my likeness after the rest and true as any on the shadow'd wilds,

It coaxes me to the vapor and the dusk.
I depart as air, I shake my white locks at the runaway sun,
I effuse my flesh in eddies and drift it in lacy jags.
I bequeath myself to the dirt to grow from the grass I love,
If you want me again look for me under your boot-soles.

In those lines, taken by leaps and bounds from *Song of Myself*, Whitman's first and longest piece of sustained declamation, it is often hard to say whether the 'I' that is speaking is Whitman himself or some elemental voice of nature endowed with self-consciousness. In fact it is both. Whitman's super-self was a combination of egotism and immense natural force and sympathy. He flung the two together and tried to make them one. And he convinced himself that they were one and that others could make them one as he did.

I know perfectly well my own egotism, (he wrote)
Know my omnivorous lines and must not write less,
And would fetch you whoever you are flush with myself.

But in prose he acknowledged the partial nature of this selfhood, writing that his purpose was 'to express by sharp-cut self-assertion, One's Self, and also, or maybe still more, to map out, to throw together for American use, a gigantic embryo or skeleton of Personality'.

To throw together an embryo or skeleton was an odd conception for a poet to have of his function. No poet before him would have wanted to map out an embryo, however gigantic.

Consciously or unconsciously poets have always wanted to create something organically complete, which would go on living an independent life of its own in the imaginations of men. The agony of the poet has always lain in his failure to create this whole world in miniature, his purest joy when a real child of his being is born.

Whitman apparently never suffered in this way. Yet he could not help wanting to get a whole world into his verse, to create the kosmos that he said he was. So he set about collecting all the materials of his world which he could lay hands on and indefatigably packing them into a poetical portmanteau which could be endlessly enlarged. In this way he did gather together the substance of the American society of his day in all its phases, and of the New World in all its sweep of landscape, as he put it, and oceanic spread.

That was a remarkable achievement, more remarkable perhaps than the egotistic gospel he declaimed or the 'chants of Dilation or Pride' in which he indulged in the intervals of cramming something more into his trunk.

And his world *was* actually embryonic. The States of Whitman's day were in transition between an agricultural and an industrial economy. His life coincided with the change over from a pioneering and patriarchal society to one of ruthless capitalism. The Civil War speeded the process and, if it speeded up also the liberation of the slave, secured the triumph of corrupt and selfish interests and of those who used the catchwords of Democracy to pile up profits for themselves. It had been a struggle between manipulators of two forms of servitude, the slave and the machine. And the machinists won.

Whitman was an ageing man when the Civil War began. He was physically maimed when it ended. So that although in his *Democratic Vistas* he later denounced the corruption he could not help seeing, his roots were in the rural Long Island of his childhood and the still provincial Brooklyn of his youth. He was too old to come to critical grips with the capitalism and its industrial machinery through which mankind was already heading for destruction. Temperamentally, too, he was incapable of it. He was equally unable or at least unconcerned to come to critical grips with what was dubious in his own loudly trumpeted ego.

The need to do so was never urgent, because self-consciousness had not eaten into his physical well-being any more than profit-seeking had as yet eaten, in his young days, into the healthy, energetic body of American society. He had grown up in a world in which, however tempestuous the underlying forces, individuals were still in vital relation to one another and to the deep tides of nature, in a world too, that was felt to possess infinite spiritual and material potentialities. Here, as he wrote, was

not merely a nation but a teeming Nation of nations,
Here the doings of men correspond with the broadcast doings of the day and night,
Here is what moves in magnificent masses careless of particulars,
Here are the roughs, beards, friendliness, combativeness the soul loves,
Here the flowing trains, here the crowds, equality, diversity the soul loves.

It was natural in such a world to believe that all which was required was to cast off the bonds with which a decaying civilization elsewhere, with its traditional forms and conventions, had shackled the spirit of man. And his view of art as merely a loose channel through which natural impulse and feeling, ideas and observation might flow revealed the same blindness to the fact that to be really natural, whether in poetry or life, is the supreme and the most difficult art.

In fact his own desire to spring from his lines into his reader's arms was so extreme because he was in some ways inhibited. In the fully realized poetic act the materials of life are absorbed and recreated by the imagination. And Whitman's omnivorous appetite for mere things imperfectly digested, his habit of endlessly cataloguing them with more or less of suffused feeling, sprang from his inability to act sufficiently upon what he passively received. It was as if he had to pile facts up to fill a void within or as a counterpoise to something infinite and abstract in his ego.

His love, at times morbid, of his own body, betrayed the same need, the need of correcting the dizziness of abstraction by clinging to the concrete, whether it was the 'fat that stuck to his own bones' or the bodies of other men 'moving magnificently in masses'. Because this kind of clinging could never really satisfy him, because his ego still remained lonely and homeless, 'flying those flights of a fluid and swallowing soul', of which he boasted, it was from his yearning for death as the resolver of all 'tension' that his purest poetry flowed.

2

But before considering what death meant to Whitman or the insufficiencies of his gospel of egotism, let us recognize gratefully what a spring, what a river, what an ocean of life flowed through him. How did it come about? He made no secret of that. Come, he said, 'loaf with me on the grass. I loaf and invite my soul.' And the lines in which he described what has usually been considered his deepest mystical experience sprang out of a transparent summer morning's loafing.

'Swiftly arose then,' he wrote,

> And spread around me the peace and knowledge that pass all the argument of the earth,
> And I know that the hand of God is the promise of my own,
> And I know that the spirit of God is the brother of my own,
> And that all the men ever born are also my brothers, and the women my sisters and lovers,
> And that a kelson of the creation is love,
> And limitless are leaves stiff or drooping in the fields,
> And brown ants in the little wells beneath them,
> And mossy scabs of the worm fence, heap'd stones, elder, mullein and poke-weed.

Every gospel of brotherhood must have its roots in an experience of unity, of identification between a single separate being and all Being, loved as the universal source of life and in its minute particulars. And every work of art crystallizes in a thousand oblique and allusive ways a like experience.

This was how Whitman experienced it. And he called it the joy of simple physiological being. He resigned himself to nature, he loafed and was at ease. He let the worrying mind sink back into the primeval depths from which it had emerged and was ready to turn and live with animals that were so placid and self-contained.

In doing this he had a diffused sense of being part of everyone and of them being part of him. So that nothing was any longer rank in his eyes or to be condemned, no body which was not spirit, no offence which was not forgivable, no goal which was not attainable.

And there was that in him, he felt, and in every man and woman, which was a God, not so much knowing good and evil as oblivious of them. 'Divine am I inside and out', he cried, 'and I make holy whatever I touch or am touch'd from.'

Whitman owed something of this belief to Emerson and other transcendentalists of his day. But he proclaimed it in his own way and it sprang in essence out of that experience of a 'peace and knowledge that pass all the argument of the earth'.

To what was valid in that experience we owe all in *Leaves of Grass* that breaks down barriers, all that melts the bonds of fear between man and man, and between life and death, and between the soul and those great tides that flow through the whole vast kingdom of nature from the stone to the star.

So that in reading some of Whitman's lines we can indeed cry,

> We are Nature, long have we been absent, but now we return.

To that same experience we owe an added strength to believe even in these dark days in a city of Friends,

> invincible to the attacks of the whole of the rest of the earth,

and the continual reminder that

> no man has ever yet been half devout enough,
> None has ever yet adored or worship'd half enough.

Through it we are shamed out of any moral exclusiveness, remembering the lines *To a Common Prostitute*, which so shocked the respectable of Whitman's day.

> Not till the sun excludes you do I exclude you.
> Not till the waters refuse to glisten for you and the leaves to rustle for you, do my words refuse to glisten and rustle for you.

And through it we hear not only the terrible trumpets of war, as Whitman sounded them in *Drum-Taps* over the tramping host, but the word too, which resolves all the pomp and horror and insane blindness of war in a vision of simple human truth,

> Word over all, beautiful as the sky,
> Beautiful that war and all its deeds of carnage must in time be utterly lost,
> That the hands of the sisters Death and Night incessantly softly wash, again and ever again, this soiled world;
> For my enemy is dead, a man divine as myself is dead. . . .

All this and much more flowered out of that summer morning's loafing on the grass and from Whitman's power to renew the peace and knowledge that then possessed him and live in it and speak out of it.

But because there was a flaw in that experience, there was a flaw also in what he wrote. One need not be a Puritan to be a little suspicious of that loafing on the grass as the basis of a gospel of life. Not that loafing on the grass is a bad thing. So far as it means a letting go of the tight anxious will, of the petty self that wants to snatch at or impose itself on life, to exploit nature, to wield power at other people's expense, it can be the beginning of everything good.

Every true mystic has practised such a surrender and every artist in the day to day exercise of his craft. But the surrender, if it is to be fruitful, is itself a kind of action. And all who have tried it know that to act out of inaction, which is out of a new and true centre in the self, is the hardest thing to do and costs much practice.

As a young man Whitman had been a craftsman in a small way both as a printer and a carpenter. But he insufficiently applied the lessons of these manual crafts to his gospel of egotism. And so he failed to see that loafing on the grass, even the kind of loafing which suffused his being with such a sense of peace and knowledge, might be a losing of the self without a real finding of it.

He was undoubtedly peculiar in this way. He had as remarkable an aptitude for floating on his back in the ocean of life as in the actual sea. It was more than a physical aptitude. He relaxed into an act of faith and love. That was why people liked to be with him. He helped them to share in that act of faith and love, to believe, not by an effort of mind, but by the grip of his hand, his large slow movements, and a kind of harmony and ease that were his atmosphere, that life was good and they were good and there was nothing to fear or be ashamed of, and that time being infinite, there was leisure to enjoy a host of things and the commoner the things, the better.

This was Whitman's secret as a man and he wrote *Leaves of Grass* chiefly because he wanted to share it with hosts of people whom he could not reach in the body. In the end he succeeded up to a point. But only up to a point, because there is much in what he wrote which fails to express his secret, which in fact makes us doubt whether he was 'the new man' that people like Edward Carpenter, John Burroughs and Maurice Buck believed him to be.

If so, why those 'prophetical screams' that jar upon an ear attuned to the mystery and truth of things? Why the assertive clamour with which he proclaims that the self is real and unassailable? And why that occasional doting over the 'lusciousness', as he called it, of himself?

The fact is that there was a feud in Whitman, that 'vehement struggle so fierce for unity in one's self' to which he once confessed. But he never really faced it. He forgot it when he loafed and he was so peculiarly constituted that despite the feud he could as a man live on the whole happily and helpfully through his sympathies.

But the conscious ego in him, which was lulled to sleep at such times, awoke when he began to write. When it screams such words as 'I find no sweeter fat than sticks to my own bones', it proclaims its satisfactions as infantile. But when it commands us equally to pride and sympathy, it is not so easy to detect the falsehood that is mixed with the challenging truth.

Put most simply, Whitman never really faced the fact of evil. He thought he had.

'I am he', he wrote,

who knew what it was to be evil,
I too knitted the old knot of contrariety,
Blabb'd, blush'd, resented, lied, stole, grudg'd,
Had guile, anger, lust, hot wishes I dared not speak,
Was wayward, vain, greedy, shallow, sly, cowardly, malignant.

Yes, he knew *about* evil in himself and others. But he never really knew it as the publican knew it when he beat his breast or as Gerard Hopkins when he wrote:

I am gall, I am heartburn. God's most deep decree
Bitter would have me taste; my taste was me.

There can, of course, be an egotistic obsession with evil more destructive of life and virtue than self-indulgence. And Whitman let in some bracing and cleansing air on the sin-haunted and sex-haunted underworld of Puritanism.

But his gospel of egotism as distinct from the primal, elemental egotism of life of which he could be a great poet, fails to be a true gospel of selfhood in the degree that he evaded the conflict in himself both inwardly through lack of introspection and outwardly by merely diffusing himself over a multitude of things.

To-day it is tragically clear that without real penitence, which is equally distinct from luxuriating in a sense of sin or merely professing penitence, there can be no hope of brotherhood. A self-righteous democracy is a contradiction in terms. For every sin not freely and wholly acknowledged man suffers and will always suffer a compulsory judgment, until he learns through self-judgment that only by transcending the principle of judgment and embracing the impulse of forgiveness will judgment be no longer used against himself.

Whitman was no judge. He even said that every time he criticized a man or a book he felt as if he had done something wrong. But he accepted the good in life too easily as what he once called that 'jolly, all-round time — with the parsons and the police eliminated'.

You may do well enough without the parsons and the police.

But if the good you trust in has not been tested in the fires of self-knowledge, if the fact of evil in yourself and in the world has not been deeply suffered and so forgiven, then your faith, however enthusiastically you proclaim it, may momentarily excite and refresh people, but it will fail them in a crisis.

Whitman's gospel is apt to have that effect. Events have discredited his optimism grimly enough. Admittedly he claimed only to be a pioneer and pathfinder. And there was a grand simple compulsion in his summons to his 'tan-faced children'.

> O you youths, Western youths,
> So impatient, full of action, full of manly pride and friendship,
> Plain I see you Western youths, see you tramping with the foremost,
> Pioneers! O pioneers!
>
> Have the elder races halted?
> Do they droop and end their lesson, wearied over there beyond the seas?
> We take up the task eternal, and the burden and the lesson,
> Pioneers! O pioneers!
>
> All the past we leave behind,
> We debouch upon a newer mightier world, varied world,
> Fresh and strong the world we seize, world of labor and the march,
> Pioneers! O pioneers!

It was enough for him to be stepping out into an unknown future. And of Democracy he wrote in his 'Democratic Vistas': 'I cannot too often repeat that it is a word the real gist of which still sleeps, quite unawakened. . . It is a great word, whose history, I suppose, remains unwritten, because that history has yet to be enacted.'

For him the word was the more intoxicating because it was as yet unenacted. It was a talisman which promised a magical future and vistas of human expansion. He never wanted to define it. For that would have cramped his own need of expansion and his style as a singer of it in 'high tones'.

It would have made it less easy to contradict himself with careless exultancy.

> Do I contradict myself?
> Very well then I contradict myself
> (I am large, I contain multitudes).

For the poet who had warned the New World against going the way of the Old when he wrote: 'We fear that we shall be too willing to avenge our injuries by war — the greatest curse that can befall a people', could cry in his *Drum-Taps*:

> Thunder on! Stride on, Democracy! Strike with vengeful stroke!
> And do you rise higher than ever yet O days, O cities!
> Crash heavier, heavier yet O storms! You have done me good,
> My soul prepared in the mountains absorbs your immortal strong nutriment . . .
> Now I no longer wait, I am fully satisfied, I am glutted,
> I have witness'd the true lightning, I have witness'd my cities electric,
> I have lived to behold man burst forth and warlike America rise.

Such contradictions are part of the flux of life and therefore natural to a poet of the flux, to one who was content with making what he called 'the poems of emotion, as they pass or stay, the poems of freedom' — the freedom to ride the waves of unpondered impulse, to reflect the moment or the hour, to be everything or nothing.

Whitman's verse is a great ocean in that sense. He was wonderfully responsive to whatever tide or current of feeling or of events was flowing strongly in his environment. He could say justly enough — 'what the world calls logic is beyond me: I only go about my business taking on impressions — reporting impressions'.

We may question whether more is not required, if not of a poet, of one who would proclaim a new gospel of life as Whitman did. The seer does indeed abandon the defensive positions of the logician and moralist but only to reach down to the real conflict at the heart of things which he seeks to resolve. Only so can he affirm convincingly the goodness beyond or latent in things evil. Only so, if he is a poet, can he really create his own form.

Whitman never wholly succeeded in doing either. His verse for the most part remained as half-formed in its abundant energies as the continent which it celebrated. So did the man who, he promised, was to be 'cohered out of tumult and chaos' in his *Leaves* and prefigure a new world of comradeship.

That man was, of course, an enlargement of himself. And we see in him very clearly the conflict that is always being waged in us between spirit, so infinite in its claims, and the limited natural man. The more acute this conflict is, the more the spirit is driven to assert itself in the limitless pretensions of the ego, while at the other extreme the actual physical world is reduced to mere matter to be exploited.

In Whitman the split was never so acute as this. But it was visible enough in the two modes of his verse, the vaunting assertions of his ego on the one hand, the mere catalogues of things, on the other. Whitman never wholly succeeded in reconciling spirit and matter, though no one has proclaimed more loudly the need of doing so. And no one made a braver attempt to descend upon the materialism of the nineteenth century and lift and fill it with the meanings of the spirit.

We know now where that materialism has brought us. It has brought us to an abyss. And though Whitman can encourage us to believe in the possibility of a better world beyond it, he has less to say which will help us to get out of it. The bridge he threw across it seems too often to end in thin air. As D. H. Lawrence wrote:

> Over the precipice, blue distances, and the blue hollow of the future. But there is no way down. It is a dead end.

Not quite perhaps. But certainly Walt's exultant carolling as he stands on the edge of the precipice sounds rather falsetto to those who are lying bruised and battered at the bottom of it. We have or should have learnt that Democracy is not be be achieved or maintained by expansive affirmations of humanitarian sentiment. In its completion it can be nothing less than the 'beloved community' to which all the great religions have pointed.

Whitman professed himself as indifferent to the religious as to the art forms of the past. But he wrote that 'the attitude of literature and poetry has always been religion — and always will be', and he claimed himself to be the prophet of a new religion of comradeship.

There was something necessary and not to be explained away merely as the ignorance of an uneducated mind in his rejection of existing literary categories and religious systems. For both were decadent. But he never seems to have recognized what an immense responsibility such a rejection imposed upon the individual man and woman, who were to enjoy the freedom of a life dedicated to brotherhood merely by following their expansive instincts as genially as he himself liked to do.

It is true that the Civil War and its aftermath opened his eyes to the vicious channels into which expansive feeling might flow even in his own America. But to the end of his life he tended to encourage the belief that Democracy meant an outward merging without an inner change.

Yet though a mature integrity speaks more humbly and with a more inward utterance than his, he is a prodigious affirmer of the good in man and nature. And in the verse in which he wooed death he came nearest to that resolving of conflict in conflict itself which is the magic and the revelation of great poetry. It was for him characteristically more of a dissolving than a resolving, a dying to all the differences and distinctions which compose the problems of life and which demand for their creative solution a sensitive adjustment of the self to the infinitely varied demands of people and things. But in the negative mode of surrender to death or what he called ebbing with the ocean of life he came nearer losing and finding himself in the rhythm in which life and death are one than when he forced the note of life in celebrating his ego.

His love of death was akin to his love of the sea and in one of his greatest poems, *Out of the Cradle Endlessly Rocking*, originally called *A Voice from the Sea*, the two loves became one, as he recalled the most poignant experience of his boyhood, the singing of the mocking-bird from Alabama that on moonlit nights, perched close to the waves on a moss-covered stake, sang to the mate he had lost. 'O you singer solitary', he wrote,

> Never more shall I escape, never more the reverberations,
> Never more the cries of unsatisfied love be absent from me,
> Never again leave me to be the peaceful child I was before what there in the night,
> By the sea under the yellow and sagging moon,
> The messenger there arous'd, the fire, the sweet hell within,
> The unknown want, the destiny of me.
> O give me the clew! (it lurks in the night here somewhere)
> O if I am to have so much, let me have more!
> A word then, (for I will conquer it.)
> The word final, superior to all,
> Subtle, sent up — what is it? — I listen;
> Are you whispering it, and have been all the time, you sea waves?
> Is that it from your liquid rims and wet sands?
>
> Whereto answering, the sea,
> Delaying not, hurrying not,
> Whisper'd me through the night, and very plainly before day-break,
> Lisp'd to me the low and delicious word death,
> And again death, death, death, death.

Another bird, a hermit-thrush, sang the same song fifty years later when the lilac was in bloom and Lincoln dead.

> Come lovely and soothing death,
> Undulate round the world, serenely arriving, arriving,
> In the day, in the night, to all, to each,
> Sooner or later delicate death.
> Prais'd be the fathomless universe,
> For life and joy, and for objects and knowledge curious,
> And for love, sweet love — but praise! praise! praise!
> For the sure-enwinding arms of cool-enfolding death.

Dark mother always gliding near with soft feet,
Have none chanted for thee a chant of fullest welcome?
Then I chant it for thee, I glorify thee above all,
I bring thee a song that when thou must indeed come, come unfalteringly.

Over the tree-tops I float thee a song,
Over the rising and sinking waves, over the myriad fields and the prairies wide,
Over the dense-pack'd cities all and the teeming wharves and ways,
I float this carol with joy to thee O death.

There is no doubt that this was 'the song and all songs' for Whitman and that he was a great poet in the singing of it. Death may have been for him in one aspect a 'Dark mother' in whom he sought escape from the cost of growing up and the tension of a life-long adolescence. But when he sang of her, as at his best when he sang of life, the impulse and the meaning were more than that.

For behind the homely man, plain and easy to know, with his capacity for simple happiness and for being at home with simple people, was an elemental being who, whether he chanted of life or death, drew upon a primal fount. There was in him something of the grandeur of the primeval, something, as Burroughs put it, that might have belonged to the first man.

There is no way back to Eden and its pristine virtue. But Whitman retained more of this virtue than most men do. From it sprang the unspoken meaning in many of his *Leaves* and his power to transmit living impulses through the ideas he declaimed or the waves of actuality in which he bathed.

A real poet or prophet always expresses more than he is aware of. He is the instrument of unknown powers. Whitman at his best was such a poet, one who had a genius for making himself hospitable to life and for discovering greatness and harmony, where before was thought no greatness, in the most ordinary people and things.

Essentially perhaps he was more of a pioneering prophet than a poet — one of those men who, once in a long long while, issue forth and are their own law and break through the hardened crust of custom and convention, and voice certain elementary powers and truths, which an old civilization is stifling.

It is for us to take those truths in the right way and incorporate them in the life, personal and social, of our day. That was what Whitman wished his readers to do. Words for him were never important in themselves, were perhaps not important enough. They were but a channel along which a new life and a new faith might flow. Through them he would shake us out of our sloth our dead habits, our mental or moral smugness. That was the life-work he conscientiously set himself to do — to release men into comradeship with life. Once released and with their feet planted in the common earth, they could begin to build freedom into something. He was little concerned about the building himself. Characteristically the only building he took a close interest in was his own tomb.

But if on his 'open road' there is no 'Hill Difficulty' or 'Doubting Castle' to test the moral sinews of the pilgrim, it runs through the wide spaces and teeming cities of a continent, and throbs with the energies and exploits, the courage and conviviality of labouring men.

It points, too, to a goal, however imperfectly defined, when politics shall be brotherhood and men and women rejoice in each other's selfhood because they have found in themselves that which is the root of all courage and contentment, and which makes the ordinary divine.

III

THE AUGUSTAN CITADEL

THE editor of the *Oxford Book of Eighteenth Century Verse* remarks in his preface that our attitude to that century is still in process of readjustment, and that the verdict of the nineteenth century is now before the twentieth for revision.

The verdict of the nineteenth century was a muffled echo of the impassioned revulsion of the Romantics. 'Poetry', wrote Wordsworth, 'is like love, a Passion.' Or again it is 'the language of men in a state of vivid sensation'. It shatters 'the surfaces of artificial life' and the pride of 'self-applauding intellect', that delights to trade

> in classic niceties,
> The dangerous craft of seeking term and phrase
> From languages that want the living voice
> To carry meaning to the natural heart . . .

And Keats with all the force of an imagination eager to

> prepare her steeds,
> Paw up against the light and do strange deeds
> Upon the clouds

uttered his famous protest against those 'dismal soul'd' who

> were closely wed
> To musty laws lined out with wretched rule
> And compass vile; so that ye taught a school
> Of dolts to smooth, inlay, and clip, and fit,
> Till, like the certain wands of Jacob's wit,
> Their verses tallied.

We need not spend more time upon the indictment. It is more exhilarating to abuse your father and perhaps your grandfather than to acknowledge what you owe to them. And it is often necessary to effective self-expression.

The Victorians had less excuse. Most of them drew back in alarm from the strange deeds which the Romantic imagination had done upon the clouds. They preferred the safety of sentiment and morality to the creative hazards of that Liberty in whose name alarming as well as sublime things had been done. Yet though they compromised, they were too close to the Romantics to do justice to the eighteenth century.

We can see now that the new discoveries in feeling and sensation, which the Victorians inherited from the Romantics, were but part of an effort to extend and unify human consciousness. From this effort the Victorians as a whole drew back. To-day, however, we recognize that there can be no going back except to the real roots of things and that the Victorian compromise was an insincere evasion with fatal consequences. We see how desperately necessary is the reintegration of conciousness for which the greatest of the Romantics strove. But we see also how costly it is, how it challenges and divides the natural man, until in the conflict between the instinctive and the rational life he longs to return to 'the mother swamp, the primal sea', and yet knows, in the words of a modern poet, that

> the grappled soul must still remain,
> Still choose to think and understand beneath
> The very grinding of the ogre's teeth.

The poets of the eighteenth century, with the exception of those who were haunted by melancholy or mania, could still think without being conscious of the grinding of the ogre's teeth.

But the interest which we can derive from them to-day lies not only in the balance which they achieved by accepting rational limits, of which we can wistfully appreciate the advantage, while compelled ourselves to overstep them, but in the gradual infusion of that orderly awareness with feelings and ideas which were bound before long to shatter its bounds. This infusion can be most clearly traced through the lyrical output of the century, because the lyric, being at first an outcast among the correct disciples of Dryden, attracted to it all the freer spirits of the time.

These men do not boast the magisterial manners of a Pope, and so their humble efforts to loosen the self-conscious fetters which bound the feet of poetry have received less than their due.

2

Viewed then from this standpoint such catchwords as 'the tyranny of Pope' or 'the domination of the heroic couplet' are superficial. Style in poetry is significant as the means by which a poet organizes and crystallizes his experience. Ideally it is more than that. It is the very movement and modulation of the experience itself. In the rhythm and cadence of poetry the very pulse of the poet's inner being beats. The perpetuation, however, of such catchwords as those just cited is due to approaching eighteenth-century poetry with a preconception that what virtue it possesses is that of a style existing in its own right as the accepted mode of a period.

All periods do of course have their predominant mode and idiom and in some the prevailing convention is more powerful and pervasive than in others. Certainly there was more formalism in the eighteenth century than in some. But the formalism itself was an intrinsic attitude to life which was not only subtly different in different poets, but which, in society at large, as the poets reflected or foreshadowed it, was being undermined by a growth of sensibility. The domination, not of the heroic couplet, but of restrictive reason and of a moral complacency which assumed too easily that the individual mind and the laws of the universe were in harmony, was gradually giving way. The defences behind which poets had guarded themselves against the starker truths of life and the deeper and less manageable truths of their own natures were, as the century advanced, rapidly crumbling. Reality, like a rising tide filtering through many channels, was breaking in.

The catchwords of academic criticism miss the graduations of this change in the spiritual climate of the age. It has long, for example, been an accepted dogma of criticism that Pope bestraddled his age like a crippled Colossus. But it would be truer to say that he represented rather a last refinement of the age of Dryden than the fertile forces of his own. His influence on the mere versifiers of the century was potent, as the influence of Tennyson was on the versifiers of his day and century. But even on the poets who were his contemporaries it has been greatly exaggerated; on those who succeeded him it was inconsiderable; and where, as in Crabbe, his heroic couplet recurs forty years after his death, it was put to the service of a theme which the urban Pope would have found distasteful and unworthy of the Muses:

> I grant indeed that Fields and Flocks have charms,
> For him that gazes or for him that farms;
> But when amid such pleasing scenes I trace
> The poor laborious natives of the place,
> And see the mid-day sun, with fervid ray,
> On their bare heads and dewy temples play;
> While some, with feebler heads and fainter hearts,
> Deplore their fortune, yet sustain their parts,
> Then shall I dare these real ills to hide,
> In tinsel trappings of poetic pride?
> No; cast by Fortune on a frowning coast,
> Which neither groves nor happy valleys boast;
> Where other races than those the Muse relates,
> And other Shepherds dwell with other mates;
> By such examples taught, I paint the lot,
> As truth will paint it and as bards will not.
> Nor you, ye Poor, of letter'd scorn complain,
> To you the smoothest song is smooth in vain;
> O'ercome by labour and bow'd down by time,
> Feel you the barren flattery of a rhyme?

Pope, of course, occupies a significant place in his century. But the criticism of life which his couplet embodied was not typical of the century as a whole.

In Pope the intellect preserves a gratifying but impoverishing mastery over the sensibility. But the impulse behind much of the poetry of the eighteenth century is a protest, often subconscious, but growing in intensity and volume, against such impoverishment.

The citadel of 'reason', which was also for the more languid spirits a 'castle of indolence', was in fact throughout the century under siege from without and, more insidiously, from within. Augustan 'reason' was a kind of elegant common sense and the cult of a decorous mean as a safeguard against excess of feeling. Certainly sentiment had begot many inanities to justify caution. But to set reason against emotion was to reduce it to a shrunken faculty, at best capable only of reflective comment or disciplinary action.

Thus we find Sir Joshua Reynolds bidding 'Reason' (in the sense of logic) preside over Imagination which he conceived only as a fanciful faculty. But real imagination transcends the mere logic of the mind in a creative reason of its own. The reason of such imagination is not nature 'methodiz'd', as the Augustans desired, but humanized and spiritualized. It was towards this ideal, this release from the partial and the cramped, that the sensibility of poets slowly and tentatively moved. Johnson might make a weighty or Goldsmith a half-hearted attempt to mend the breaches in the citadel. But they failed. And nature struck at them from within. Swift's lacerated heart, Gray's melancholy, Shenstone's hypochondria, Johnson's thwarted tenderness and terror of death, were all proofs of the penalties that dog an arbitrary check upon feeling. Life, mocking their logic, their abstractions and personifications and pseudo-classic correctness, now by one channel, now by another, seeped in and foretold an irresistible tide.

The characteristic temper of early eighteenth-century poetry may be best defined by a few quotations. John Pomfret, for example, who died two years after the century had begun, described in a poem entitled *The Choice* a scheme of life which seemed to him ideal.

He would have 'a private seat' within reach of some fair Town, 'Built uniform, not Little, nor too Great'.

> It should within no other things contain,
> But what were Useful, Necessary, Plain:

But among these were the works of Horace, Virgil, Juvenal and Ovid, and of such Moderns as were 'Men of steady Sense'.

He would 'Live Gentilely, but not Great', and possess

> As much as I cou'd moderately spend,
> A little more, sometimes t'Oblige a Friend . . .
> A frugal Plenty shou'd my Table spread;
> With Healthy, not Luxurious Dishes Fed.

His wine-cellar should likewise be small but choice, and serve to whet the wit, but never cloud or intoxicate it. Two friends would satisfy him, and both should be

> Brave, Gen'rous, Witty, and exactly Free
> From loose Behaviour, or Formality;
> Airy, and Prudent, Merry, but not Light,
> Quick in Discerning, and in Judgment right . . .
> Obliging, Open, without Huffing Brave,
> Brisk in Gay Talking, and in Sober, Grave.
> In their Society, I cou'd not miss
> A Permanent, Sincere, Substantial Bliss.

But lest the Bliss of male conversation should prove too substantial, and because

> there's that Sweetness in a Female Mind,
> Which in a man's we cannot hope to find,

he would also choose

> Near some Obliging, Modest fair to live.

But not too near. Against the risk of the 'sweetness in a Female Mind' cloying his palate, against the disconcerting caprice of the feminine disposition, he would take every precaution; and if, as he approached old age he should require any feminine attention, he is careful to say that he would depend on

> Some Kind Relation, (for I'd have no Wife).

Indeed a wife, with the qualities which he demands of his 'Modest Fair' would prove far to seek.

I'd have her Reason all her Passions sway
Easy in Company, in Private Gay;
Coy to a Fop, to the Deserving Free,
Still Constant to her self, and Just to me . . .
I'd have th'Expression of her Thoughts be such,
She might not seem Reserv'd, nor talk too much.

The antitheses in this poem, such as 'Airy, and Prudent, Merry, but not Light' are not mere tricks of diction. They conform to an ideal, the ideal of the mean. To balance one impulse by its opposite, enthusiasm by good sense, generosity by prudence, desire by discretion, and so preserve a mastery over life and an assured poise in yourself—that was the choice of John Pomfret and of many of his contemporaries.

They qualified every feeling, every impulse, every taste. For they felt that indulgence led to excess, and that in excess the individuality was dissipated. They desired above all things to possess themselves.

And just as in civilization they saw only a small citadel of culture in a brutish world, dependent in fact on the social and economic well-being of a rising individualistic middle-class, so they conceived of poetry as a pattern of good sense and elegant sobriety imposed upon the rebel instincts.

This attitude to life may not command our admiration to-day, but it deserves the respect of an age which for the most part is without any art of life whatever. This is doubtless a consequence of the necessary collapse of middle-class individualism, which in the nineteenth century was to become the moneyed self-aggrandizement of traders and industrialists. Out of the spiritual and social vacuum so created a new art of life, more deeply rooted in reality and no longer dependent on social privilege, may eventually take shape. Meanwhile, however, chaos is only held in check by the clamps of mechanic order.

But in the eighteenth century, men could still aim at poise and completeness. Their success in achieving their aim was largely due to confining experience to the easily manageable. But they did, many of them, realize an enviable balance. And balance, however maintained, is laudable. For, as Cowper was to write,

> To find the medium asks some share of wit,
> And therefore 'tis a mark fools never hit.

The attitude to 'Nature' of these poets, as we shall see, was throughout an index of the balance they strove to maintain between rationality and sensibility. In the earlier part of the century 'Nature' and 'God' were for many of them almost synonymous, although they might formally preserve the separate terms. Newton's system and the 'natural philosophy' associated with it seemed to have reduced the mysterious and dangerous cosmos to manageable order. The unruly potencies of the universe were revealed by physical science to be subject to law of which God was the majestic but controllable dispenser. Hence the extreme shock of the Lisbon earthquake which showed that neither God nor Nature were as law-abiding as was comfortably supposed. Human nature, too, after two centuries of religious wars, was enjoying a period of comparative civil peace, so that optimism about man was for the time as inviting as optimism about God.

It was only towards the end of the century that with the French Revolution, the dispossession of craftsmen and small-holders, and factory enslavement, tragic reality broke through once more and could not be overlooked. Then William Blake who suffered the full impact of these ills turned upon the 'religion of Nature', whether scientific or pseudo-Platonic or genially sentimental, and denounced it as a delusion. For him, the natural world and human nature, so far as it partook of that world, had to be redeemed by a reality beyond it, by the divine imagination which was for him the organ of super-Nature, the Son born of the Father in every human soul.

But Blake was so much ahead of his times, as he was of most of his romantic successors, that his vision has only begun to be accepted in our own day which in its spiritual bankruptcy is in such desperate need of it. In the first half of the eighteenth century a superficially civilized existence based on moral control in the individual, corroborated by the law and order discovered by science in the constitution of the universe, seemed acceptable enough.

And so the balanced antitheses in which such poets as John Pomfret clothed their verse and which Pope perfected, was not a mere structural convention. It was a criticism of life, a formal expression of the belief that

> If Reason rules within, and keeps the Throne,
> While the inferior Faculties obey,

happiness was assured.

Yet even in the early years of the century it was not an unquestioned belief. Prior, for example, in his *Epitaph* on 'Saunt'ring Jack, and Idle Joan' riddled it with delicate raillery.

> Their Moral and Oeconomy
> Most perfectly They made agree:
> Each Virtue kept its proper Bound,
> Nor Trespass'd on the other's Ground.

And the consequence was this:

> Nor Good, nor Bad, nor Fools, nor Wise;
> They would not learn, nor cou'd advise:
> Without Love, Hatred, Joy, or Fear,
> They led — a kind of — as it were:
> Nor Wish'd, nor Car'd, nor Laugh'd, nor Cry'd:
> And so They liv'd; and so they dy'd.

More solemnly in *Love and Reason* he proclaimed the frailty of Man, insensibly betrayed by his own delusion of self-sufficiency and security.

> Seeing no Danger, We disarm our Mind,
> And give our Conduct to the Waves and Wind . . .
>
> We weave the Chaplet, and we crown the Bowl,
> And smiling see the Nearer Waters roll;
> 'Till the strong Gusts of raging Passion rise;
> 'Till the dire Tempest mingles Earth and Skies; . . .

O mighty Love! from thy unbounded Pow'r
How shall the human Bosom rest secure? . . .

We think we see thro' Reason's optics right;
Nor find, how Beauty's Rays elude our sight . . .

Against this nearest cruelest of Foes,
What shall Wit meditate, or Force oppose?
Whence, feeble Nature, shall We summon Aid,
If by our Pity, and our Pride betray'd?
External Remedy shall we hope to find,
When the close Fiend has gain'd our treach'rous Mind,
Insulting there does Reason's Pow'r deride,
And blind Himself, conducts the dazl'd Guide?

It is not the attractiveness of rational control which Prior questions but its too conscious cultivation. If a balance of impulses be a gift of nature, he can applaud it, as in his charming *Jinny the Just* whose

Will with her Duty so equally stood
That seldom oppos'd she was commonly good,
And did pretty well, doing just what she wou'd.

But Jinny's happy antithetical conduct of life, he is careful to note,

answered the end of her being Created.

It was not a system imposed upon life and so did not conflict with that 'Fate', that force of Nature, against which, Prior regretfully admitted, an Augustan façade of elegance and propriety was a flimsy protection.

Yet the system was so comforting to self-esteem and within limits so realizable, that it was long before poets abandoned it. And in Pope, in the perfected cunning of his interlocked antithesis and the bland complacence of his *Essay on Man* it found its apotheosis.

He who could arrange words to balance each other with such grace and propriety found it easy to attribute to the Creator of the Universe a kindred aptitude:

Cease then, nor Order *Imperfection* name:
Our proper bliss depends on what we blame,
Know thy own *Point*: This kind, this due degree
Of blindness, weakness, Heav'n bestows on thee.
Submit — in this, or any other Sphere,
Secure to be as blest as thou canst bear:
Safe in the hand of one disposing Pow'r.
Or in the natal, or the mortal Hour.
All Nature is but Art, unknown to thee;
All Chance, Direction which thou canst not see;
All Discord, Harmony not understood;
All partial Evil, Universal Good:
And spite of Pride, in erring Reason's spite,
One truth is clear, Whatever Is, is Right.

This statement of faith corresponds superficially with that deeper affirmation of Life which so many Romantics were later to utter. Yet between Pope's falsetto 'Whatever Is, is Right' and Blake's sonorous 'For every thing that lives is Holy' lies a gulf of disillusionment, mental warfare and imaginative conversion.

Pope could affirm the living order of the Universe so blandly because he viewed it externally and provincially. He fancied God making it as he made his own verses, with as orderly a precision and as polished a clarity.

To him no high, no low, not great, no small;
He fills, He bounds, connects, and equals all.

It was this projection of his own accomplishment and decorum into the Universe itself that explains Pope's composure and that of so many of his contemporaries. For him the Deity was, like Viscount Bolingbroke, an admirable Augustan gentleman,

From grave to gay, from lively to severe,
Correct with Spirit, eloquent with ease,
Intent to reason, or polite to please.

But the more men obeyed his injunction

Know then thyself, presume not God to scan,

the more they discovered in their nature cravings, high and low, which Pope's Universe could neither contain nor satisfy.

In his practice as a poet, as distinct from his rational and deistical theory, Pope was a man of more singular sensibility than romantic critics have often recognized. But the self-possessed agreement between God and Man, the balance between reason and sentiment, which he had achieved by curtailing both, was becoming invalid. A more direct feeling for life was quickening beneath the orderly surface of Augustan manners, a sense, too, of the transcendent, of the indifferent, and even of the hostile in Nature.

It was some time before cracks appeared on that glazed surface. Devotees of Nature and even Methodists, after the rise of the Evangelical Movement in 1740, reconciled their transports at first, not unsuccessfully, with a decorous tradition. Yet the foundations of the structure so neatly and suavely adjusted had given way. The antithesis in all the most vital poets of the middle and later eighteenth century, with few exceptions, was abandoned. For the balance which it expressed was no longer a reality and men were seeking uneasily and often sentimentally for a new harmony in poetry and a new religion in life.

3

A more real 'Nature' crept into the Augustan consciousness by way of the garden and the country-seat.

A favourite theme of the time was the contrasted charms of country and of town. They were still such near and accommodating neighbours that the contrast was very conciliatory. They had yet to be alienated by that industrialism over the cradle of which Dyer hung in such innocent admiration:

So appear
Th' increasing walls of busy Manchester,
Sheffield, and Birmingham, whose Redd'ning fields
Rise and enlarge their suburbs. Lo, in throngs,
For ev'ry realm, the careful factors meet,
Whisp'ring each other. In long ranks the bales,

> Like war's bright files, beyond the sight extend.
> . . . Pursue,
> Ye sons of Albion, with unyielding heart,
> Your hardy labors: let the sounding loom
> Mix with the melody of ev'ry vale.

Thirty years later Cowper was to write very differently of merchants who,

> unimpeachable of sin
> Against the charities of domestic life,
> Incorporated, seem at once to lose
> Their nature, and disclaiming all regard
> For mercy and the common rights of man,
> Build factories with blood, conducting trade
> At the sword's point, and dyeing the white robe
> Of innocent commercial justice red.

But so long as men could cherish a belief in the consonance of the sounding loom and 'the melody of ev'ry dale', so long could they try to blend a rational urban consciousness with that feeling for nature which could not be denied.

That feeling grew in intensity and in dimension as the town became a scar of smoke and steam and of sweated humanity in the countryside.

Most of the poets of the eighteenth century, however, were not shocked by the ugliness of industrialism to seek in Nature a philosophic cure for their pain. It was not from commercial ugliness but from the artificiality and glitter of the town, that they sought rural retreats.

Goldsmith, indeed, might lament the decay of 'Sweet Auburn, loveliest village of the plain' and attribute it to the licence of accumulated wealth. Cowper might scold the town for its corrupt morals and pursuit of pleasure, but the primary impulse even in these was to hymn the praise and heighten by contrast the delights of 'blest retirement'.

Later, poets were to flee to Nature in search of a lost Eden of innocent anarchy, but these poets at first sought her with the conscious aim of soothing their nerves and enhancing in 'lowly Dale', by 'River Side', or on 'Woody Hill', that art of life which was still their chief concern.

Their garden-craft and their terror of anything approaching the elemental in Nature prove how jealously they guarded their sense of order against unruly forces. Did not Cowper shrink even from the wildness of the South Downs and Gray draw the blinds of his carriage against the worst terrors of the Lake District? And since

> we receive but what we give
> And in *our* life alone does Nature live,

these poets could still impose their ideal upon her elementalism, could select, from all she had to offer, her sedative influences. As Thomson could write:

> Men, woods and fields, all breathe untroubled life.
> Then keep each passion down, however dear.

They felt indeed the climate of the time to be too cultivated and yet they valued their culture. They only wished to freshen it, to forget Society-crushes in the quiet of garden-paths and studious glades, to forget and yet not lose their self-sufficiency.

So, even as early as 1713, we find the Countess of Winchilsea writing:

> Give me, O indulgent Fate!
> Give me, yet, before I Dye,
> A sweet, but absolute Retreat,
> 'Mongst Paths so lost, and Trees so high,
> That the World may ne'er invade,
> Through such windings and such Shade,
> My unshaken Liberty.

There was nothing abandoned in the Liberty which they sought. It was a liberty to relax while preserving their self-awareness intact, to feel without endangering their powers of exact observance or of hearing. 'And falling Waters', writes the same poetess, 'we *distinctly* hear', and although 'silent musings' may urge her mind to seek

> Something too high for Syllables to speak,

she restrains the impulse which would shatter the approved mood of inward equilibrium:

> When a sedate Content the Spirit feels,
> And no fierce Light disturbs, whilst it reveals.

The capacity to focus with fine sensitiveness an object without penetrating it was perhaps the outstanding quality of their defect. Pope, of course, possessed it to a remarkable degree, as in the famous description of the dying Pheasant:

> Ah! What avail his glossy, varying dyes,
> His purple crest, and scarlet-circled eyes,
> The vivid green his shining plumes unfold,
> His painted wings, and breast that flames with gold.

But it is found in a score of lesser poets too, in the vivid wintriness for example of Ambrose Philips' couplet:

> The frighted Birds the rattling Branches shun,
> That wave and glitter in the distant Sun.

We find then poet after poet thus submitting their jaded nerves to the gently reanimating quiet of the country. They are convalescents recovering from an illness which is not yet serious enough to demand a more radical treatment.

Like William Somervile they derive 'ease of body blest, and peace of mind', or like Mathew Green they

> place their bliss in mental rest,
> And feast upon the food possesst,

or with William Whitbread they invoke

> The still small voice retirement loves to hear;

while John Armstrong discusses the influence of nature in a poem entitled *The Art of preserving Health.*

Nature responds to their appeal. Insensibly they recover tone. Mathew Green in his *A Cure for the Spleen* sketches a very similar scheme of life to that of John Pomfret in *The Choice* forty years earlier. But how much richer in the sap of life is his verse!

> And may my humble dwelling stand
> Upon some chosen spot of land;
> A pond before full to the brim,
> Where cows may cool, and geese may swim;
> Behind, a green like velvet neat,
> Soft to the eye, and to the feet. . . .

The aim is still composed, but the poet's senses are no longer veiled by the mind's bland decorum.

And with sympathy for the country is born sympathy for the countryman, a sympathy still, maybe, tinged with patronage, but sincere in its revulsion from smooth-cheeked and smooth-tongued urbanity. 'Sometimes at eve', wrote John Armstrong,

> (for I delight to taste
> The native zest and flavour of the fruit,
> Where sense grows wild, and takes of no manure)
> The decent, honest, chearful husbandman
> Should drown his labours in my friendly bowl;
> And at my table find himself at home.

There are many examples among writers in our own day of attempts to reinforce a sensibility, rendered listless by over-cultivation, by grafting it on a wild stalk. But conditions in the eighteenth century did not exasperate the need as they do now. The culture which divided poets from the soil was, despite all its accomplished formality, superficial.

Such a poet as Gay for example, despite his literary refinement, was at home with the humours of village life, which, though often rude, had also their decorative conventions. He could write, for example, with bucolic zest in *Blouzelinda's Funeral*:

> To her sweet mem'ry flow'ry garlands strung,
> O'er her now empty seat aloft were hung.

With wicker rods we fenc'd her tomb around
To ward from man and beast the hallow'd ground,
Lest her new grave the Parson's cattle raze,
For both his horse and cow the churchyard graze.

Now we trudg'd homeward to her mother's farm,
To drink new cyder mull'd, with ginger warm.
For gaffer *Tread-well* told us by the by,
Excessive sorrow is exceeding dry.

While bulls bear horns upon their curled brow,
Or lasses with soft stroakings milk the cow;
While paddling ducks the standing lake desire,
Or batt'ning hogs roll in the sinking mire;
While moles the crumped earth in hillcocks raise,
So long shall swains tell *Blouzelinda's* praise.

Yet few eighteenth-century poets had preserved as well as Gay their ability 'in ale and kisses to forget their cares', and their rediscovery of the countryman implied rather a growing understanding of his cares, of his hard life and his homely integrity, than a relapse into bucolic manners.

This understanding was as sure a sign of quickened sensibility as the new quality of their experience of nature. When Gray wrote of the unmemorized poor that

Chill Penury repress'd their noble rage,
And froze the genial current of the soul.

he had ceased to view the country as a classical estate. When Colley Cibber wrote of a blind boy:

O say! what is that Thing called Light,
Which I can ne'er enjoy;
What is the Blessing of the Sight,
O tell your poor Blind Boy!

he had crossed the border of Blake's kingdom of imagination with its inescapable question:

Can I see another's woe,
And not be in sorrow too?

The good sense of the age may still have prevented the poets from advancing deep into this kingdom. But it also restrained their expanding sympathies, for the most part, from dissolving into sentimentalism. They might romanticize the peasant, as Thomson does in describing the effect of a rainbow on a rustic:

> He wondering, views the bright enchantment bend
> Delightful, o'er the radiant fields and runs
> To catch the falling glory; but, amazed,
> Beholds the amusive arch before him fly.

But they never exploit the miseries, or make a doctrine of the virtues of the poor.

4

The change, then, in the spiritual climate of the century is felt first in this growing tenderness of mind, a tenderness for animals and green places, for the poor and outcast or an evening sky. This tenderness was not a discovery of Bowles, whose plaintive self-pity, despite Coleridge's youthful infatuation for him, lacked just the masculine quality that is the virtue of this age, nor even of Collins or of Cowper.

It could not free itself at once from neo-classical conventions. When Ambrose Philips writes of Miss Charlotte Pulteney in her Mother's arms:

> Simple maiden, void of art,
> Babbling out the very heart,
> Yet abandon'd to thy will,
> Yet imagining no ill,

his words lack the evocative veracity of Coleridge's

> A little child, a limber elf
> Singing, dancing to itself,
> A fairy thing with red round cheeks,
> That always finds, and never seeks. . . .

THREE ADDRESSES

When Robert Blair writes:

> Sudden! he starts, and hears, or thinks he hears
> The sound of something purring at his Heels:
> Full fast he flies, and dares not look behind him,

he lacks the power to evoke horror which made Shelley fall fainting on the floor at the words —

> Like one that on a lonesome road
> Doth walk in fear and dread,
> And having once turned round, walks on,
> And turns no more his head,
> Because he knows a frightful fiend
> Doth close behind him tread.

When Thomson writes of frost at night:

> but to the sedgy Bank
> Fast grows, or gathers round the pointed stone,
> A crystal Pavement, by the Breath of Heaven
> Cemented firm; till, seiz'd from Shore to Shore,
> The whole imprison'd River growls below.
> Loud rings the frozen Earth, and hard reflects
> A double Noise;

the words are but a tinkle compared with Wordsworth's:

> From under Esthwaite's splitting fields of ice
> The pent-up air, struggling to free itself,
> Gave out to meadow-grounds and hills a loud
> Protracted yelling, like the noise of wolves
> Howling in troops along the Bothnic main.

When William Oldys thus addresses a fly:

> Busy, curious, thirsty Fly,
> Gently drink, and drink as I;
> Freely welcome to my Cup,
> Could'st thou sip, and sip it up;
> Make the most of life you may,
> Life is short and wears away.

his sentiment is near to triteness compared with Thomas Hardy's meditative brooding in *An August Midnight*:

> 'God's humblest, they!' I muse. Yet why?
> They know Earth — secrets that know not I.

Yet here and in poem after poem of this century a new sensibility is defying the best endeavours to 'revive the just Designs of Greece' or mimic the odes of Horace.

Such a poem for example as John Langhorne's *The Evening Primrose* opens in the approved style of one of 'Nature's votaries'. We have the personified abstractions, 'ENVY's lurid eye' and 'AMBITION's losing game'; we move in 'Eden's vale' and listen to 'the voice of vernal gales', and then suddenly the acquired hardness of a poetic convention melts at the enchanted touch of the evening hour:

> Didst thou, Shepherd, never find,
> Pleasure is of pensive kind?
> Has thy cottage never known
> That she loves to live alone?
> Dost thou not at evening hour
> Feel some soft and secret power,
> Gliding o'er thy yielding mind,
> Leave sweet serenity behind;
> While all disarm'd, the cares of day
> Steal thro' the falling gloom away?

Many examples could be given of this 'soft and secret power' inducing in the self-centred intelligence the yielding grace of sympathy. We find it again in the following lines from John Brown's poem *Night*:

> Nor voice nor sound broke on the deep serene,
> But the soft murmur of swift-gushing rills,
> Forth-issuing from the mountain's distant steep,
> (Unheard till now, and now scarce heard) proclaim'd
> All things at rest, and imag'd the still voice
> Of quiet whispering in the ear of Night.

One more example must suffice. It is Thomas Russell's poem *The*

Maniac, of which the theme is that of the betrayed country-girl so beloved by the Romantics. Here again we find, at first, examples enough of the conventional diction which we should expect from an Oxford don of the time.

We read of 'passion's tender tale'; we read that

> Young Julia still was fair:
> The rose indeed had left her cheek,
> The lily still was there.

But then suddenly we enter a new world of experience, a world which is as old indeed as the ballads and as young as the young Keats and Wordsworth:

> When thirst and hunger grieved her most,
> If any food she took,
> It was the berry from the thorn,
> The water from the brook . . .
>
> From ev'ry hedge a flower she pluck'd,
> And moss from ev'ry stone,
> To make a garland for her Love,
> Yet left it still undone.
>
> Still as she rambled, was she wont
> To trill a plaintive song,
> 'Twas wild, and full of fancies vain,
> Yet suited well her wrong . . .
>
> Oft too a smile, but not of joy,
> Play'd on her brow o'ercast;
> It was the faint cold smile of Spring
> Ere Winter yet had past.

This 'Smile of Spring' coming and going with all Spring's caprice across the winter of Augustan discontent lends a new charm and vitality to the poetry of the second half of the century.

Not all, however, could ease so pleasantly the bonds of the constrictive reason. Collins, Cowper and Smart reveal the darker side of the conflict between thought and repressed feeling, between the civilized but cramped ego and its unconscious depths. In Smart, indeed, the depths opened to the heights in the greatest religious poem of the century, *A Song to David*. But even for him the abyss of melancholy and madness yawned perilously close.

When Joseph Warton in the Preface to his *Odes* expressed his conviction in 1747 that 'the fashion of moralizing in verse has been carried too far' and that 'invention and imagination' should be 'the chief faculties of a poet', he hardly visualized the forces which a really creative imagination unleashed or the havoc they could work, if foiled.

Every birth into a new order of consciousness and being has its perils. It may be a long sickness, a fever, or a shattering convulsion. In some of the great poets of the Romantic Movement the truth of this was to be more manifest than in their immediate predecessors who were less imaginatively compelled. But to be half-committed to a new creative adventure was to be poised between death and life, the known which had lost its savour and the terrors and intoxicating allurements of the unknown. It was to be preyed upon by imagination instead of being released into a new oneness of faculty through it.

Only a few of these poets suffered the extremity of that state, but the shadow of it haunted many of them, even the moralizing Edward Young, the piety of whose *Night Thoughts* triumphed with difficulty over his pessimism.

More often, however, reason enlarged itself without attempting to plunge into a new and dangerous dimension. Men's minds were being quickened with ideas. Elegant pretensions yielded before generous conceptions of a better world; private moralizing was caught up by a moral enthusiasm which demanded that the chains not merely of poetic convention but of mean self-interest should be broken.

Here again the new idealism could not burn away all the dross of 'poetic' artifice. Akenside can still sing of 'the tenants of the warbling shade' in the poem in which he writes of a mind enlarged and enriched by communion with Nature:

would the forms
Of servile custom cramp her generous pow'rs?
Would sordid policies, the barb'rous growth
Of ignorance and rapine, bow her down
To tame pursuits, to indolence and fear?
Lo! she appeals to nature, to the winds
And rowling waves, the sun's unwearied course,
The elements and seasons: all declare
For what th'eternal maker has ordain'd
The pow'rs of man: we feel within ourselves
His energy divine: he tells the heart,
He meant, he made us to behold and love
What he beholds and loves, the general orb
Of life and being; to be great like him,
Beneficent and active.

There are other passages in *The Pleasures of Imagination* which recall *The Prelude* more intimately. There are the lines, for example:

O ye Northumbrian shades, which overlook
The rocky pavement and the mossy falls
Of solitary Wensbeck's limpid stream;
How gladly I recall your well-known seats
Beloved of old, and that delightful time
When all alone, for many a summer's day,
I wander'd through your calm recesses, led
In silence by some powerful hand unseen.
Nor will I e'er forget you: nor shall e'er
The graver tasks of manhood, or the advice
Of vulgar wisdom, move me to disclaim
Those studies which possess'd me in the dawn
Of life, and fix'd the color of my mind
For every future year.

Wordsworth's acknowledgment of Nature's moral power is weightier and more intimately personal, because he had fought his way to faith through deeps of disillusionment, unplumbed by Akenside.

Nevertheless the kinship of this poet with Wordsworth and his shadowy exaltations and intimations is as undeniable as Wordsworth's debt to him.

5

I have said nothing of another kind of tenderness which flowed into the religious verse of the eighteenth century, into the hymns of Watts and of Wesley, of Byron and of Cowper, and rolled in a wave of liturgical ecstasy through the *Song to David* of Christopher Smart.

Evangelicism, as the history of Cowper painfully attests, could prove a dangerous stimulus. But in reaffirming the realm of Darkness, the fact of sin and the mystery of redemption, it restored to imagination a dimension without which the poetic Platonism of, for example, Henry Brooke in his *Universal Beauty* lacked root and depth. And although the loyalty to reason characteristic of many of the Deists deserved a profounder laureate than Pope, Deism at its best was always too egocentric a creed. The rediscovery that 'God moves in a mysterious way', that reality at its heart is incommensurable, was necessary to revitalize experience, even if it shook the unsure foundations of some men and made fanatics of others.

But here again the formal tradition proved its virtue in restraining the excesses of religious revivalism and preserving a dignity in devotional self-surrender. What could be more free, for example, from the mawkish enjoyment of a sense of sin, so typical of many Salvationist hymns, than John Byrom's

My Spirit longeth for thee,
   Within my troubled Breast;
Altho' I be unworthy
   Of so divine a Guest.

Of so divine a Guest,
   Unworthy tho' I be;
Yet has my heart no Rest,
   Unless it come from Thee.

I have said nothing too of the revival of the ballad and the folk theme, which linked the vernacular to the academic as it had in Elizabethan times. Yet a century which can boast of Allan Ramsay and David Mallet, of Henry Carey and Jean Elliott, of William Julius Mickle and John Logan, had something more than an antiquarian and dilettante interest in balladry, could feel down, in a few at least of its poets, to the common soil from which any culture that is to be strong and racy must spring.

These poets, as we should expect, have more sympathy for vernacular sentiment and humour, than for that vernacular melodrama which requires the force of primitive conviction to raise it to tragic dimensions. Yet how captivating in its country humour is such a ballad as Allan Ramsay's *A Dainty Sang*:

> *Jocky* said to *Jenny*, *Jenny* wilt thou do't,
> Ne'er a fit, quoth *Jenny*, for my tocher-good;[1]
> For my tocher-good, I winna marry thee,
> E'en's ye like, quoth *Jocky*, ye may let it be.
>
> I hae gowd and gear, I hae land enough,
> I hae seen good owsen ganging in a pleugh;
> Ganging in a pleugh, and linkan o'er the lee,
> And gin ye winna tak me, I can let ye be.
>
> I hae a good ha'house, a barn and a byre,
> A peatstack 'fore the door, we'll make a rantin fire;
> I'll make a rantin' fire, and merry sall we be,
> And gin ye winna tak me, I can let ye be.
>
> *Jenny* said to *Jocky*, gin ye winna tell,
> Ye shall be the lad, I'll be the lass my sell;
> Ye're a bony lad, and I'm a lassie free;
> Ye're welcomer to tak me, than to let me be.

Finally there are those two miracles of forgery, Chatterton's and Macpherson's, which played their part through their very unreality in releasing men from the conventional and disposing them

[1] 'tocher' means 'dowry'.

to accept the imaginatively real. The immense success of *Ossian* showed how eager for food the contemporary imagination was.

6

In what way, then, is the verdict of our century upon these poets likely to differ from that of our predecessors? It will differ surely in point of emphasis. Hitherto the emphasis has tended to be on the exclusive balance which Pope perfected and on the finely organized but conventionalized diction which expressed it.

That balance, as I have tried to show, was the preliminary and for some time dominating condition of eighteenth-century experience. It was, too, in some ways a balance which we can envy, if we cannot wholly admire, and it made for felicities of form, both in life and poetry. But it was a balance achieved by excluding too much that is essential to a warm and vivid humanity. And generally the poets of the century were too human to sustain it.

Our emphasis therefore is likely to lie increasingly on the forces which disturbed, strained to breaking point, and at last destroyed this balance. So long as the movement was only one of sentiment, the balance could be preserved while being softened. But when imagination began to supervene, the precariously poised structure cracked.

And this will modify our conception of the Romantic Movement too. We shall see it less as a sudden miracle of liberation than as the breaking of a wave which had been gathering for more than fifty years out of the deeps of human longing and dissatisfaction, and not merely gathering but overcurling now here, now there, as a wave does in its advance, in broken edges that caught the rays of a rising sun and glistened with a new light of vision.

We shall see the eighteenth century not as the schoolroom of a prescribed classicism or of an accomplished sobriety, but as a nursery of sensibility. And in the knowledge of all the pain and perplexity in which heightened sensibility involves man, of the burden of the mystery which poets were once again to be called to bear, we shall yet delight to mark the motions of that overruling necessity which drew these poets from a provincial security towards the hazards of the imaginative life, towards words unsoiled by conventional usage, and towards

> truth, by no peculiar taste confin'd
> Whose universal pattern strikes mankind.

PART TWO

POETS AND POETRY

I

THE CULT OF SYMBOLISM

IN art, as in religion, there is always danger when experience hardens into doctrine. That doctrine, in its turn, can clarify experience and clear the way for new experience is equally true. And it would be folly to deny its importance. Every great age of poetry, in modern times at least, has had the backing of fine criticism, and the idea that a poet ought not to know what he is doing but should be seized incontinently by the Muses is only half the truth of the matter.

The trouble, however, with many modern poets is that their knowledge is wrongly placed. They know too much of the surface and too little of the depths. Instead of their knowledge springing out of the realm of mystery, upon which every poet must draw, and taking form through the conscious faculties, the process is reversed. It is self-conscious intelligence which applies its analytical scalpel to the little that it can wrest from the hidden depths and carves out of it arbitrary forms.

This fissure between inspiration and intelligence is the disease of modern life which poetry inevitably reflects. Nor is there any short-cut back to health. The fracture of imagination which can be seen and felt in the split between heart and head cannot be healed by any simple relapse into the primitive. The perversities of an uncentred intelligence, the malady of an ingrown self-awareness, or the violent incoherence which betrays an inner frustration represent a phase of consciousness which cannot be evaded but only outgrown. Real poetry, however simple or complex its content, is a proof of an integrated response to life in the poet and a test of a like capacity at one remove in the reader.

And who more than poets should be aware of the need of such integration or in the vanguard in labouring for it? For as Blake wrote, 'if it were not for the Poetic or Prophetic character the Philosophical and Experimental would soon be at the ratio of all things, and stand still, unable to do other than repeat the same dull round over again'.

That poets within the realm of their own art have been intensely aware of this need during the last half-century and are aware of it to-day, no one could deny. And fairness demands that in all discussion of the difficulty, often exasperating, of much modern verse, the difficulty of the problem to be solved should be recognized. The problem may perhaps be best approached by way of symbolism, an aspect of poetry with which modern poets have been deeply preoccupied and of which a recent writer has remarked truly enough in reference to eccentric or esoteric symbolism in the poetry of Yeats that 'art is not "liberated from life" by being made unintelligible; and any symbol the interpretation of which is known only to the few initiated is death, not to the despised common life, but to the poetry'.

Yet the problem is more complex than these words convey.

Yeats himself, in the essay which he wrote in 1900 on 'the symbolism of poetry', did not in fact suggest that the symbolical was unintelligible, nor did the illustrations which he gave from Burns, Nash and Shakespeare. At most he argued that 'the form of sincere poetry, unlike the form of the popular poetry, may indeed be sometimes obscure, or ungrammatical, as in some of the best of the *Songs of Innocence and Experience*, but it must have the perfections that escape analysis, the subtleties that have a new meaning every day'. And earlier he spoke of symbolism as 'a return to the way of our fathers, a casting out of descriptions of nature for the sake of nature, of the moral law for the sake of the moral law, a casting out of all anecdotes and of brooding over scientific opinion'.

All true forward movements are also recoveries of something which has been lost or dangerously overlooked. And in its initial impulse at least this was so with the Symbolist Movement which originated in France in 1885 under the leadership of Jean Moréas.

It was a movement against externalities of all kinds—realistic, moral, scientific or picturesque. In intention at least it sought to restore the sovereignty of imagination. The Symbolists claimed to be more truly objective than the Parnassians, who had earlier declared war on a poetry of vague personal emotion. For while the Parnassians, amongst whom Baudelaire himself was at one time numbered, were concerned primarily with objective precision and refinement, the Symbolists to whom Baudelaire really belonged and of whom Verlaine, Rimbaud and above all Mallarmé were disciples, claimed to reconcile the outer and the inner worlds in a new dimension of experience, to think, as Mallarmé strove to do, 'with images rather than ideas, with words rather than sentences'. For the sentence has a logical structure with which evocative words can dispense.

Their claim was seldom, however, wholly valid. What they did achieve was to reassert the value of the personal in aesthetic experience against the abstract impersonality of scientific reason. To the Symbolists, as Mr. Edmund Wilson has written in his *Axël's Castle*, 'all that is perceived in any moment of human experience is relative to the person who perceives it, and to the surroundings, the moment, the mood'.

This emphasis upon the person who imaginatively perceives and not, as with the Naturalists, upon the facts perceived, could develop in a Symbolist of a later generation, Paul Valéry, into an explicit discarding of ordinary intelligibility, as when he wrote that 'there is absolutely no question in poetry of one person's transmitting to another something intelligible that is going on in his mind. It is a question of creating in the latter a state whose expression is precisely and minutely that which communicates it to him'.

Such a statement does not imply, of course, that poetry should be meaningless. Indeed there is an affinity between it and Stendhal's definition of style as being 'to add to a given thought all the circumstances fitted to produce the whole effect that the thought ought to produce'. Valéry claims that poetry should communicate something more essential than thought, though thought is a necessary element in it, that it should express and provoke a particular state of awareness.

The Symbolist Movement was, in fact, as Mr. Bowra has pointed out, essentially mystical, and Mallarmé was its high priest.

The Absolute of aesthetic perfection, which he worshipped and called 'L'absence' because it could never be captured in words or in fact, corresponds to the nameless and ineffable One of which the religious devotee, if he is asked to define it, can only say 'not that, not that'. To communicate a supernatural reality through images drawn from the world of sense but transformed so as to evoke the inward and the invisible was the Symbolist's aim. And because of all arts music comes nearest to expressing the inexpressible and is farthest removed from conscious rationality, he strove to translate thought, as nearly as words allowed, into sound, or to convert it into some other immediate sensation.

It is in this sensationalism that an aesthetic mysticism differs from a religious mysticism. The religious mystic, who experiences a spiritual world which transcends the senses, must also, if he would communicate his experience, convey it by means of images. So far as the world he sees is expressible, it is, in the exact meaning of the word, a transfigured world and can only be revealed through a transfigured language, that is through images which are not merely reflections of the world with which the senses are ordinarily familiar, but which are figures of the more real world which true imagination each moment recreates.

But the vision of the religious mystic is not primarily, still less exclusively, aesthetic. Perfect beauty is for him the form in which perfect charity, humility and truth manifest and cannot be found in separation from these. And so his love of beauty is far less likely than that of the artist to be tainted by a hunger of the senses for mere aesthetic satisfaction.

But aestheticism is equally alien to the imagination of great poets or artists. They, too, have used a truly symbolical language and recreated the world in their vision. They, too, have acted as mediators between an eternal realm and a temporal which they would reconcile. We have only to think of Dante declaring in the final canto of the *Paradiso* how, as he gazed upon the Eternal Light, his purified sight surpassed language as do the images of a dream of glory of which it is possible to record only a single spark; or of Goethe requiring Faust to visit a land of mystery, outside space and time, where reign 'The Mothers', if he would bring Absolute Beauty, personified in Helen, into the common ways of men. Or again Milton, exquisite artist as he was of what the senses love, conceived the characters, landscape and incidents of *Paradise Lost* as but shadows and symbols, 'Archetypes', as Jung would call them, of 'things above the world'.

Admittedly each of these was an epic poet who could turn to mythology to aid his imagination in transfiguring the actual and interrelating the two realms of experience, existence and being. Rationalism in the modern world has largely destroyed the suggestive power of traditional mythologies. And so the poet has had to create his own myth as well as his own symbolical language, as Villiers de L'Isle Adam did in *Axël's Castle* or Kafka has in our own day. Such myths inevitably lack the universality of the myths which were rooted in the imagination of a whole people, even if a single poet originated them.

And the French Symbolists in their efforts to restore the poetic stream, which had been diverted into a shallow materialistic reservoir, to its true spiritual channel inevitably suffered from the strain of fighting a hostile environment. Their imagination could find so little ground in the actual world to rest upon that they were always in danger of becoming, like the Keats whom Moneta reproved, 'a dreaming thing, a fever of thyself'.

Imagination was so beleaguered and outcast in the world in which they lived that, like Axël, they were tempted to dismiss the solicitations of life with the remark: 'Our servants will do that for us.' This divorce of imagination from actuality contained within it the seeds of its own decay. For a healthy imagination mediates between the realms of spirit and of nature, and needs to be faithful to each. But it did reflect an extreme need of the period. Poets are or should be the sensitives of their time. And a time that denies the spirit is one in which inevitably they suffer most, and in which they are driven, if they are to be true to their vocation, to reaffirm the reality of imagination at all costs.

Since the eighties and nineties of the last century the need has become even more acute in a world in which the artist is everywhere tempted, bribed, or compelled to be a propagandist of social creeds or of political programmes based on unscrupulous expediency. The gulf between the values of the artist, who must be concerned first and last with the human soul, and an industrialized society which would sacrifice that soul to mechanical efficiency has yawned wide. To harmonize the two worlds, the inner and the outer, to conquer and redeem the discord and conflict in both has become even more difficult and costly, and the serious poet has tended more and more to be thrown back upon his own spiritual resources in a private world of his own.

It may be, indeed, that for some poets this is necessary work, that, like the extremer religious contemplatives, their task may be to explore the depths and heights of the inner world and maintain communion with it in a time of distracted externality. The imagery which expresses such an inward vision is inevitably esoteric to those who live on the individual and social surface and whose literature is journalism. The more prevalent journalism has become, the more has the serious writer been driven into the fastnesses of his own soul where the popular mind cannot follow him. Yet his original purpose has not necessarily been one of escape into an ivory-tower, though some writers have ended there. If his need has been, in Valéry's words, 'to lead men where they never before have been', to extend the limits of human experience and expression, that has always been the need and the achievement of imagination.

In art, as a Russian poet of our own day, Boris Pasternak, has said, 'the man is silent and the image speaks'. The image is the voice of that true personality, the deep and central ground of being, of which the ego, with its sentiment or its rationality, is but a sundered part. Religion has always laboured to cherish and recreate that integral selfhood. But organized religion itself in modern times has lost much of its power to do so.

The Symbolist poets, therefore, took up the task which the Churches were too faithless to perform. In the materialistic nineteenth century spiritual vision had become so dimmed that art itself, no less than religion, reflected the divided consciousness and its shallow naturalism. It had abandoned its true vocation which was one not of reason, but of revelation. The true poet, like the true mystic, lives by faith, not by reason, though his faith expresses a higher and purer reason. To reveal, not to record or define, to be a seer and a maker of a perceived reality, in which the seeing self and the thing seen become one, was the lost art which the Symbolists were intent on recovering. As Mallarmé wrote, 'to name is to destroy, to suggest is to create', and the world he created or strove to create was so intensely personal that it was impersonal too, with the impersonality not of analytical science, but of a kind of transcendental feeling that reconciled two orders of reality normally opposed.

The Symbolist poets, however, in their struggle to transcend reflective sentiment or merely rationalizing intelligence, tended to lose touch with that centre in the heart which links us with human experience. Unlike the mystic, who aspires to the 'unitive way', they concentrated too exclusively upon the aesthetic faculties and so fell into a one-sideness of their own. By cultivating a certain kind of sensibility and intensely refining it, they not only lived in a world of their own imagining, which every creator must do, but translated into it too little of the content of the actual world. The pursuit of such eclectic refinement can only lead to a spiritual hot-house, to the merely artful or the wilfully recondite.

So great, however, was the influence of the Movement upon English poets at the end of the century that Mr. Arthur Symons could write in his *The Symbolist Movement in Literature* that 'here in this revolt against exteriority, against a materialistic tradition; in this endeavour to disengage the ultimate essence, the soul, of whatever exists and can be realized by the consciousness; in this dutiful waiting upon every symbol by which the soul of things can be made visible; literature, bowed down by so many burdens, may at last attain liberty and its authentic speech'.

Alas! Real liberty was not to be so easily won. But in estimating the preciosities into which the Symbolist Movement to some extent declined it is well to remember how great was the pressure of materialism and externality which it challenged. In theory at least and in the practice of its greatest exponents it reaffirmed the inward value without which the external object is only a thing of use or of passing pleasure. It renewed, too, the relation which has always existed in true poetry between the dream and the fact, the immediate sense of things and the entranced contemplation of them.

For symbolism, as has been said, is necessarily the language of every imaginative writer. And it was the vital functioning of imagination that the Symbolists sought to restore. No Movement, however, could do that. And it was just because it became a Movement that symbolism tended to be pursued as a private end instead of an integral necessity. It became a cult, and Mallarmé's profession of 'an Idealism which (in the same way as in fugues, in sonatas) rejects the "natural" materials, and, as brutal, a direct thought ordering them', became a pretext for cultivating as spiritually suggestive any sensation, however abstruse or perverse.

2

In England, however, in the nineties the cult was largely imitative and superficial. The real revolt against the uncreative came later. It began in the years immediately before the war of 1914 in the group of poets, painters, sculptors and philosophers, of whom T. E. Hulme was the dynamic centre, and who called themselves *Imagists*. It was a temperate and highly disciplined revolt. For Hulme was as anti-mystical as he was anti-romantic and anti-humanist. His classicism, if it can be so called, was one-sided, was Apollonian and on guard against the dangers of Dionysian inspiration. He stressed the finiteness, the limit of man, and in maintaining a clear separation between the human and divine, he did encourage in poetry what he described as its great aim, 'accurate, precise and definite description'.

He thus, as Mr. Herbert Read has said, incited those who acted on his theory, notably Mr. Ezra Pound, to introduce 'a clearer tone into poetic expression'. But valuable as this was and true as Mr. Pound's affirmation may have been, that 'it is better to present one image in a lifetime than to produce voluminous works', the Imagists tended to evade the whole problem of discovering a really creative language by concentrating on a part of it, exact description. And this was implicit in Hulme's arbitrary denial of the infinite and the subjective because they had previously been sentimentally indulged.

Nor, since the Imagists, has any really successful attempt been made to grapple with the problem that the Symbolists did truly raise. The revolt against the external and the commonplace has continued, but in its most notable exponents it has been a predominantly intellectual and highly sophisticated revolt, infected during the years after the first world war with disillusionment or more recently with a conviction that the existing framework of society must be shattered and a new relation between it and the artist spring up before the forms of art can become organic.

There have, indeed, been original attempts to create new forms in art itself prophetic of a new personal and social reality, notably in the creed and practice of Surrealism with its striving to release the energies of the unconscious from the stranglehold of the conscious, or in the group of 'apocalyptic' poets who have laboured to reinvoke the myth to counter the machine. But if the Surrealists have for the most part reduced art to the anarchic utterance of a neurotic confessing to a psycho-analyst, the 'Apocalyptics' have yielded too often to emotional rhetoric. Neither have as yet succeeded in laying the cerebral curse of their time, in bringing together the sundered halves of being which are crying to be reunited.

We see this failure notably exemplified in a modern poet of no school but his own, W. H. Auden, a poet of exceptional virtuosity who has become more and more preoccupied with the need of outgrowing the intellectualism which splits experience into the two worlds of private dream and impersonal fact, of innocence or disgust. 'Can I learn to suffer', he writes in one of his latest poems, 'without saying something ironic or funny on suffering?' The dilemma of the clever modern mind could not be more pathetically or piquantly stated. In his latest poems he borrows for his own uses two already existing mythologies, those of Shakespeare's *Tempest* and of the Christian mystery as it unfolds from Advent to the Flight into Egypt. In so doing he reduces the imaginative depth of both to the agitated complexity of his own uncentred mind.

But he knows what he is doing and his disability. Again and again we find him brought up starkly on the edge of the abyss which opens before the disintegrated soul.

> We are afraid
> Of pain but more afraid of silence; for no nightmare
> Of hostile objects could be as terrible as this Void.
> This is the Abomination. This is the wrath of God.
> Alone, alone, about a dreadful wood
> Of conscious evil runs a lost mankind. . . .

Again and again, too, as if to nerve himself for the plunge into a self-liberating reality which he cannot yet take, he affirms its necessity:

> Believe your pain: praise the scorching rocks
> For their desiccation of your lust,
> Thank the bitter treatment of the tide
> For its dissolution of your pride,
> That the whirlwind may arrange your will
> And the deluge release it to find
> The spring in the desert, the fruitful
> Island in the sea, where flesh and mind
> Are delivered from mistrust.

This is the deeper motive underlying the intellectualism which still agitates brilliantly and mordantly but often trivially the surface of Mr. Auden's verse. It is the star which the three wise men, as he portrays them, follow to discover how to be truthful, living and human. And occasionally it can give to his writing a tenderness in which 'the derisive whistle of the awful schoolboy' ceases to be heard, in which the mind comes home to the heart, or wisdom bridges, however tenuously, the gulf between psychology and poetry.

3

Behind all Movements, then, or creeds or theories or social frustrations lies this problem of the artist himself. The modern poet with a few notable exceptions, has failed to create a symbolism which is profound and yet not obscure because he has failed to reach that level in himself at which the complexities of a conscious intelligence are redeemed in a new simplicity. The demands of the complex and the simple are equally imperative. Neither can be denied without loss of reality. Yet although there is a sense in which all real poetry unveils its deepest meaning only to the initiated, Keats's maxim remains true that unless poetry come as naturally, meaning organically, as leaves to the tree, and is as appreciable to any sensitive reader as such, it had better not come at all.

Poetry is natural speech in the highest sense. It only seems unnatural because we have never developed the capacity to be natural and so to speak naturally in that pure creative sense. Consequently its naturalness is inevitably and unforgettably strange to us. But it is not obscure or inscrutable without an elaborate commentary. An enjoyment of Milton's poetry may be the highest reward of scholarship, but it can be enjoyed without such scholarship. Blake's *Songs of Innocence and Experience* may be and are full of the veiled mystical and metaphysical meaning which Mr. Foster Damon and other learned researchers have brought to light. But they sing themselves into the heart and mind of a child.

The sure sign of a true symbolism would seem to be that it carries within it layer upon layer of meaning, speaking at different levels of understanding to all, withholding itself from none but those who have no ears to hear. That is why we can return again and again to great poetry and measure our progress in experience by the deeper and subtler meaning we find in its essential simplicity.

But when in any poet or school of poets we find the complexity on the surface, barring our approach to inner depths and proclaiming its own clever or fantastic ingenuity, we may be sure that the secret of wholeness, in which the ordinary life of men is never despised but rather illuminated, has been lost. A true symbol is a sign of an inward and a spiritual grace. But those who flaunt their signs, like banners embroidered with strange devices, have little to signify.

For a too-conscious pursuit of originality is itself fatal to the end desired. Carried to its extreme it demands the creation of an entirely new vocabulary and syntax, as in James Joyce's later work. Words are symbols and if through dull usage they have lost their symbolic power, it is due to the mental abstraction which has drained vitality out of them. It is not necessary for all poetry to be intensely keyed or to express the high passion of spiritual contemplation, or there would be no place for fine descriptive or reflective verse, for the poetry of lyrical sentiment or of sensuous delight. There are many degrees of experience and each can have its own relative integrity, which will be reflected in the form and texture of the verse, even if its imagery is not highly metaphorical or mythopoeic. Keats's axiom that poetry should surprise by a fine excess, and not by singularity, and that it should strike the reader as a wording of his own highest thoughts, and appear almost a remembrance is the true reproof to all false strain.

But because the modern poet lives in a world of strain in which imagination, far from rising, progressing and setting like a sun over a world in tolerable health, has to pierce through an enveloping murk of mechanical abstraction and destruction before it can enlighten, he can hardly avoid the singular and the eccentric. In such a world and amid such stresses of heart and mind, the challenge of contemporary reality is inescapable. A world crying out for a radical creative redemption inevitably demands poets who respond to its need. A conflict has to be resolved, a dark night traversed. For the true poet suffers the agonies of humanity no less sensitively than he shares its seasons of calm weather or of expansive energy.

We may hope humanity will, in time, outgrow its present discord and rebuild its social life on firmer foundations. But meantime, the culture of the past, so far as it survives, has no roots in the daily life of people. The poet's task is to find and feed more roots in himself, to be a forerunner of unity and harmony, and to build a true bridge between the future and the real culture of the past. The bridge between the present and the past has been broken, and consequently mankind is careering without direction along a way that violates the sanctity of life more and more. All true culture is rooted in a reverence for life and in a love and a wisdom that cannot exploit it.

It is this culture that the modern poet is called to recover in himself and in his art, and so reveal the way by which life itself may again become an art and flower anew, not only in men's souls, but in their social relationships and practices. He cannot achieve this by striving to restore the modes of other centuries which possessed a true culture. It is the spirit which animates all real culture, however various its manners, which has to be reborn. The spirit can be safely left to dictate its own new form. But to renew that spirit even in a single poem demands a real rebirth in the contemporary poet. Not for him can be pleasant exercises in urbane reflection or moral musings or even such heart-cries of romantic feeling as were authentic in poets of other and kinder times, to whom the miseries of the world were not yet known as miseries that would not let them rest.

Romantic love can speak authentically in a contemporary poet, as can a meditative philosophy, but only if they speak with a new voice, pure of the taint of self-indulgence, and through a consciousness that has suffered the pain of things, yet risen through pain to reaffirm the true victory over pain.

The awareness of this necessity, as of the deep division into which life had fallen, first clearly showed itself in the poets of the Romantic movement. Their effort to speak a new language was not a mere matter of poetic diction, as the poetry of Blake and Wordsworth and Coleridge attests. The diction could only be revitalized by an inward change, a determination to replant the tree of poetry in the simple human depths from which it had sprung and from which a creative imagination must draw its sap.

The impulse failed in their successors. Indeed Mr. T. S. Eliot has even suggested that since the seventeenth century, when poets 'possessed a mechanism of sensibility, which could devour any kind of experience', there has been 'a dissociation of sensibility from which we have never recovered'. This dissociation became perhaps most apparent in the poets of the mid-Victorian age, in the very violence with which Browning fought against it and the lyrical moralizing which Tennyson indulged. And it gave a false emphasis to Arnold's definition of poetry as 'a criticism of life', 'mainly on the side of morality', as it gave an imaginative poverty to the actual tone and texture of much of Arnold's own poetry.

The truest poetry is only a criticism of life in the sense that it is a re-creation of life and of the world from what they appear to the practical, self-interested consciousness, or, as Coleridge called it, to the primary imagination. It is this world, which, in Coleridge's phrase, the secondary imagination, which is the symbolizing imagination, 'dissolves, diffuses, dissipates in order to re-create'.

A great modern poet, Rilke, has also stressed again and again this need of the imagination to re-create, to transform. Indeed, it was the very heart of his endeavour. 'All these appearances and things', he wrote, 'ought to be comprehended by us in a most fervent understanding and transformed. Transformed? Yes, for our task is to stamp this provisional, perishing earth into ourselves so deeply, so painfully and passionately, that its being may rise again, "invisibly", in us.'

To seek among visible things, as Rilke put it elsewhere, 'equivalents for the vision within', or, more simply, 'to look at each thing properly and ask it about the beauty it possesses', is the impulse out of which a true symbolism grows. And that such an impulse involves a surrender of the acquisitive will, modern psychologists like Ribot, in his 'Essai sur l'Imagination créatrice', have also testified.

In their revolt against moral preoccupations or reflective opinion in verse the Symbolists rightly rejected unimaginative states of mind. And their more intellectual successors have often realized the necessity of restoring to poetry its contact with the ordinary life of man even when they have proved their incapacity in practice to do so.

But success in this can never come by conscious pursuit of the ordinary as a reaction from the intellectually complex. The unity with the outward common life, seen in all its essential uncommonness, can only spring from an achieved unity within, in which consciousness regains its unconscious depths, its 'unknown modes of being', and sorts out, as reason alone never can,

> the dark mysteries of human souls
> To clear conceiving.

For the true poet, words are transformed because his vision transforms the world. They may be quite ordinary words he uses, just as the world is ordinary until it is really seen. But both become extraordinary in his vision. This vision has, of course, different degrees of intensity. And so has his language. All poetry is in some degree symbolical because its language conveys the poet's imagination of objects. But between descriptive poetry that informs us of sensuous details and unifies them by simile and rhythm, and the metaphorical poetry which penetrates beyond comparison and equivalence until objects cease altogether to stand over against each other and, as Wordsworth said, 'unite and coalesce', there is a difference only in the degree of creative tension achieved.

In Shakespeare pre-eminently metaphor has become what Mr. Middleton Murry has called 'a mode of apprehension'. The transforming process, the taking up of ordinary life into the vision of the imagination is complete. A new world is created out of the actual and it speaks its own language, the figurative speech in which the actual becomes the real.

So to re-create the world is the task which lies now as ever before the poet. And if he can pay the inner price, without which such a task can never be fulfilled, he will create a symbolism which opens the doors of vision instead of baffling the ordinary mind. He will do more. He will inspire others who are working in a more concrete and resistant medium to re-create the world too.

II

GERARD HOPKINS: A CENTENARY TRIBUTE

THE peculiar circumstances under which the star of Gerard Hopkins's genius was hid from the general eye of poetry-seekers for nearly thirty years after his death at the age of forty-five make it hard to credit that July 28th, 1944, marks the centenary of his birth. A poet who revitalizes the medium of his art as he did may well seem to belong to the present because the present treads most close upon the future and an inspired originator breaks through to the future and at the same time strikes back to the fresh springs of genius in the past. Hopkins did both. In this sense he was in the forefront of poetry's unfolding and broke clean through the decorous Victorian ranks.

Yet even if his poetry had been published thirty years earlier, it is doubtful whether it would have found acceptance sooner or much influenced the course of poetry meanwhile. Certainly he extended the resources of the English language in rhythm and texture, a rare gift indeed to practising poets, but a rare test too. The idea that our modern psychological conflicts make us sufficiently akin with him to appropriate his technique is ingenuous. The extreme tension which Hopkins endured and from which he wrung creative expression of so fine and explosive a quality was on a level to which only genius and sainthood dare aspire. His poetry cannot be separated from the spiritual vocation which he so clear-sightedly embraced. As Mr. F. R. Leavis has observed in an essay devoted to an appreciation of his language: 'Hopkins's genius was as much a matter of rare character, intelligence and sincerity as of technical skill; indeed, in his great poetry the distinction disappears; the technical triumph is a triumph of spirit.'

Few poets, in fact, have lived so intensely in the spirit as Hopkins. His entry into the Order of Jesus at the age of twenty-four inevitably raised problems and caused difficulties which poets have not usually to face. But it is possible to exaggerate the effect upon him of the Jesuit training and practice, and useless to deplore on aesthetic grounds the step he took. He was a man destined by nature for extreme asceticism of one kind or another. And despite all the hindrances to poetic expression which his vocation imposed and his own excessive scruples enlarged, he chose what his genius needed.

The choice may have limited his genius, may even have starved it of common human experience which it needed as ballast to its own skyward straining and thrown him too nakedly upon the intricacies of melody and pattern or what he called 'inscape' in poetry. Yet this was so powerful a bent in him that in any circumstances it could hardly have been other than it was. Being so essentially lyrical and devotional by nature he chose a path most calculated perhaps to intensify his vocation in verse as in religion.

Doubtless in his later years, as his letters to Dixon show, he felt with one part of his nature the want of publication, the discouragement of a spirit given in poetry, but not received by his contemporaries. Probably, however, in any event this discouragement would have been his. He was as alien to the idiom of his time as to its spiritual lethargy. And his recoil from tentative efforts by Dixon or Bridges to make his verse known sprang at bottom from an innate conviction that 'there is more peace and it is the holier lot to be unknown than to be known', a doctrine that may well sound strange in modern ears.

But it was more than doctrine. It was the confession of one who all his life sought both peace and perfection, as only a soul stretched between extremes and too absolute for any easing compromise can seek them. The two stanzas which Bridges printed under the title *Heaven-Haven* ended with the lines:

> And I have asked to be
> Where no storms come,
> Where the green swell is in the havens dumb,
> And out of the swing of the sea.

But in its original form, as extracted from Hopkins's early diaries, the poem continued thus:

> I must hunt down the prize
> Where my heart lists.
> Must see the eagle's bulk, render'd in mists,
> Hang of a treble size.
>
> Must see the green seas roll
> Where waters set
> Towards those wastes where the ice-blocks tilt and fret
> Not so far from the pole.

He called the poem *Rest*. But for so intrepid a spirit there was no rest except at the peak of sustained endeavour and at the unattainably ideal pole of being. He could not rest even in the mysteries of the religion to which he assented in mind and heart.

To him the very essence of such mystery was that it contained in a sort of counter-poise the explicable and the inexplicable, leaving some men, as he wrote to Bridges about 'the dogma of the Trinity',

> all their lives balancing whether they have three heavenly friends or one — not that they have any doubt on the subject, but that their knowledge leaves their minds swinging; poised, but on the quiver. And this might be the ecstasy of interest, one would think.

'Poised, but on the quiver' — such was his habitual state, treading a tight-rope between immensities of height and depth and intensely conscious at times of his precarious stance.

> O the mind, mind has mountains; cliffs of fall
> Frightful, sheer, no-man-fathomed. Hold them cheap
> May who ne'er hung there.

Those who have blamed the Jesuit discipline for the tormenting depression and sense of aridity of his last years had as well blamed Hopkins himself. Doubtless physical causes contributed, the uncongenial atmosphere of Dublin, the wearying monotony of examination work on which he so anxiously spent himself. But it is all of a piece with his character. A life lived on the stretch was almost bound to end on the rack. Ten years earlier he had cried:

> When will you ever, Peace, wild wooddove, shy wings shut,
> Your round me roaming end, and under be my boughs?
> When, when, Peace, will you, Peace? I'll not play hypocrite
> To own my heart: I yield you do come sometimes; but
> That piecemeal peace is poor peace. What pure peace allows
> Alarms of wars, the daunting wars, the death of it?

The peace of the true mystic was never within his hold. His was an apprehensive mind, which, outside the realm of sight and touch and even sometimes within it, strove to force experience into too sharp a focus. He lived too alertly in the mind and strove too avidly after perfection in life and art to let the unconscious unfold its mystery within him.

Yet his lack of inward ease was the very condition of his unmatched awareness of the natural world, if also of the over-stress which is felt at times in the violent twists and turns of his idiom. His problem was always how to subdue sufficiently the inordinate uprising of his spirit, the pride and fire of his unique individuality. This was the need which, after eight years of self-suppressing silence, he voiced with such shattering force in the poem in which he found himself as a poet:

> I did say yes
> O at lightning and lashed rod;
> Thou heardst me truer than tongue confess
> Thy terror, O Christ, O God;
> Thou knowest the walls, altar and hour and night:
> The swoon of a heart that the sweep and the hurl of thee trod
> Hard down with a horror of height:
> And the midriff astrain with leaning of laced with fire of stress.

Only one whose spirit could soar so high could feel so vividly the horror of height, of a spiritual void. In this 'The Windhover', one of his greatest poems, is at once a superb rendering of the flight of a bird and an allegory of his own being, ecstatically caught upwards in 'the roll, the rise, the carol, the creation', but adoring the Power that bent and bowed him down to a finer, richer purpose.

> Brute beauty and valour and act, oh air, pride, plume, here
> Buckle! AND the fire that breaks from thee then, a billion
> Times told lovelier, more dangerous, O my chevalier!

This counter-poise of opposites is the very principle of his poetry as of his being. It is reduced to its starkest elemental and moral terms in *Spelt from Sibyl's Leaves,* and in the last tragic sonnets the upward rise of his spirit has been almost quelled. But in the poems which lay between them and *The Wreck of the Deutschland* how tinglingly the balance of earth-awareness and heavenward flight was sustained!

All Hopkins's poetry is breath-taking proof of the trembling susceptibility of his senses. But he had, also, the finest chastity of mind and heart. Hence his fear of what was so 'dearly and dangerously sweet' to him and even of exercising the art in which his sense of physical intimacy with Nature was so ecstatically heightened. Dixon might argue that God surely meant him to use the talent which he had given him. But in the pleasure which he derived from it Hopkins feared lest he was not using it purely for God, lest he was giving back beauty to 'beauty's self and beauty's giver' with some taint of false personal relish.

Such scruples may have been excessive, but they have a place in an artist's conscience as well as a saint's. As a saint Hopkins sought to consecrate the beauty of Nature in Christ 'in whom all that beauty comes home'. Only so dare he love and praise her as he must. Opinions will differ as to the degree of his success in doing so. In certain poems at least the Christian reference may seem little more than a gloss upon an instinctive rapture. But how pure the rapture was, even when most earth-loving, as in the octet of the sonnet, *Spring*:

Nothing is so beautiful as spring —
  When weeds, in wheels, shoot long and lovely and lush;
  Thrush's eggs look little low heavens, and thrush
Through the echoing timber does so rinse and wring
The ear it strikes like lightnings to hear him sing;
  The glassy peartree leaves and blooms, they brush
  The descending blue; that blue is all in a rush
With richness; the racing lambs too have fair their fling.

Certainly Hopkins's poetry is a unique example of sensibility bridled by a finely masculine mind and thereby brought to a most rare focus. But between the two extremes of God and primal Nature, the two poles of spirit and sense that magnetized his being, stood Man. And in his later poems it was to man that he was increasingly drawn, to Felix Randal the farrier and Harry Ploughman, and those young creatures, the Bugler boy or the Brothers, whose 'chastity in man sex fine' he loved as he loved in Nature

A strain of the Earth's sweet being in the beginning
In Eden garden.

It would be interesting, were there space, to contrast the quality of this love of his with Whitman's, with whom he acknowledged his affinity but only as 'extremes meet'. In the poetry in which he expressed it the poet and the priest combined more happily than elsewhere. But here, too, the tension was not relaxed. There was no 'loafing' in his love of youth and young manhood. The enraptured sense he had of 'innocent mind and Mayday in girl and boy' and of the 'handsome heart' dearer than handsome face heightened his anxiety lest time and sin should mar them and natural beauty fall from grace.

His dread of spiritual disaster went beyond those he immediately loved. Like Carlyle, whose principles he hated but whose genius he admired, he was shocked and saddened by Victorian industrialism. He was proud to be an Englishman, and the degradation of his countrymen wounded him to the quick. Writing to Dixon of his Liverpool and Glasgow experience he declared his 'truly crushing conviction' not only of the misery of the poor in general, but 'of the hollowness of this century's civilization'. It issued in his poetry as a cry of lamentation and dread at the inveteracy of the power of evil in the 'dear and dogged man' he loved.

Yet as the sestet of the sonnet *God's Grandeur* proclaimed, infinitely more real to him than all the evil of the world was the purity of the realm of spirit, whether it manifested as 'the dearest freshness deep down things' or as 'the Holy Ghost' brooding over the bent world 'with warm breast and with ah! bright wings'.

Of this realm he was supremely the poet, and no English poet has perhaps more radiantly found the world of spirit in the world of Nature than he. His technical originality would need an article to itself. Yet it is inseparable from what he so intensely was. Few poets have controlled the spontaneity which possessed them more subtly. His achievement in bringing poetry closer to living speech while creating and maintaining significant design went altogether beyond his attempts to explain it in terms of prosody. But he knew the dangers of such novelty and boldness as his and confessed that even for those who read, as he insisted they should, with their ears as well as their eyes, his style was at times excessively singular. 'It is the vice of distinctiveness to become queer. This vice I cannot have escaped.'

Nor did he. The compression or ellipsis native to his darting spirit puts at times an undue strain on the reader panting at his heels; or the music is too consciously and anxiously contrived. Yet these are but the occasional defects of inimitable qualities. If there is overstrain in Hopkins it is due to an access of spirit which the poor flesh could hardly contain. He has been compared in the quality of his genius with such different poets as Milton, Donne and Shakespeare. But perhaps the best comparison is his own 'Caged Skylark':

As a dare-gale skylark scanted in a dull cage
  Man's mounting spirit in his bone-house, mean house, dwells —

And the freedom of the two realms of earth and heaven for which he so unsparingly strove in life and song is crystallized in the last lines of the poem:

> Man's spirit will be flesh-bound when found at best,
> But uncumbered: meadow-down is not distressed
> For a rainbow footing it nor he for his bónes rísen.

But for him that resurrection and reconcilement was an experience too intoxicating, too heavenly for the taut senses to bear, beyond the quivering moment, here on earth. His peace was 'piecemeal' to the end.

III

THE CONFLICT OF PRIEST AND POET IN HOPKINS

THE degree to which a poet must be of his time is hard to measure in the person of Hopkins. The posthumous fame which he has won since Bridges in 1918 bid his spirit

> Go forth: amidst our chaffinch flock display
> Thy plumage of far wonder and heavenward flight!

led at first to a curious and rather complacent assumption that he was a 'modern' poet born, unfortunately for himself, out of due time, but at last earning the appreciation of his peers. Even Bridges was reproved for not being modern enough to value his technical originality at its true worth and for being so laggard in publishing his verse. Of late, however, opinion has swung rather the other way and critics, discomfited by convictions expressed in Hopkins's letters which sound oddly old-fashioned in the contemporary ear, have begun reminding us that he was a Victorian. One such passage is worth quoting because it reveals the context of values within which his poetry flowered.

> I quite understand [he wrote to Bridges] what you mean about gentlemen and 'damfools'; it is a very striking thing and I could say much on the subject. I shall not say that much, but I say this: if a gentleman feels that to be what we call a gentleman is a thing essentially higher than without being a gentleman to be ever so great an artist or thinker or if, to put it another way, an artist or thinker feels that were he to become in those ways ever so great he wd. still essentially be lower than a gentleman that was no artist and no thinker — and yet to be a gentleman is but on the brim of morals and rather a thing of manners than of morals properly — then how much more must art and philosophy and manners and breeding and everything else in the world be below the least degree of true virtue.

Only a Victorian, perhaps, could still put a gentleman so high in the scale of human achievement and Hopkins was careful to add that the quality of a gentleman was 'so very fine a thing that it seems to me one should not at all be hasty in concluding that one possesses it'. Newman, in his famous definition of a gentleman, was obviously of the same mind.

The important thing, however, was that while Hopkins was of his time and class in the terms in which he measured merit, he gave to these terms, like all true poets, a significance which is true in any age. In Hopkins the timeless quality was his, both as a poet and a religious. Outwardly, as a priest-poet, he strove to bridge the gulf between poetry and religion which had gone on deepening since the Renaissance. Yet it remained in the depths of his own nature and as reflected in the conflict between his poetic impulse and the self-denying austerities to which he submitted as a Jesuit. No one can measure the extent to which that conflict impoverished or enriched his poetry, though the last sonnets reveal its anguish, or such a cry of impotence as is found in a letter of January 12th, 1886: 'All impulse fails me: I can give myself no sufficient reason for going on. Nothing comes: I am a eunuch — but it is for the kingdom of heaven's sake.'

In the end it may have seemed so. Even in the years of his richest production we have a sense of a poet driving himself too hard, of an almost unbearable excitement, superbly mastered. But it was not his religious devotion in itself that was at fault, still less that 'chastity of mind' of which he wrote that it 'seems to lie at the very heart and be the parent of all other good, the seeing at once what is best, the holding to that, and the not allowing anything else whatever to be even heard pleading to the contrary'. He may have practised his ideal too rigorously. But his lesson to modern poets consists as much in the purity of his self-dedication as in his technical originality.

'So few people', he complained once, 'have style, except individual style or manner.' The one he earned; with the other he was lavishly endowed. Yet some of his most startling innovations, as Dr. Gardner has so industriously shown,[1] were rooted in the

[1] W. H. Gardner: *Gerard Manley Hopkins (1844-1889)*.

past. Even his 'sprung rhythm' existed not only in Welsh poetry and in Langland and Skelton, but in Shakespeare and Milton. His imagery, diction and syntax, too, had close affinities with Chaucer and Spenser and above all with the 'metaphysical' poets.

There could, however, be no better proof that real style is inimitable than the verse of those who have tried to play the sedulous ape to Hopkins, and who have only succeeded in reflecting his mannerisms. This is not to say that his verbal and metrical originality has not influenced in less obvious ways the verse of the last twenty years. It undoubtedly has and its influence is likely to grow. Yet the revolt against the prosody in common use in English verse for three centuries had already begun before Hopkins's poetry was published in 1918. His example undoubtedly strengthened this revolt, but it is well to remember that in the whole structure of his thought and imagery Hopkins belonged to another age, and that his adoption into ours, through an accident of long delayed publication, is misleading.

Equally misleading has been the undue concentration on the technical side of his verse. The innovations he introduced into metre, Mr. Herbert Read has suggested, have prevented more than anything else the appreciation of his poetry. Certainly they have tended to encourage the idea that his poetry belonged to one compartment of the man walled off from that in which he worked and prayed as a Jesuit priest. This the poetry itself refutes.

But the idea that the poet could cease to be the priest in his poetic activities was congenial to a generation which tended to assume either that poetry might be a substitute for religion or that they must necessarily be at loggerheads. Bridges's prime concern with his friend's metrical audacities and lack of interest in, if not actual antipathy to, the spiritual core of his life began the log rolling in this direction. And although the publication of Hopkins's letters and of his note-books and papers have done much to counter such a view, Dr. Pick was the first to show in his book[1] a real understanding of the unity of poet, priest and Jesuit in Hopkins. As a Catholic, Dr. Pick may have tended at times to

[1] JOHN PICK: *Gerard Manley Hopkins, Priest and Poet.*

affirm this unity too confidently. But such affirmation uncovers more meaning than the secular assumption of disabling discord.

The first and last impression of Hopkins's verse is one of intense originality. No poet, perhaps, has ever had a sharper sense of the unique, of things 'counter, original, spare, strange'. His poems were wrought out of this stabbing awareness, and he was fully conscious of it, as a passage which Dr. Pick quotes from his commentary on the Spiritual Exercises of St. Ignatius sufficiently declares. He had opened his commentary (Dr. Pick writes) with a consideration which he had long felt: the sharp individuality or 'self-bent' which he found in all things, the beautiful uniqueness of the inscapes about him. He proceeded to express in a dozen different ways the distinctiveness of self; and human nature he found 'more highly pitched, selved, and distinctive than anything in the world'. And he concluded:

> Nothing else in nature comes near this unspeakable stress of pitch, distinctiveness, and selving, this selfbeing of my own. Nothing explains it or resembles it, except so far as this, that other men to themselves have the same feeling . . . searching nature I taste *self* but at one tankard, that of my own being.

'This unspeakable stress of pitch' — the phrase epitomizes the quality of Hopkins's poetry. It epitomizes, too, his aim as a religious. The pattern of perfection which he set before himself as a Jesuit throbbed with the same unspeakable stress. Like St. Thomas he maintained that each thing striving after its own perfection strives to attain the likeness of the divine. As a religious he strove to attain this likeness in himself. As a poet he strove equally to re-create nature in the image and glory of God, and as such in its divine uniqueness which the clouded vision of sinful man has lost.

His poetry, therefore, cannot be dissociated from his religious quest without impoverishing its meaning, even if we admit that the way he uses the English language must be a first consideration. His poems, in Dr. Pick's words, are 'really love poems'. They tell 'the story of the relationship of his soul to God'.

In a general way this would be granted by the least perceptive or most secularly prejudiced reader. But Dr. Pick is no generalizer. He founds his claim on the Spiritual Exercises which, as a Jesuit, Hopkins studied, meditated and practised for twenty-one years, which became a part of his life and attitude, and gave direction to all he experienced, thought and wrote. His poems, Dr. Pick insists, were moulded and shaped by his personal practice of these Exercises. 'They influenced his most exuberant and joyous poems; they were part of his sufferings and desolation.'

The claim may seem excessive to those who regard the discipline of poetry as sufficient in itself. Such discipline may, indeed, be sufficient, if there be a deep devotion to reality behind it. But this devotion and dedication were in Hopkins governed by his Jesuit training. In the popular mind such training is supposed to deny or cripple the play of the poetic impulse. Hopkins himself, by destroying, when he joined the Society, all the verse he had written may have fostered this assumption. That, however, was only part of an initial act of self-dedication to the religious life. Though the problem of satisfying the impulses of his genius as a poet within the framework of his Order was often difficult, the prime difficulty lay in his own high scruples. The Order, if it severely limited the range of his poetry, greatly intensified it. In this intensification the Spiritual Exercises, acting upon a nature so tensely poised in itself between the sensuous and ideal, played a principal part.

In giving, therefore, a succinct account of these exercises, and of their purposes and meaning, Dr. Pick has provided something of real value to the understanding of the perfection which Hopkins sought both as a poet and as a man, though his claim that without knowing something of them we can hardly know the priest-poet is questionable.

The most valuable light they throw is upon the direction given by them to his temperament at its most sensitive point of tension. From his youth upwards Hopkins was haunted by a fear that his attachment to beauty was inordinate. In his first year at Oxford he was drawn momentarily towards the aestheticism which had begun as a counter-movement to the growing rationalism. Only momentarily however. He knew beauty too vividly upon his senses and had too chaste a mind 'at the tip of the senses', to borrow Mr. Eliot's phrase, to find reality in aestheticism. But the problem of integrating his craving for beauty in a spiritual vision which at once included and transcended the physical was to test him all his life.

It is arguable that the extreme religious vocation which he embraced exacerbated this conflict by enforcing too strict an asceticism upon the extreme sensuous awareness which is a true poet's birthright, until in the end it killed 'the roll, the rise, the carol, the creation'.

Yet it was before he became a Jesuit that he inclined to deny the natural world and all the shape, texture and colour of it to which he was so ardently susceptible. It was in an Oxford poem, *The Habit of Perfection*, that he wrote,

> Be shellèd, eyes, with double dark
> And find the uncreated light:
> This ruck and reel which you remark
> Coils, keeps, and teases simple sight.

Or in another poem of the same period, after acknowledging 'the glories of the earth', he lamented,

> Yet like a lighted empty hall
> Where stands no host at door or hearth
> Vacant creation's lamps appal.

Upon this Dr. Pick comments:

> Such an attitude had very naturally resulted in a pseudo-mysticism or pseudo-asceticism in which the young Hopkins tried to cast off his body, to live only in the spirit. This results in that puritanism which is really manichean in its implications. Now whether the young Hopkins was indulging in this heretical view of man or whether he was starting on the purgative path of a true asceticism, which for a time severely disciplines the senses, so that they may be purified and fully realized, is really unimportant. The important thing is that he did advance to a new vision of the world and of man in which he saw 'God in all things and all things in God', and

in which the physical universe became 'word, expression, news of God'.

There is no reason of course, to assume that Hopkins would never have advanced to this new vision if he had not entered the Society of Jesus. The need to do so was inherent in the intense contraries of his nature. And however far he advanced, the tension always remained and he saw ever more painfully the conflict between the divine and the earthly in himself and in the world, a conflict only to be resolved, as religion taught him, by divine grace.

That there were times when he almost despaired of such grace and when his sense of the pain of a divided universe was stronger than his intuition of a power that unified it, is apparent in his poems, above all perhaps in the last sonnets, wrung from him in a time of spiritual desolation, or in the stark vision of fell opposites confronting under the night in *Spelt from Sibyl's Leaves*:

> Heart, you round me right
> With: Óur évening is over us; óur night|whélms, whélms, ánd will end us.
> Only the beak-leaved boughs dragonish|damask the tool-smooth bleak light; black,
> Ever so black on it. Óur tale, O óur oracle! Lét life, wáned, ah lét life wind
> Off hér once skéined stained véined variéty|upon, áll on twó spools; párt, pen, páck
> Now her áll in twó flocks, twó folds — black, white;| right, wrong; reckon but, reck but, mind
> But thése two; wáre of a wórld where bút these|twó tell, each off the óther; of a rack
> Where, selfwrung, selfstrung, sheathe- and shelterless,| thóughts agáinst thoughts ín groans grínd.

If we needed a proof that Hopkins, by becoming a Jesuit, did not practise an asceticism injurious to his art as a poet, we have it, Dr. Pick argues, in the quality of the poetry which followed those seven years of dedicated silence, above all in *The Wreck of the Deutschland*, the poem in which he broke into utterance with a spiritual power, reverberating in every line and word, gathered in those years of inner concentration.

But was the preliminary detachment from the things of sense, which his training as a Jesuit imposed, so altogether beneficial to him as a poet, even if it was only, as Dr. Pick writes, 'a negative aspect of a very positive thing', the purifying of the senses as organs of experience? The paradox of detachment and attachment implicit in this hard task must always be particularly difficult for the artist. And Hopkins strove to maintain it at the highest pitch. In religious language he strove to see all things and all men in Christ. Blake called it seeing them in the divine imagination. For both of them Christ played 'in ten thousand places'.

In this the goal of poetry and religion are one, whether it is named an imaginative or a sacramental view of nature. And for both the unity sought is one that contains the true tension of opposites. At times the anguish and ecstasy of this tension in Hopkins is so extreme as to be almost morbid. Certainly he never ceased to feel the danger of the mortal beauty which ravished him, and the need of its continual redemption by the eternal. 'To what serves mortal beauty', he wrote,

— dangerous; does set danc-
ing blood — the O-seal-that-so| feature, flung prouder form
Than Purcell tune lets tread to?| See: it does this: keeps warm
Men's wits to the things that are . . .

But it does more than this. It is 'heaven's sweet gift' to earth, whose beauty is completed in grace.

What do then? how meet beauty?|Merely meet it; own,
Home at heart, heaven's sweet gift;|then leave, let that alone.
Yea, wish that though, wish all,|God's better beauty, grace.

Hopkins, it would seem, never for long succeeded in 'owning, home at heart, heaven's sweet gift', or in letting that alone. And it is at least questionable whether the Jesuit discipline helped him quite so admirably as Dr. Pick claims, towards a realization of 'God in all things and all things in God'.

When Newman congratulated him on entering the Society of Jesus, he wrote, 'Don't call "the Jesuit discipline" hard; it will bring you to heaven.' But what Hopkins needed above all was to reconcile heaven and earth, to redeem the contraries in his being.

The austere Jesuit discipline may not have been the best means to this end. It may well, through the too-exclusive concentration on the spiritual world which it encouraged, have tightened up a tension, which needed easing. The vital human impulses in Hopkins were thus too much pent up and straitened and when he so rarely released them in poetry, they burst out with the shattering force of an explosion, notably in *The Wreck of the Deutschland*, though the explosion was under masterly control.

Creative imagination in its fullest and finest range is not explosive, is not even a controlled explosion. It is a marriage of opposites. And this is equally true whether it manifests in a saint or a poet. Christianity, in its fear of lapsing into a featureless monism, an absorption of individuality in the One, tends always to overstress the duality of experience and the gulf between man and God. The Christian, therefore, hardly dares admit that he is at peace with God and with himself, since to do so would be to suggest that he was sinless, and not, as he is even at his best, a sinner in need of God's unfathomable love and forgiveness.

But the mystics of all faiths, while acknowledging this, have in that acknowledgment found peace with God and with themselves. Indeed Eckhart could declare that 'whoso does not attain to being one with God in spirit is not a really spiritual man'. And to be one with God in spirit is also to be in harmony with God's nature, which includes the natural world redeemed by imaginative vision and no longer dreaded or wrongly desired through selfish attachment.

Hopkins was not a mystic. He was rather a noble scholastic, in whom pride of intellect and intense physical sensibility strove for a concordat under the unrelaxed control of a lofty spiritual will. The Jesuit discipline confirmed and fixed this strained complex in his being. Whether a less hard discipline or a richer or at least wider human experience would have released him into a deeper unity, it is impossible to say as it is useless to conjecture. He was of those who are compelled to take the Kingdom of Beauty as of Heaven by violence, because there was division in his soul.

In an undergraduate essay on the subject of 'Health and Decay in Art', he wrote:

> Perfection is dangerous because it is deceptive. Art slips back while bearing, in its distribution of tone, or harmony, the look of high civilization, towards barbarism. Recovery must be by a breaking up, a violence.

Never perhaps was that more true than in Hopkins's lifetime when Victorian art and life, despite a show of order and prosperity, were already slipping back. Hopkins, as his letters show, was vividly conscious of this, and it was one of the causes of the extreme tension under which he lived, but not the primary one.

That was in himself, in the conflict which no Spiritual Exercises could resolve, between the twin impulses of self-expression and of self-effacement of which poetry encouraged the one and religion evoked the other. Throughout his adult life, therefore, he had to maintain a precarious poise between two vocations, each of them spiritually intense. Others have reconciled them without self-torment, but it was not in his nature to do so. And those readers who complain that the stress of his verse is over-great, or at least too continuously pitched at an extreme, have some reason for their complaint.

A too sharp focus can be as much a defect in art as vagueness, and there are times when it is not so much the indolence of Hopkins's reader as a lack of imaginative contemplation in the poet which provokes the feeling that he is overstraining the language and the medium of his expression.

There was an element of ecstatic avidity, of which he himself was uneasily aware, in the stress of an emotion, that, as Mr. Charles Williams has written, 'seems to utter all its words in one'. The spring of his genius was too tightly coiled. But this was a defect, if defect it was, of supreme qualities. From it sprang a poetry as ecstatically articulated, as finely sensed and noble-minded, within its own limits, as any in our English tongue.

IV

THE DREAMING MIND

'I HAVE dreamed in my life', says Cathie in *Wuthering Heights*, 'dreams that have stayed with me ever after, and changed my ideas; they have gone through and through me like wine through water, and altered the colour of my mind.' That, surely, comments Mr. de la Mare, 'is the very voice of Emily Brontë herself'. And, he adds, 'with due qualification, this has been my experience also'.

His poetry is sufficient testimony of that. For no modern poet has hovered so hauntingly between the worlds of dream and fact or reconciled them so magically. The regret that has so often blended with the magic is itself proof of the region where his imagination is most at home. No one, indeed, could be better qualified than he to introduce us to the realm of dreams and familiarize us with its atmosphere. In this delightful book[1] he performs that service to perfection.

The realm which he surveys in his fascinating introduction, and to the qualities and features of which he calls a host of witnesses in verse and prose in the anthology which follows, is a very extensive one. Its chief landmarks, as he describes them, are sleep and its associations, dream and the state of dreaming, the Unconscious and its fringes, fantasy and the imagination, the art and genius that reveal their value and significance, and Death, either as incredible end or as inscrutable beginning

But these are only the major divisions of a province that includes a score and more of particular viewpoints, alluring or alarming, at each of which we are invited, either with Mr. de la Mare himself or with others who have gone that way, to linger and learn.

There are Day-dreams, for example, those musings of the mind over which sleep has not quite cast her veil nor wakefulness subdued to narrow ends. There is Night, of which modern life does its

[1] WALTER DE LA MARE: *Behold, This Dreamer.*

best to cheat us, the tide of darkness at least as mysterious, in Mr. de la Mare's words, 'as the tides of the Seven Seas', when after rain 'the leaden minute-drops from leaf to leaf sharpen the quietude, arrest the listener behind the ear', or when 'the recurrent onset and lulling of the wind is less like a mere formless noise than the accents of a voice roaming through a world countless centuries before the spirit of man stirred its dust'.

There is the Moon, who instead of dazzling 'pacifies, invites us in', and yet whose reflected beams have mysterious potencies for good and evil. There are the other worlds blissful or terrifying, and of as many kinds and conditions as there are states in our waking life into which we go away in sleep, a whole universe in which reality and unreality, vision and hallucination intermingle. There is insomnia and the beds on which we lie, the sleep of childhood and the lover's dream, the silent pool within the soul from which a fountain of new life may spring, and the perennial problem of reconciling *Animus* and *Anima*, reason and imagination.

These are but some of the aspects of the dreaming faculty. Indeed, it would be hard to set limits to the world which dreams inform. Not only are we ourselves such stuff as dreams are made on, but the whole manifested universe, as those have testified who have seen deepest into it, is the unfolding of a dream. Whether we locate the fount of life's inspiration in the sub-conscious or the super-conscious, whether, to borrow Mr. de la Mare's imagery, we are concerned to keep the cellar locked, in which a 'Blatant Beast, with virtues of its own nature', is confined, or to listen to the marvellous song of the 'caged bird in the attic', it is from a region beyond the pale of our waking consciousness that all the power and virtue of our being come.

The poet has always known this, has agreed with Mr. de la Mare when he says that it would be nearer the truth to say 'we are thought into' than 'we think'. To him the mind is in the service of the imagination, the mysterious faculty of this unmapped region, and 'every imaginative poem, as we allow it to use us, itself resembles in its onset and in its effect the experience of dreaming'.

Any sensitive reader of poetry will confirm this claim. And

since poetry is the language of dream, whether revealing or fantastic, it provides the greater part of Mr. de la Mare's anthology, the prose in it being chiefly intended 'to indicate, like a finger-post, what for the most part it so inadequately exemplifies'. In writing thus Mr. de la Mare scarcely does justice to some of the prose which he includes, whether imaginative like Hardy's description of Egdon Heath in November twilight, or transcripts of actual dreams, or, in varying measure expressive and explanatory, passages from the mystics or philosophers.

But poetry is the distillation of dreams as prose can never be, though to-day a certain kind of dreaming has notoriously fallen into other hands than the poets'. The dreamer, as Mr. de la Mare has to confess, has fallen from his high estate. He is no longer venerated as once he was; while the diviner, if he existed to-day, 'would probably combine his office with that of Psychologist to the Crown, rather than, as might be assumed, with that of the Poet Laureate'.

The split between imagination and reason and the specialization of the latter is characteristic of our day. It is, we may admit, a necessary phase in our self-knowing. But in sharpening the focus of our conscious minds we have grievously contracted their range, so that reaches, wide and deep, of visionary knowledge which man once plumbed by a kind of dreaming, if never perfectly possessed, remain to be recovered by human experience.

The psycho-analyst's interpretation of dreams is the most obvious example of this shrinking of vision combined with a determination to bring the world of mystery under human rule. Mr. de la Mare treats the psycho-analyst with respect, but in pointing out that there is scarcely an object around us that cannot be conceived of as a symbol figurative of anything with which the waking mind is deeply concerned he emphasizes the arbitrariness of a science which so often limits that concern to sex or infantile sensations.

As he has written in a poem on 'Dreams':

> O Poesy, of wellspring clear,
> Let no sad Science thee suborn,
> Who are thyself its planisphere!

All knowledge is foredoomed, forlorn —
Of inmost truth and wisdom shorn —
Unless imagination brings
Its skies wherein to use its wings.

For him as a poet even the most fragmentary of dreams may hint at a variety of meanings, significant according to the quality of the imagination which interprets it. For it is, as he writes, 'what in our brooding hearts we think of anything and what we feel about it that matters, rather than the thing itself'. And, paradoxically, it is only by dreaming anew that we can interpret a dream. For as with everything else we value and delight in, 'what we dream into it, divine in it, is what counts most. That gone, wasted, there is nothing left remarkable in it, not even its moonshine'. What is partial, therefore, in psycho-analysis is due to the defeat of the dreaming by the waking mind. For the waking mind, unless it dreams, is limited by the prejudices and interests of the ego, however impartial it may strive to be.

Yet the dreaming mind, it must be confessed, is as often tainted by the same interested party and can be wildly irresponsible. Hence the grave judgments passed upon it by such moralists as Johnson, who have feared that even 'a temporary recession from the realities of life to any fictions', if often indulged, may lead to 'an habitual subjection of reason to fancy'. For imagination may be indulged no less than reason, and as flagrantly distort or diminish reality.

A whole section of Mr. de la Mare's anthology, the most prosaic but not the least interesting, is devoted to the uneasy relationship of these two faculties. But he forbears himself, as a wise dreamer, to go into the problem deeply or to attempt to distinguish, for example, fancy from imagination.

But it is perhaps a pity that in such explanatory passages as he has included he has confined himself to Western writers. For the Eastern seers have undeniably explored the realm of dreams far more thoroughly than we in the West have yet succeeded in doing. Our determination to be vigilantly conscious has for the most part prevented us from penetrating far into regions that can only be experienced by an extended consciousness. It is just this extended consciousness which the Eastern seer has cultivated by inward concentration, thereby carrying reason with him into the very realm of mystery and reconciling in the visionary eye the powers of waking and the dreaming mind.

We need not accept all he reports, perhaps too precisely, of the different planes of that world from the most lofty and lucid to the treacherous marshes where the senses breed phantoms to ensnare the spirit. But if our dreaming is ever to be more than magical reverie, an enchanting or alarming picture-show, over which we have little control, if it is to be that visionary seeing which is both being and knowing in a new dimension, we need to cross, after long preparation maybe, a frontier in ourselves beyond which the existing order of sleeping and waking is reversed. We need to enter that country in which, as is written in the *Bhagavad-Gita*, the darkness and hiddenness of true being, which is night to all born beings, is changed, for the enlightened sage into luminous day, while the day of the ordinary consciousness, in which men act and believe themselves awake, is seen as a night of troubled sleep to the seer who has awoken from it.

Mr. de la Mare makes no claim to such revolutionary seership. But he does confess that he has spent in sleep a far more active and adventurous existence than has been his outward lot in the waking day. And many of the dreams which he describes so vividly are of unusual interest, as for example, that of the murder, without a trace of conscience or motive in it, which he dreamed that he committed and which had its sequel in a dream of many years later, or of the face, the most beautiful that he had ever seen, which he continued to see poised in the air above him after he had woken, just as at another time the music of an enchanting voice also persisted into waking life and was even overheard by a niece who was staying in the same house.

Mr. de la Mare describes these dreams without any 'irritable reaching after fact and reason'. He muses upon them, but he is a dreamer by virtue of his capacity to be in uncertainties; and none of his dreams it would seem, has been of that dramatic and life-changing order which he recalls in such historical examples as those of Pascal, Descartes and Cowper, not to say of Nebuchadnezzar and St. Paul. Yet they have given him sufficient assurance that in sleep we can enter not merely a limbo of treacherous twilight, but 'another order of life, and one of an infinite value and efficacy'.

It is, however, not so much from sleep, 'the most modest, the most benign of self-effacements', or from his little squirrel-hoard of strangely mixed nocturnal experiences that he derives his deepest conviction of the value of dreams, but from the arts of all the ages, the works of all men of genius and the testimony of the mystics.

Dream, as he points out, has been not merely a literary device in English poetry from the days of 'Pearl' to those of Tennyson. It has been its transfiguring principle, as it has of the imagined characters of drama or fiction. The most sensible and practical of poets, Chaucer and William Morris, for example, are among the greatest dreamers, and no realist can be a poet unless his imagination re-creates the actuality which he depicts.

At the other extreme, the problem for the visionary is to clothe the perfect dream in sufficient earthly substance, and Dante and Shakespeare in their different ways are the supreme examples of the capacity of genius to dream in the ideal world while its eyes are open in the real and to express the tragic conflict of the two visions in the redeeming light of a divine comedy.

But however far poets may fall short of such supreme unifying of the life of the senses in the light of imagination, there can be no authentic poetry in which, as Mr. de la Mare puts it, 'life itself and everything in nature which the desire of the mind and the pining of the heart most covet and delight in' are not continually being compared, however unconsciously and implicitly, with what is after their own pattern and quality in dream. And at the heart of it, revealed past reason, is 'an unearthly rapture, a desire that will perish in the having, the vision of the immortal beyond change'.

That vision, uncentred in the human heart, may lead to weak fantasy and the very evanescence which it claims to contradict. But it is the touchstone, as it is the magic source, of the reality which the rhythms and incantations of poetry evoke. Love and death are pre-eminently its ministers. For the lover is in a dream and death promises a state of dreaming, though in that sleep of death what dreams may come must, on this side of the gulf, give us pause. Yet both open a way to a Beyond for which the soul hungers in the toils of the flesh.

We need not, however, confine dreaming to such primal themes. Or rather, love and death meet and mingle in and penetrate every moment of poetic experience, so that all true poems owe their origin, as Mr. de la Mare writes, 'to a graft of the waking mind on the wild and ancient stock of dream'. There are few things, whether near or remote, of which poets have not dreamed. The sound of a scythe has enchanted them as deeply as the evening star. And each, with Keats, has cried after the enchantment he has failed to hold,

> Was it a vision, or a waking dream?
> Fled is that music: — Do I wake or sleep?

V

CHRISTIAN VERSE

RELIGIOUS emotion, as Lord David Cecil remarks in his Introduction to this Anthology,[1] is the most sublime known to man. But he goes on to admit that, in Christian Europe at any rate, it has not proved the most fertile soil for poetry. If religious poetry were merely the expression of emotion, however sublime, there would be nothing unexpected in this. But even in the best of the hymn-writers it has been something more. At its truest and greatest, of course, it embodies the intensities of spiritual experience, and there is a sense in which all the greatest poetry in the world is profoundly religious, because it strives to establish a relation between the human and the Divine, to establish, as Rilke put it, 'new outposts in the mystery and darkness that surround us', and at the same time to be a channel by which transcendent values may irradiate the world of matter and of sense.

Even, therefore, with the limitations imposed upon his choice in an anthology devoted exclusively to Christian verse, Lord David's task as editor, in deciding what to include, cannot have been easy, and he is to be congratulated in erring, if at all, rather on the side of strictness than laxity. His difficulties and how he has faced them are well illustrated in the person of Blake, of whom he writes:

> It is doubtful whether he should appear in a book of Christian verse at all. If he was a Christian, he was certainly a heretic. His surprising gospel, with its admiration for all positive feelings, its horror of any kind of prohibition or asceticism, is at odds both with the doctrines of every important branch of Christianity and also with Christ's own teaching. But Blake, whether he would or no, was soaked through with Christian thought: Christian symbols are an essential part of his native language. And he was exquisitely responsive to certain phases of Christian sentiment.

[1] *The Oxford Book of Christian Verse.* Chosen and edited by Lord David Cecil.

For those to whom Christianity is more than a body of established doctrine, to which all personal experience must conform, and who see in dogma itself something which evolves as spiritual insight deepens, this admission of Blake into the Christian fold may seem gratuitously cautious.

Lord David is far surer, for example, of Browning's Christian credentials, because Browning restated two approved beliefs, those in the necessary imperfection of man and in the self-sacrificing love of God, in terms that were at once original and acceptable to orthodoxy. Yet it is difficult not to regard Blake as more essentially and prophetically Christian than Browning.

The difference between poetry and conformity is even more apparent when we compare Blake's verses with those of some of the many minor poets included in the anthology, whose orthodoxy demands no scrutiny; with such lines as these, for example, by the nineteenth-century poet Digby Mackworth Dolben:

> Bid all fear and doubting
>   From my soul depart,
> As I feel the beating
>   Of Thy Human Heart.
>
> Look upon me sweetly
>   With Thy Human Eyes
> With Thy Human Finger
>   Point me to the skies.

But the impossibility of limiting an anthology of Christian verse to the orthodox is even more formidably exemplified in the person of Milton, despite his apparent dependence on Biblical mythology, than in that of Blake. Milton, Lord David boldly asserts, was essentially neither a Christian nor a religious poet, though he made religion his subject. He was a 'philosopher rather than a devotee' and 'theology to him was a superior branch of political science'. He valued the Stoic rather than the Christian virtues, and regarded pride not as a vice, but as the mark of a superior nature.

The *Nativity Ode*, if not the *Morning Hymn of Adam and Eve*, reveals more of a Christian temper in Milton than Lord David will allow. But it is as a supreme poet, whose essential paganism the pale Galilean had certainly not subdued, that he has his inevitable place in this anthology.

The same is true in miniature of such a poet as Herrick, who, as Lord David happily puts it, 'lays his little garlands of rose and daffodil on the altar of the Virgin as gaily as a classical shepherd making a libation to Aphrodite'. Or it may be a flower that he bids a pretty child bear

> Unto thy little Saviour;
> And tell him, by that bud now blown,
> He is the *Rose of Sharon* known:
> When thou hast said so, stick it there
> Upon his bib, or stomacher:
> And tell him, (for good handsel too)
> That thou hast brought a whistle new,
> Made of a clean straight oaten reed
> To charm his cries, (at time of need:). . . .

Lord David is perhaps more kindly inclined towards such pretty garlands, which may not much enrich our spiritual experience but form a welcome relief to 'celestial sublimities', than he is to such sublimities when expressed by poets who never claimed to be Christian.

He includes, for example, only a sonnet by Shakespeare, 'Poor Soul, the centre of my sinful earth', and rightly enough, nothing by Keats or Shelley. Wordsworth is represented by the sonnet to King's Chapel and (a happy choice) by *Devotional Incitements*. Neither the *Ecclesiastical Sonnets* nor *The Excursion* which might seem an obvious field of Christian verse are drawn upon.

This is typical of the combination of sensitive taste and firm but flexible Christian standards which governs Lord David's choice and prevents him from being seduced by the varieties of religious experience as such, however eloquently versified. Coleridge, for example, is represented by *A Christmas Carol*, the sublime *Hymn before Sunrise in the Vale of Chamouni*, and by his *Epitaph* on himself, but by no passage from the *Religious Musings*.

Inevitably Lord David overlooks some verses which will strike other readers as more essentially Christian and better poetry than some which he has included, particularly perhaps among the moderns. Hardy's two lyrics, *After Reading Psalms xxxix, xl* and *Surview*, for example, might well have found a place, despite their author's explicit agnosticism. And the book would have been richer in the sixteenth century for Henry King's *A Contemplation upon Flowers* or *Exequy on his Wife*, even if they only express an exquisite Christian temper.

On the whole, however, without too literally interpreting his terms of reference, but also without welcoming verse, however sublimely religious, which is not distinctively Christian, Lord David has produced an anthology that has a character of its own. Certain poets stand out in it by the power with which they have melted the traditional Christian doctrines in the cauldron of their own experience and re-created them as passionate realities. And it is on this ground that Lord David is perhaps right in giving first place among English Christian poets to Donne, because he alone is equally interesting as Christian and as poet.

Poetry is born of conflict and of the struggle to resolve such conflict at ever deeper levels of integrity. It is the lack of this inner tension which makes pseudo-mystical verse so vapid. But of all faiths Christianity has stressed most insistently, in its doctrine of sin and atonement, the necessity of this conflict at the heart of human experience. It is, therefore, a religion which we should expect to express itself powerfully in poetry. In the degree that it has failed to do so, as this volume often shows that it has, it is because this conflict has ceased to be a vital reality to the poets concerned or has been arrested and conventionalized at a certain point.

The danger of this happening is of course inherent in any conformity to a creed. The doctrine assented to becomes a substitute for costly experience instead of a formulated mystery within which such experience can be concentrated, striking new and deep roots in the soil of life. The most obvious sign in Christian verse of such creative poverty is the trite use of Biblical or liturgical symbols, although the true poet can, of course, charge these in every age with new and impressive vitality.

But there is another reason why Christian poets have tended too often to recoil from the unguarded reality with which any poet who would speak the language of imagination rather than of elevated feeling must grapple. Lord David draws attention to it when he writes:

> The New Testament conception of God is so much more elevated than that of the Old that the devout person feels it profane to show himself in all his earthly imperfections before Him. He will allow himself to express only unexceptionable sentiments, love, reverence, humility: will voice no aspiration save for a purer soul and stronger faith. As for using any but the most decorous language to express his feelings, the very idea horrifies him . . . The writer does not say what he really feels, but what he thinks he ought to feel: and he speaks not in his own voice but in the solemn tones that seem fitting to his solemn subject.

To prefer seriousness, still more solemnity, to truth is a common failing in the devout, from which the saint on the other hand has always been refreshingly free. But saints generally live poetry rather than write it and are too deeply involved in the spiritual struggle to indulge in virtuous sentiments.

The tendency, however, for minor Christian poets to write out of only a part of their natures, the part which they regarded as moral, rational and respectable, becomes apparent, chiefly after the Reformation when the whole realm of sense became increasingly suspect. The Catholic tradition has never encouraged a false bias against the senses. And the virtue of this acceptance is found not only in the medieval poetry in this collection, with its tender, homely reality, but in the metaphysical or mystical ecstasies of Donne, Crashaw and Vaughan. Indeed, strained and eccentric as were many of the conceits and raptures of the seventeenth-century metaphysical poets, compared with the limpid folk-simplicity of the medieval carol, the tradition of a religious poetry, which was an ecstatic love-poetry, may be said to have died with them, although here and there a voice was to recall it. Protestantism had, of course, its own virtues, but it represented a split in the integrity of human experience which was inevitably reflected in the quality of Christian verse, whether in the rational piety or generalized descriptions of the eighteenth century or the crude doctrinal passion, leavened with much tender feeling, of the hymn-writers of the Evangelical Movement.

Of the Christian poets of the nineteenth century, too, it is significant that the best of them, Patmore, Hopkins, Christina Rossetti and Francis Thompson (not to say Newman) were Roman Catholic or Anglo-Catholic. And in Hopkins we have perhaps the clearest example of the poetic virtue that springs from a true tension of rich sensuousness and spiritual austerity.

To read through this anthology, is, indeed, to perceive not only different notes in the common chord of Christian experience, but the weakening and thinning of that chord and a restoration, in some measure at least, during the last eighty years of its full tonal value. An anonymous seventeenth-century poet wrote in 'The Invitation':

> Lord, what unvalued pleasures crown'd
>   The days of old;
> When Thou wert so familiar found,
>   Those days were gold; —
>
> When Abram wish'd Thou couldst afford
>   With him to feast;
> When Lot but said, 'Turn in, my Lord',
>   Thou wert his guest . . .
>
> What, shall Thy people be so dear
>   To Thee no more?
> Or is not heaven to earth as near
>   As heretofore?

Such a lament is characteristic of the modern rather than the medieval poet who, being nearer to earth, was also nearer to heaven, and to whom even sin and hell were rather homely religious verities than the torments of a will consciously divided against itself. The writer of a fifteenth-century lyric could find even in the Fall itself an occasion of blessedness:

> ne hadde the appil take ben,
> the appil take ben,
> ne hadde never our lady
> a ben Hevene qwen.
> blyssid be the tyme
> that appil take was!
> therefore we mown syngyn
> *Deo gracias.*

We can read to-day in such symbolism an unconscious spiritual wisdom, as a result of which medieval religious verse was lyrical as it has never been since. Heaven for the medieval poet was not a state of the soul to be philosophically pondered or morally expounded. It was a clearly pictured place to be loved as spontaneously as earth was loved in spring and summer and fall. Since Christ had laid in a manger at Bethlehem, had hung on Calvary and risen on Easter morning, Heaven was no longer far from earth nor, despite its ancient terrors, was Hell. Both, in the common mind, had been humanized and almost domesticated. Heaven had its kind, familiar figures, the Virgin and Child, the Angelic choir, the shepherds and the kings on bended knee with ox and ass. And if Hell had its demons, they, too, were half-humanized, while for the faithful their power had been forever trampled underfoot.

Religion sprang up warm in the heart and the senses from roots in the common soil of life, its sufferings and its joys. It flowered in the imagination of the people as naturally as lady's smock and eglantine in the hedgerows, as holly and ivy, as 'the rose Mary, flour of flours'. And from heaven it came to them, not with thunder and lightning, but

> As dew in April,
> That falleth on the flour.

To be without religion would have seemed as unnatural to a man of the Middle Ages, whether clerk or peasant, as to be without the birds of the air or even the air itself. For its spirit sustained their lives almost as unconsciously as the air they breathed.

We cannot but regret the passing of this childlike acceptance, this devotional innocence, which made the greatest mysteries homely and personal and which sang so tenderly its faith because it had not begun to question it. But the time of questioning had to come, the loss of unity, personal and social, and of the goodly glee which warmed the hearts of men in a world that lacked so many material comforts and exacted so much toil and drudgery.

In the solitary depths of the individual soul heaven had to be lost and found again, and hell had to yawn that it might be more radically redeemed. Wisdom had to become conscious at the cost of a naive integrity. The apple had to be eaten to the core that 'Hevene's Qwen', the divine *Sophia*, might one day be fully known. Christian experience, as crystallized in these verses, becomes more and more individual and temperamental. Yet its impulse is ever towards that completion of individuality in the really personal, that marriage of Heaven and Hell, which is enshrined in the mysteries of the Incarnation and the Atonement, when they are truly interpreted.

In a very real sense, to be a true Christian involves the same struggle for integrity as to be a true poet. And although the great poet always transcends the limits of his age, this collection of Christian verse is a mirror which reflects the spiritual temperature of different times as well as the varieties of religious temperament.

Few will quarrel with Lord David's claim that religious poetry rose to its greatest height in the seventeenth century in the Caroline School of devotional poets who were Donne's direct descendants or with his view of Herbert as the most complete exponent of the peculiar genius of the English Church. How much this was due to the individual genius of the poets or to the religious climate of their age, it would be idle to inquire. But it is at least significant that the Catholic tradition and the Puritan impulse were more happily and vitally balanced then than they have ever been since, and that it is towards a restoration and renewal of this balance that many Christians have been working since the days of the Oxford Movement.

More questionably Lord David considers the second half of the nineteenth century to be the second outstanding epoch of religious poetry in England. But its flowering was Roman Catholic rather than Anglican, and our own period, apart from Mr. Eliot and Miss Ruth Pitter, the latter of whom he surely overvalues as a religious poet, has little distinctive to show. If out of suffering we are to rediscover as a people the reality of religious experience, there will certainly be poets to express it. But the more real that rediscovery is, the more certain is it to create new symbols for eternal truths and to be Christian by virtue rather of its universality than of any exclusive doctrine.

Yet how hospitable to diverse genius and talent the Christian faith can be, this anthology amply testifies. It contains, indeed, a sprinkling of the insignificant. Yet among the smaller voices are many that sound notes of singular charm and purity. And catholic in the truest sense is the choir which can incorporate the cool sublimity of Spenser, the burning piety of Southwell, the decorative grandeur of Drummond, the homely pungency of Quarles, the dewy freshness of Traherne, Dryden's didactic strength, Smart's enraptured rhetoric, Addison's reasoned piety, Newton's fervid and Cowper's stricken faith, Arnold's spiritual homesickness and Bridges's philosophic calm.

VI

DONNE'S *HOLY SONNETS*

WHEN in August 1617 Ann Donne died, worn out with poverty and childbearing, her husband, to quote Walton's words, 'buried with his tears all his earthly joys in his most dear and deserving wife's grave, and betook himself to a most retired and solitary life'.

During the seventeen years since that 'first strange and fatall interview' which had led on to the secret marriage deplored by Walton as 'the remarkable error of his life', Donne had passed through crisis after crisis of sickness and worldly disillusionment. Yet if his marriage had wrecked his ambitions, it had brought to his passionate nature some sense of rest and security. The triumphant assurance of reciprocated love which sounded in *The Anniversarie*,

> Who is so safe as wee? Where none can doe
> Treason to us, except one of us two,

was sustained in deeper tones through all his mature love poetry. The hatred of the senses' inconstancy by which he had been obsessed, the fever of desire and the revulsions from it, the thwartings and jealousies which he expressed with such naked candour in the *Songs and Sonnets* of his youth, were resolved in a marriage of mutual trust which satisfied both body and mind.

Secure in this harmony, the problem of the interaction of body and mind in all experience, which fascinated Donne throughout his life, had no longer seemed quite so insoluble. Indeed, as such poems as *Aire and Angels* or *The Extasie* show, his experience of love and marriage was peculiarly enriched by the very tension of passion and intellect which had previously torn his nature in half.

It has been remarked that he was always too self-obsessed to see even the woman whom he loved except as in some sense a mirror of himself in the act of loving. But at least in his love for his wife he had, in a measure, reconciled the diverse cravings of his nature and so been able to defer, save in certain crises of illness, the harder problem of reconciling them in the face of death. In her he had found a haven from what was to him the fever of the love of women. But it was only in January 1615 and then because he had had to abandon at last all hope of secular preferment that by entering the ministry of the English Church he found a corresponding haven within which to reconcile, so far as he could, his mind and heart in the love of God.

And despite the *Essays in Divinity* which he wrote to convince himself that he was 'worthy and competently learned to enter into Holy Orders' and the noble prayers which they contain, it is doubtful whether he experienced conversion at all deeply until after his wife's death. At least her death threw him back upon himself and into the arms of religion with a violence which Walton described as being 'crucified to the world'.

The first fruits of that crucifixion are the *Holy Sonnets* written in the desolate months which followed. He himself in the seventeenth of them described how his wife in dying had carried upward his love from earthly to heavenly things. But characteristically he ended the sonnet by confessing to God that

> though I have found thee, and thou my thirst hast fed,
> A holy thirsty dropsy melts mee yett.

His appetite for heavenly good was in fact as insatiable as it had been for earthly bliss, and it was far harder to satisfy. For one of such strong and rooted passions, conversion was inevitably an agonizing and never completed process. Certainly, however much it had turned his nature in a new direction, it had not changed or resolved its conflict. Rather conversion for him renewed a conflict which had been to some extent assuaged in the self-giving, spiritual and physical, of married love. The widower who turned away from the world, the flesh and the devil was the more intensely conscious of the prison of himself and of the desperate need of escaping from it into the loving wholeness of God. It was, therefore, unmistakably the same man who now wooed God as had in his 'idolatrie' wooed his 'profane mistresses'. He was subject in his new devotion to the same burning moods and humours as in his old.

> As ridlingly distemper'd, cold and hott,
> As praying, as mute; as infinite, as none.

The tormented reality of his Divine Poems and sermons as well as their moments of sublime release were due to the fact that he never attained to the state of Grace, the liberation of self into Self, which is the crown of the mystical life. How fiercely he struggled to break out of prison is nowhere more powerfully expressed than in the fourteenth of these *Holy Sonnets*, in which he bade God punish him like a pugilist:

> Batter my heart, three person'd God; for you
> As yet but knocke, breathe, shine and seeke to mend;
> That I may rise, and stand, o'erthrow mee, and bend
> Your force, to breake, blowe, burn and make me new.

The hammer blows of the monosyllables here proclaim how physically Donne hungered after the spiritual, as does the imagery of the concluding lines:

> Take mee to you, imprison mee, for I
> Except you enthrall mee, never shall be free,
> Nor ever chast, except you ravish mee.

The riddling intellect, he knew, could never by itself touch ultimate reality. He had come nearest to it hitherto through the passion of love. But to reach the heart of reality, to rest in it, needed now a passion of faith. And strive as he would to surrender, he had to confess that reason in him, which should be God's viceroy, was itself as much in bondage to his ego as were his physical senses. And this bondage found now its chief expression in the fear of death.

The fact of death was continually present to the medieval mind in a way that it is not to the modern, and Donne, despite his omnivorous study of the new learning remained essentially medieval in his ideas, finding in the 'new philosophy' of the Renaissance signs rather of the world's decay than of its rebirth. But his fear of death was irreducibly his own. In the appalled contemplation of death and of what might come after death his egoism made its last stand, as he viewed with equal horror his past enslavement by the flesh and the dreadful necessity of putting it off.

It is the predominant theme of the *Holy Sonnets* in which he fights again and again for faith against the 'sinne of feare' to which he confessed in his *Hymne to God the Father*, a fear not merely of relinquishing his grasp upon the body which was the instrument of his ego, but of passing out of it into nothingness or worse. The theme is stated in the very first sonnet, recurs continually throughout the series, and reaches its climax in the two magnificent sonnets, VII and X, in the first of which he summons the dead to the Last Judgement with a trumpet blast, only to bid them sleep again as he takes comfort in the assurance that pardon is to be had even now by him who can learn to repent; and in the second of which with inimitable audacity he faces his great enemy and turns the tables on him, since death, too, is slave to chance and kings and desperate men,

> why swell'st thou then?
> One short sleepe past, wee wake eternally,
> And death shall be no more; death, thou shalt die.

In the preceding sonnet he had asked:

> But who am I, that dare dispute with thee
> O God?

Yet to struggle with God, to assault him with questions and demands, appeals and intercessions, was the only way in which Donne could come near to the reality he sought and ease the frenzy of his mental solitude. Just as in his earlier years he had never been a poet of ideal beauties but of actual truths wrung imaginatively out of life in the warfare of sense and intellect, so now he enjoyed no immediate sense of God but only the agonized doubts, the ecstatic hopes of pursuing Him.

Of death itself he could write: 'I would not have him merely seise me, and onely declare me to be dead, but win me, and overcome me.' And in the power of his indomitable egotism he challenged God, too, to overcome him. It is this determination to fight his spiritual battle through to victory or defeat (and in that battle defeat is a condition of victory) that gives to these *Holy Sonnets* so compelling a reality, whether in lines of noble resonance or in the broken music of a naked thinking heart.

To feel Donne's poetry you have to think it. But the intellectual pattern of his meaning was so charged with feeling in these sonnets that there was no room for fantastic conceits. They embody in a small space and with unforgettable intensity the drama of us all who fear the death that we long to die.

VII

DOROTHY WORDSWORTH

'I MAY sum up her character as a companion', wrote De Quincey in concluding his famous word-picture of Dorothy Wordsworth, 'by saying that she was the very wildest (in the sense of the most natural) person I have ever known.' Yet, ironically enough, the only portrait of Wordsworth's 'exquisite sister' which has come down to us is that of a benign old lady in a bonnet. And perhaps one reason why she has had to wait so long for the biography which she would certainly have deprecated is that her life, even more than her brother's, has seemed to present such a depressing anti-climax.

The two lives were bound together by the deepest ties of affinity and devotion, and inevitably they conformed to a similar basic pattern. There was a miraculous flowering period in both of them. In Dorothy's it extended roughly from the September morning in 1795, when she set out with William from Bristol to Racedown, to the October evening in 1802, when she returned with him and his bride to Grasmere. There were, indeed, radiant hours in her childhood and girlhood, and there was, in the year following her brother's marriage, the tour in Scotland on which something of the old rapture was recovered. But with her return from that tour the existing evidence had suggested that the Dorothy whom De Quincey drew became more and more entangled in petty domestic circumstance until her gipsy wildness and darting sensibility, still manifest in 1807, were submerged in the anxious labours of a devoted aunt.

But although a feeling of anti-climax will probably persist, even after reading Professor de Selincourt's biography,[1] it will be very much modified by the new material which he has been able to incorporate and by his balanced and perceptive interpretation of each phase in Dorothy's life. Praise could hardly be too high for

[1] ERNEST DE SELINCOURT: *Dorothy Wordsworth.* A biography.

the skill with which he has selected from Dorothy's *Journals* and letters and the correspondence of others or for the sympathetic, yet just, temper of the narrative in which so much original material is embedded. The last twenty years of cruelly protracted illness he has rightly regarded as a posthumous life, but of the sixty preceding years he can claim that though Dorothy's 'capacity for suffering was commensurate with her capacity for joy, and her instinct for entering into the lives of others intensified both, she was yet essentially happy'.

With this claim few, after reading this book, will quarrel. Certainly the new evidence it contains lends little support to those who have looked on Dorothy 'as a pathetic figure and an object for commiseration'. She had a genius for self-devotion and she concentrated that devotion upon her brother. With characteristic modesty, combined as it was in her with that self-respect which really humble people always possess, she wrote to Lady Beaumont when she was twenty-two: 'I have not those powers which Coleridge thinks I have — I know it — my only merits are my devotedness to those I love, and I hope a charity towards all mankind.'

Five years later she replied even more explicitly to Lady Beaumont's entreaties that she should take herself seriously as a poet.

'Do not think [she wrote] that I was ever bold enough to hope to compose verses for the pleasure of grown persons — Descriptions, Sentiments, or little stories for children was all I could be ambitious of doing, and I did try one story, but failed so sadly that I was completely discouraged . . . Looking into my mind I find nothing there, even if I had the gift of language and numbers, that I could have the vanity to suppose could be of any use beyond our own fireside, or to please, as in your case, a few partial friends; but I have no command of language, no power of expressing my ideas, and no one was ever more inapt at moulding words into regular metre.'

Dorothy's 'partial friends' have multiplied far beyond the circle of relatives and acquaintances since she wrote this, and her *Journals*, her *Recollections of a Tour made in Scotland*, and her account of the tragedy of the Greens, have disproved her assertion that she had no command of language where her sensations and her sympathies were concerned. Her passionate simplicity of heart, upon which no intermeddling subtleties of mind encroached, and her 'exquisite regard for common things' dictated her language. Unconsciously she commanded it, as the experience of the moment commanded her. To quote her brother's lines:

> She welcom'd what was given and craved no more;
> Whatever scene was present to her eyes,
> That was the best, to that she was attuned;

— attuned so intimately that what she saw lived and moved with its own life in her sensing of it, as in this characteristic passage of her Journal:

'We rose early. A thick fog obscured the distant prospect entirely, but the shapes of the nearer trees and the dome of the wood dimly seen and dilated . . . It cleared away between ten and eleven. The shapes of the mist, slowly moving along, exquisitely beautiful; passing over the sheep they almost seemed to have more of life than those quiet creatures. The unseen birds singing in the mist.'

The only order such a passage has is that of a sequence of impressions received and recorded. But what nature gave was so lovingly accepted that we feel a day palpably unfold as we read.

To be so faithful to fact and yet to divine its magic was proof of an abnormally pure sensibility. In the earlier *Journals* her sensibility was so passive to nature that her own feelings and imagination seldom intruded. But later she could re-create more actively what she saw, as in this description of a favourite birch-tree:

'It was yielding to the gusty wind with all its tender twigs. The sun shone upon it, and it glanced in the wind like a flying sunshiny shower. It was a tree in shape, with stem and branches, but it was like a spirit of water. The sun went in and out and it resumed its purplish appearance, the twigs still yielding to the wind, but not so visibly to us. The other birch trees that were near it looked bright and cheerful, but it was a creature by its own self among them.'

Or again there is her impression of the waves on Rydale lake:

'I sat a long while to watch the hurrying waves, and to hear the regularly irregular sound of the dashing waters. The waves round about the little Island seemed like a dance of spirits that rose out of the water, round its small circumference of shore.'

In both passages the forms of nature, so exquisitely caught in their trembling motion by her senses, are humanized and spiritualized by the imagination.

In recording such experiences there is no doubt of her command of language. But when nature or some concrete human incident were not there to appeal directly to sensibility and imagination, she could neither create nor consciously compose. In this she was, as she confessed, 'only half a poet'. And although her close companionship with her brother quickened her poetic susceptibility, as her own 'perfect happiness of soul' restored his poetic faith, her appreciation of his creative power was so intense because it supplied what she herself lacked.

This, of course, was only one factor in their mutual devotion which had its roots from childhood in an instinctive affinity which never weakened or wavered, and of which Professor de Selincourt is the first to reveal the full intensity.

2

When she was in her seventeenth year Dorothy wrote to her friend Jane Pollard: 'I am very sure that love will never bind me closer to any human being than friendship binds me to you, my earliest female friend, and to William, my earliest and my dearest male friend.' And again, a few weeks later: 'It is enough for *you* that I am likely to have the happiness of introducing to you my beloved Brother. You must forgive me for talking so much of him, my affection hurries me on to the subject and makes me forget that you cannot be so much interested in it as I am. You do not know him; you do not know how amiable he is. Perhaps you reply "But I know how *you* are blinded". Well, my dearest Jane, I plead guilty at once, I must be blind, he cannot be so pleasing as my fondness makes him. I am willing to allow that half the virtues with which I fancy him endowed are the creation of my love, but surely I may be excused! he was never tired of comforting his sister, he never left her in anger, he always met her with joy, he preferred her society to every other pleasure, or rather when we were so happy as to be within each other's reach, he had no pleasure when we were compelled to be divided.'

This was no schoolgirl's effusion. There was a bond between them far more compelling than that of family affection, even allowing for the 'sort of violence of affection' which both William and she habitually felt for those they loved. It had been intensified by the fate which had kept them apart, from Dorothy's sixth to her sixteenth year. The familiarities of a common up-bringing were lacking and this made them something more and less than brother and sister, and gave a lover-like fondness to those expressions of affection by William which Dorothy described as 'a thousand almost imperceptible attentions . . . a sort of restless watchfulness which I know not how to describe, a tenderness that never sleeps, and at the same time such a delicacy of manners as I have observed in few men'.

Already she was dreaming of living in a little parsonage with him, was furnishing in imagination the parlour, setting out the tea-table, and brightening the fire. If she had been engaged to him she could hardly have written more fondly or circumstantially. And so deep was her conviction, her determination, one might say, that they should live together, that even when the story of Annette was confided to her, the prospect of a French wife for William seems scarcely to have dimmed, still less halted, her hopes.

The two days' walk which she took with her brother from Kendal to Keswick in the spring of 1794, passing unwittingly the very doors of 'Dove Cottage', their later home, followed by their stay with Raisley Calvert at his remote farm-house, brought her dream very near. She was twenty-three and this brief foretaste of life together, tramping and reading and copying verses, fulfilled all her expectations. A year later Calvert's dying bequest and Montagu's need of a guardian for his little son determined the move to Racedown. The dream was established fact, and brother and sister were seldom thereafter to be parted for more than a few weeks until death parted them fifty-five years later.

She had entered, as Professor de Selincourt writes, 'the chosen vocation of her life'. And no young bride, long engaged and at last happily married, was ever more sure of her vocation or had a greater sense of loving necessity and of practical responsibility in embracing it. As a girl she had served her domestic apprenticeship with her Uncle and Aunt Cookson and their babies. But affectionate as her relationship with them had been, it had been a dependent one. Now in this far dearer relationship with her brother, who in his family's eyes had mismanaged his life so deplorably, she would be her own mistress and she determined to be equal to her charge.

'You know I am active', she wrote to her friend Jane Marshall, 'not averse to household employments, and fond of children.' At last she could love actively and practically the one being whom she adored and who needed her love most. 'It will greatly contribute to my happiness', she declared, 'and place me in such a situation that I shall be *doing something*; it is a painful idea that one's existence is of very little use, which I really have always been obliged to feel.'

Never again was she to feel that, until, with the collapse of her mental faculties forty years later, she lost the power of such feelings. Nor could fate have better served her devotion than by delaying her brother's marriage for so long, through the unresolved problem of his French mistress, Annette, and then giving him a wife docile enough to share her husband's affections with his sister, although she was well aware of the passionate tie that bound them together.

It was, as Professor de Selincourt remarks, 'a strange wedding', and there was something oddly apposite in the fact that when the party returned to the house William had Dorothy, not Mary, upon his arm, even though she had been too moved to attend the ceremony. Forty-five years later when Wordsworth lost his daughter, Dora, it was, as his equally stricken wife uncomplainingly remarked, in his attendance upon his sister that he found his only enjoyment, and when three years later he lay dying himself, Dorothy, as though by a miracle recovered her faculties and became for a brief space almost 'the Miss Wordsworth' of past days. On his death she sank once more into insensibility.

Such facts do but confirm the more intimate evidence of her *Journals* and his poems. No wife could have lived more intensely in and for a husband than she did in and for her brother. Present or absent, he was, in Professor de Selincourt's words, 'the pivot of her life'. When he is away at night, to ease her loneliness, she sleeps in his bed. She can hardly find it in her heart to throw away an apple he has bitten. As they sit together by the fire, she makes a pillow of her shoulder, reads to him, 'and my Beloved slept'. And what leagues they tramped together, up and down the 'gravel walk' at Forncett in their first reunion, or on the Quantocks with Coleridge or without, along the banks of the Wye, over the fells and hills and passes of the North, or amid the peaks of Switzerland. In all things their natures seem to have been in perfect step, their need for each other utterly mutual.

Dorothy wore herself out with anxiety for her brother's health, and to him, in youth as in old age, the thought of her death was an agony. If one of her dearest joys was the knowledge of the part she played in his poetic life, she and the 'charm of sweetness her presence breathed around' were poetry incarnate for him.

> Where'er my footsteps turned,
> Her voice was like a hidden Bird that sang;
> The thought of her was like a flash of light
> Or an unseen companionship, a breath
> Or fragrance independent of the wind.

His poems were, indeed, the fruit of their spiritual union and in the 'Lucy' lyrics we glimpse the 'strange fits of passion' that gave to his affection for this dear companion and sister a quality and a depth unique in itself and hardly distinguishable from the passion of married love.

Professor de Selincourt notes that when William was on his way to rejoin Dorothy after arranging to be married to Mary Hutchinson, he composed a poem, not, as might be expected, to his bride-to-be, from whom he had just parted, but a lyric of the tenderest passion, *Among All Lovely Things My Love Had Been*, recalling an incident in the life he had shared with Dorothy at Racedown. The thought that he should so remember her at such a time brought Dorothy 'an ecstasy of joy'. No wonder that she could write some weeks later, before Mary came to share but not divide their lives:

'My tooth broke to-day. They will soon be gone. Let that pass. I shall be beloved. I want no more', or declare to Lady Beaumont that love for William was 'the building up of my being, the light of my path.'

3.

It is in the light of this exclusive and absorbing passion that Dorothy's love for Coleridge can be rightly viewed. Many have regretted that Dorothy and Coleridge could not marry and others have supposed that she herself, had circumstances allowed, would have wished it. All feeling in Dorothy was in some degree a passion. But intensely tender as was her affection for Coleridge, it was, we can now see, never more than this.

Professor de Selincourt puts it categorically when he writes:

'That Dorothy loved Coleridge with a depth of devotion of which few human beings are capable, and that his later deterioration under the influence of opium was the most harrowing sorrow of her life, cannot be questioned; but if her life had its tragedy, it was not that she loved Coleridge, but rather that her passion for her brother was so intense as to preclude her from feeling for any man an emotion which would have satisfied the physical as well as the spiritual side of her nature. Coleridge himself must have realized this absorption in William: frank and open as she was, she could not have concealed from him the character of her feeling for either of them.'

It is even doubtful whether Coleridge's dereliction was the most harrowing sorrow of her life. It was the most prolonged.

But the most terrible blow that she ever suffered was, on her own admission, the loss of her brother John in the foundering of his ship, the *Earl of Abergavenny*, a loss of which she wrote that she could 'never again have a *perfect* — that is an unchastized — joy in this world', and that wherever she went, she would always be haunted by the memory of 'his retired virtues, his modesty, his tenderness, his deep affections'.

Here again family attachment was stronger perhaps with her, as with William, than any outside tie. And when eight years later her little nephew Thomas died she experienced the same anguish, calling it 'the hardest trial I have ever had, except when my Brother John died . . . My tears will flow, I cannot help it. The image of him, his very self, is so vivid in my mind; it is like a perpetual presence, and at certain moments the anguish of those tender recollections is more than I can bear . . . at times when I muse on a future life and on his blessedness in another world I lose all thoughts of anguish; the child becomes spiritualized to my mind. I wish I could have such musings more frequently — and longer, but alas! the image of the boy disturbs me and I weep again.'

Deeply as her tender heart suffered with and for Coleridge, his sad history could never harrow her in such a way. In the days of his defection, after the quarrel over Montagu's tactless words, she could write, 'I am sure he does not know the depth of the affection I have had for him!' But he was, then, for her a 'poor soul, sadly to be pitied'. And except in the earliest days of enraptured communion, when she and William and he, though three persons, were one soul, some element of pity coloured her affection. Pity can be a very painful emotion, and until Coleridge's own nature manifestly deteriorated, it was the nobler kind of pity, compassion, that Dorothy felt. But neither pity nor compassion have the power to possess or to wound that passionate love has.

Such love Dorothy never had for Coleridge. Even in the days of their tenderest intimacy a letter from William counted for far more with her than one from him, though later his self-pitying letters could so work upon her sympathies as to make her ill.

It is doubtful, indeed, whether Coleridge could have felt passionate love for anyone or excited it. He was, as Professor de Selincourt remarks, 'like the child who shows his love for his mother by running to her whenever he is hurt', and 'such was his charm that he seldom lacked the sympathy he craved'.

Before drugs and the incompatability of his marriage had sapped his powers as a poet he found in Dorothy and she in him the poetic sympathy in which each delighted and of which William completed the vital circuit. But as the lyrical poet waned in him and the hypochondriac waxed, it was indulgent sympathy rather than poetic which he craved. The very intensity of Dorothy's being was a reproach to him and in the placid, indulgent Sara Hutchinson he found the mother who would tend his hurts, and for a time at least fill the void in his heart.

Dorothy was only troubled by this attachment on Sara's account. If she had been capable of jealousy, Coleridge could not have excited it, because she felt passionate love only for William and knew how unalterably it was returned. Here, if anywhere, as Professor de Selincourt writes, may have been the fatal tie that deprived her nature of a normal growth, and her brother's also in a less degree. Certainly both outlived themselves, and their lives in a curiously similar way revealed, for those who find significance in such things, the ravages of repressed feeling.

But as certainly there can be little profit in conjecturing what Dorothy's life might have been if she had not loved her brother as she did. Her love for him was her dearest delight and constant comfort of which she never for one moment counted the cost. Nor would the cost have probably been less or the happiness greater if it had been lavished upon a husband and children of her own. One thing only a normal marriage and motherhood might have done for her. They might have eased the tension of feeling and the restless energy under which at sixty-four her mind at last gave way.

Yet such speculations are useless. Her highly-strung temperament was part of her genius as a like temperament was of her brother's. As with him, a haunting anxiety went with an intense susceptibility to feeling. The fierce, tenacious fondness which possessed and aged William so prematurely consumed the humbler and more devoted nature of his sister, too. At thirty-four she was grown so thin and old, according to friends, that they would not have known her, and when she was forty-eight she described herself as in face 'a perfect old woman'; her teeth all gone but three above and three below, and her 'profile as 70!'

Nevertheless she could write that she enjoyed walking as much as when she first came into Westmorland twenty years before and her pedestrian feats during the next decade confirm Maria Jewsbury's testimony that she still united 'green vigour with grey maturity'.

Physical activity was always, indeed, one of the means whereby she relieved the constant strain of her feeling, of which she could write that 'any strong emotion cures my diseases for a time, and if I am well, as surely brings them on'. She and William were such prodigious walkers for the same reason. For both, walking was a safety-valve. It lowered the inward pressure of feeling.

Later the devotion she lavished on his children served the same purpose, but far less securely, since her watchful love for William inevitably extended to his children, and with it her anxiety. In the Alfoxden and early Grasmere years, the happiest of her life though her heart 'fluttered and ached' when she came to look back on them (for 'emotion recollected in tranquillity' did not come easily to her), she could best share and sustain her brother's life through their common bond with nature and the humble folk, villagers and dalesmen, for whom she felt a sympathy more intimate and direct even than he. Such sympathy with the life of all about her continued to unite them in the years that followed. But her absorbed attention was inevitably deflected from the wider landscape to the small and crowded family circle.

The zest with which she threw herself into family life was the same which she had brought and was always to bring to sight-seeing and to cultivating the society of those whom she met on her travels. For she met 'no-one with a stranger's heart'. But in her love for William's children she was more than a devoted aunt. If she had been their mother, she could hardly have identified herself more closely with their birth or with the pleasures and pains of their nurture. This was particularly so with the first-born, Johnny, of whom she wrote with maternal ecstasy to her friend Mrs. Clarkson, 'Oh my dear friend how happy we are in this blessed Infant!' It was as if her passion for William had born vicarious fruit. Certainly no one ever came nearer to being a wife and mother without actually being either.

The endless drudgery she endured may seem to some a pitiful destiny for one so finely gifted. But it was not so to her. For she was still 'Nature's inmate', attuned 'through her humility and lowliness' to the household scene as she had been to the minute particulars of field and wood. One may regret the domesticating of 'the frank impulsive child of nature, the companion of waterfalls and mountain breezes'. One may feel that the wild grace of her being, that flashed upon those who knew her as a young woman, was sadly tamed, even as the primordial genius of her brother came to be. But it was a wildness which needed a home, if it was not to consume a being so ardent and excitable.

To such a high-strung temperament the domesticities of 'Dove Cottage' provided both an outlet and a balm. Dorothy's effusions as a baby-worshipper or what she called her nursery tales can hardly command the attention of posterity, but Professor de Selincourt is certainly right in asserting that to her, 'as to so many others of nervous, anxious temper, a baby brought that calm which is of all things the most healing', and that as she watched over her brother's infants she gained something of their serene detachment from the troubles that harass an older world. A passage in one of her letters to Lady Beaumont, at a time when she was still stricken with memories of her drowned brother, John, expresses beautifully her experience of this calm:

'The Children are now in bed [she wrote]. The evening is very still, and there are no indoor sounds but the ticking of our Family watch which hangs over the chimney piece under the drawing of the Applethwaite Cottage, and a breathing or a beating of one single irregular Flame in my fire. No one who has not been an intimate with Children in a *Cottage* can have a notion of the quietness that takes possession of it when they are gone to sleep. The hour before is generally a noisy one, often given up to boisterous efforts to amuse them, and the noise is heard in every corner of the house — then comes the washing and undressing, a work of misery, and in ten minutes after, all is stillness and perfect rest. It is at all times a sweet hour to us, but I can fancy that I have never enjoyed it so much as now that I am quite alone.'

Only the habitually agitated or excitable can know to the full the bliss of those moments when 'the heart goes home to quietness'. Dorothy was incapable of a serene detachment, but if the children she tended so devotedly had always been well, her thoughts, in her own words, would never have been tired when so employed. During her thirty years, however, of active devotion to her brother and his family she was exposed, not only to a succession of minor and major anxieties, but to the harrowing loss of two of the children upon whom she doted.

And behind and beyond the family circle was the heart-breaking ghost of the Coleridge who sailed in the *Speedwell* to Malta in April 1804, never to return. For the Coleridge who did return and who, more than two years later, reluctantly brought himself to meet his anxious friends at Kendal was, to Dorothy's consternation, 'utterly changed', was, indeed only the ghost, a dropsical ghost, of his former self. Of the divine expression of his countenance she could see no more than a faint and transitory gleam, and that but seldom. And though at Coleorton some weeks later he was more himself at first, she soon learnt that it was no longer 'in our power to make him happy'. For her that was the saddest part of the whole sad business.

Poor Coleridge could no longer respond to the ardent affections of his friends. He had too much to hide from them as from himself. It was not only his sense of failure,

> of past youth, and manhood come in vain,
> And genius given, and knowledge won in vain.

Their love might have surmounted his remorse, if, in the soil of failure, jealousy and suspicion had not sprung up too. But at times now he saw in William, besides a moralist deploring the 'sinful creature' in his friend, a successful rival in the affections of Dorothy and of Sara Hutchinson.

William, he could not but feel, was now very comfortably and respectably at home in life in a circle of adoring women, while he was a wastrel whom no woman could really love, but only pity. He reproached himself bitterly for harbouring such thoughts, but sick as he was in body and in soul, they were inevitable. The more anxiously concerned Dorothy's affection was, the more he felt it as a reproach, while William, for all his fondness, was not the best kind of man to help Coleridge to forgive himself.

For Dorothy's sake, therefore, it was as well perhaps, that the lurking distrust should have culminated at last in the miserable quarrel over Montagu's words. Painful as it was, it cleared the air. There was a certain hardness in Wordsworth as there was a lamentable softness in Coleridge. And this grew in Wordsworth as his sense of propriety did. Professor de Selincourt fails to allow for this in putting all the blame for the rupture, as he does, on the weaker party. But the account he gives both of the enduring depth of the Wordsworths' attachment to Coleridge and of the distress which he superfluously caused them is certainly convincing.

But Dorothy's life, as we have said, was rooted in her passion for her brother. It was an abnormal passion. But genius is abnormal, and is ready to pay the price for its abnormality. Certainly in expressing this passion and in the return she received Dorothy was more than satisfied.

Moreover, unlike some dominant passions, it in no way restricted her genius for friendship or that impulsive sympathy for all who were in need, which fully justified her brother's tribute that 'in tenderness of heart I do not honestly believe she was ever exceeded by any of God's creatures'.

And beneath her exquisite humanity was the pure child of nature whose elemental innocence remained throughout her long life uncontaminated by the world. Even when she was no longer in possession of her real self and, in her own words, 'too busy with her own feelings' to fix her attention or find quiet in reading, the poet or half-poet, as she would have it, still lived and felt beneath her deranged faculties. A life of devoted household tasks had not domesticated that poet as a little note to her niece, Dora, survives to show:

'My dearest Dora [she wrote], They say I must write a letter — and what shall it be? news — news — I must seek for news — My own thoughts are a wilderness "not pierceable by power of any star" — News then is my resting place — news! news! Poor Peggy Benson lies in Grasmere Churchyard beside her once beautiful Mother, Fanny Haigh is gone to a better world. My friend Mrs. Rawson has ended her ninety and two years pilgrimage — and I have fought and fretted and striven and am here beside the fire. The Doves behind me at the small window — the laburnum with its naked seedpods shivers before my window and the pine-trees rock from their base. More I cannot write, so farewell!'

'With its negative reiteration', to quote Professor de Selincourt, 'and its lilt of wild melancholy', this little note 'is drawn from a depth of suffering which seems to transcend mere personal experience, and become a lyrical lament on the irony of all human things.'

Nature, her brother had written long before, never did betray the heart that loved her, and though his vision of his sister's old age as 'serene and bright and lovely as a Lapland night' was not realized, through the troubled obscurity of her posthumous existence and of the mind that had once been 'a mansion for all lovely forms' flashed moments when 'all the birds of sky and earth are singing and all is wrapped in happy brightness'.

In the consuming ardency of her life, the fever of feeling which she could not outgrow, and was too reckless of herself to subdue as prudently as her brother did, a more curious inquirer into human nature might discover more meaning than Professor de Selincourt does. But as a biography, this is a model of its kind and will be a permanent monument to one who, if she desired anything for herself, desired only to live in the hearts of those she loved.

VIII

COLERIDGE: AN OBITUARY

(July 25th, 1934)

WHEN Coleridge died a hundred years ago to-day, he had for eighteen years been sitting, as Carlyle put it in his memorable portrait, 'on the brow of Highgate Hill . . . like a sage escaped from the inanity of life's battle'. His express contributions to poetry, philosophy, or any specific province of human literature or enlightenment had, on Carlyle's reckoning, 'been small and sadly intermittent', and his renowned talk a whispering of 'strange things, uncertain whether oracles or jargon'.

To-day it is rather Carlyle's own jargon which offends the ear and Coleridge's visionary genius which has survived the test of a century. Doubtless the practical intellects of the world still heed him as little as in Carlyle's day. But amongst inquiring spirits, amongst lovers of poetry and students of criticism, amongst those who would reconcile reason and religion, and amongst those who feel the fascination of a great soul disabled by and yet shining through a morbid temperament, Coleridge's reputation has steadily grown and was probably never higher than to-day.

Certainly few, if any, would now agree that his contributions to human literature or enlightenment were small. But his achievement as a writer has persistently suffered from what has been known of his failings as a man. In this respect, it must be admitted, modern research, and particularly the two volumes of *Unpublished Letters*, recently edited by Mr. E. L. Griggs, have tended rather to underline than to extenuate.

Yet if these letters expose somewhat damagingly Coleridge's constitutional weakness of will and the frequent self-deception in which he indulged in his recoil from unpleasant facts, they reveal, too, as almost everything he wrote does, that 'kind, good soul, full of religion and affection, and poetry and animal magnetism', whom even Carlyle could not but recognize, and of whom, after his death, Lamb wrote that 'his great and dear spirit haunts me; never saw I his likeness, nor probably the world can see again'.

The truth is that Coleridge, who was so exasperatingly culpable in his conduct of finite affairs, was in love with the infinite, and to that extent infinitely lovable. Not that this can be said of all who aspire to the infinite. But for Coleridge the infinite was no bleak abstraction. His love was of the heart as well as of the mind. It was a love of heaven, of the eternal, whose white radiance was not stained for him, as it was for Shelley, by life's dome of many-coloured glass, but was itself the sunny dome, glittering with its caves of ice, where music built it in the air, far above the sunless ocean of mortality, yet linked with that ocean by the sacred river that ran down to it through 'caverns measureless to man', and by which man might regain the heaven that he had lost.

The longing for this heaven and to feed on honey-dew and drink the milk of Paradise was the secret of Coleridge's inspiration, of the enchantment which he exercised alike as a writer and a talker, and of all his disabilities as a man.

From childhood he could find no home nor hold in a world of facts. His genius lay in his surrender of himself to a world of ideas, of dreams and images, and of melting sentiments. In this immaterial world, which he entered through the very loving weakness of his nature as well as by his metaphysical genius, he discovered his strength. Incapable of ordering concrete things, his dissolvent spirit found in the abstract and the impalpable a realm in which he could float above the heavy weight of mundane obligations. There his mind, made luminous by the rarer atmosphere in which it moved, divined the inward meaning, the subliminal shape, of things, and clothed it in a subtle, if at times obscuring, veil of transcendental logic.

He had begun to do this, as Lamb and others testified, while he was still a boy at Christ's Hospital. But the poet in him, as all the world knows, subdued for a short, miraculous season the speculative genius. The poems of that flowering time when, with Wordsworth and his sister he walked the Quantocks, are incomparable. The magic of *Christabel*, of *The Ancient Mariner* and *Kubla Khan* is beyond the reach of time or criticism. A modern critic has, indeed, found such profundities of meaning in their magic that he has described them as a little 'Divina Commedia', the first imaging Hell, the second Purgatory, the third Paradise. This is, perhaps, to read too much into their symbolism. Yet the proof of the purest poetry is that its meaning is inexhaustible. And infinite in suggestion these three poems certainly are.

But Coleridge was a homely as well as a homeless and unearthly enchanter, which explains the affection he inspired. And such tender soliloquies as *This Lime-Tree Bower, My Prison*, or *Frost at Midnight* have a quality of loving intimacy, both in their sentiment and in the strange vividness of detail observed, which will always endear them to readers.

When Coleridge assumed the lofty, impersonal tones of the professional poet, in formal Odes and Sonnets, or of the philosopher and moralist in such poems as *Religious Musings*, the magic went out of his verse. For it needed to be an intimate expression of himself, of his tenderness, of his moods of entrancement, and later, of his aching sense of failure. It was, indeed, when the poet in him was dying, or in his own belief, dead, that he composed the most moving of all his reflective poems, the *Dejection Ode*, and the lines to Wordsworth after hearing him read *The Prelude*.

Essentially, however, the poet never died in Coleridge, but continued to live and speak in the critic, the philosopher and even the pietist which he became. His life was less a 'decline and fall' than a succession of remarkable achievements in the realm of thought and imagination by a man who had long come to despair of himself and to be the despair of his friends.

We have only to survey the impressive range of his contributions to almost all the branches of philosophy and metaphysics to be convinced that abstract reasoning was not for him merely another narcotic in a painful world. For in his prose writings the Creative Reason or Imagination which he held to be the prime principle of true thought and being, and contrasted so often with the secondary 'understanding', was continually alight.

The reason which dominated the age into which he was born was not creative. Men's minds had already become estranged from the deeper faculties of being and from a world of more than relative reality. They had lost the sense of the essential interrelatedness of the material and the spiritual worlds, and the more sensitive of them had already begun to experience a 'homesickness of the soul'. Coleridge experienced it, but it quickened his vision of the infinite whole to which he felt that every finite activity should be referred. It was this relation which needed to be justified in a new way to the intelligence, and Coleridge was the first, in England at least, to undertake the task.

After a century of scientific development the need is still with us and even greater. And although Coleridge's terms may not be ours and we may think that he generalized and methodized to excess, his philosophical writings are full of luminous reasoning, of intuitions which break through the web of abstract thought and clothe themselves in the living image or the inevitable simile, and of that bringing together of the apparently unlike and separate which is one of the surest signs of genius.

This is particularly so in his literary criticism. And in depth and sureness of insight he is without doubt one of the greatest of English critics. For his lectures on Shakespeare and others, and his *Biographia Literaria* initiated a new order of imaginative criticism and gave to aesthetic theory a new basis in living experience.

The moralist and the pietist in him have probably the least meaning for us to-day, although those who will quarry in *Aids to Reflection* or *The Friend* will find some precious metal even there, while his *Table Talk* and that rare collection of comments and reflections from his unpublished note-books, entitled *Anima Poetae* are full of astonishing flashes of insight and of that subtle self-analysis which made him one of the most penetrating, if one of the most impotent, of modern psychologists.

But his vision of a Spiritual Reason in things, to which the logical mind must be subordinated if it was not to lead men astray, was neither impotent nor delusive. The truth of it is, indeed, coming home to us to-day. And it was the vision of a man who despite his weaknesses of self-deception and self-indulgence was essentially magnanimous and childlike, and who loved only less perhaps than he wished to be loved.

IX

THE DEATH THEME IN RILKE'S LIFE AND POETRY

'POETS', wrote Jung, 'are the first in their time to divine the darkly moving, mysterious currents, and to express them according to the limits of their capacity in more or less speaking symbols. They make known, like true prophets, the deep motions of the collective unconscious, "the will of God" . . . which, in the course of time, must inevitably come to the surface as a general phenomenon.'

Such true poets are rare in any age. But beyond doubt Rainer Maria Rilke was one of them. The true poet, like the true mystic, discovers with Rilke that

> there's an old hostility
> between our human life and a great work.

In him this conflict was lifelong and his efforts to resolve it are reflected in certain themes which recur again and again in his poetry and above all in the meaning which he gave to death. In the life and work of this gentle, yet resolute man, who was both Slav and Teuton, we see the mystery being enacted by which Europe, convulsed by a false death agony, a destructive death which is always the despairing reflex of a meaningless life, may one day rediscover its soul.

Death has always allured the German soul, as an abyss into which it would plunge to resolve the intolerable tension of life. At the heart even of the thought of Novalis and Schopenhauer, as of Wagner's music, is the 'Liebestod', the death-swoon which is a love-swoon, which releases from finite bonds, which intoxicates with its infinite languors. In the fanatical utterance of Hitler the same theme recurs, and death, divorced from a life which had lost its soul, is worshipped as an end. In him a tormented people, or those most conscious of frustration, rain destruction from the skies in their longing to destroy themselves. Yet the frustration so terribly manifested in the German people is to a somewhat less degree apparent in their victims and opponents. It is characteristic of Western civilization to-day which, in its incapacity for a creative revolution, has plunged inevitably into the revolution of destruction which is modern war.

Rilke foresaw this necessity very clearly during the first world war which he suffered in his soul as only one of his spiritual sensitiveness could. He hoped for a renovation, a profound change of heart, by which the world might be saved. Such a renovation, as we now so lamentably know, was never even begun. Instead the world hardened its heart, as Pharaoh did in Egypt. And the plague returned more dire and deadly than before.

But in Rilke himself that innermost renovation took place. In him an acceptance of death became an affirmation of life. The death-hunger, which the demons of pride and frustration in the German soul converted into a monstrous assault upon the already gravely threatened life of humanity, became a love of death which recreated the joy of existence.

Rilke's work is a developing whole. Even in his early poems and in the famous *Notebook of Malte Laurids Brigge*, completed in 1910 and ending one phase of his life, he was intent, in the handling and deepening of his intense sensibility, upon 'keeping life open towards death'. But it was not until near the end of his life, in the great *Duino Elegies* and the *Sonnets to Orpheus*, that his purpose was fulfilled.

The Elegies were conceived and two of them composed during the winter of 1911-12 when he was living alone at the castle of Duino, near Trieste, and while walking to and fro along the bastions, with the sea raging two hundred feet below, seemed to hear a voice crying the first words of them. But it was ten years before he completed them. For the war drove him back upon himself at a time when he seemed to be emerging from a period of poetical impotence. How could he affirm as one the pain and the joy of life in a world that was bleeding itself to death?

In February 1922, however, the moment of mature utterance

came and in an astonishing flow of creation he completed the remaining eight Elegies and fifty-five Sonnets within three weeks. In the Elegies the note of lament sounds the more strongly, in the Sonnets the note of praise. But in both the two notes are essentially one.

Rilke achieved this integral vision only after a lifetime of patient and solitary striving. No man knew better the cost of truth in painful experience or the necessity of living through suffering until it became an act of total acceptance which released the eternal springs of joy. To this goal both his life and his poetry were directed, and although he reached it in flashes of insight many years before the Elegies were completed, it was only in them and the Sonnets and a few other poems of his last years that the fruit of his sensibility ripened to perfection.

To others he might seem as a poet to have achieved in his earlier work a remarkable integrity. But he was still aware of his one-sidedness, as when he wrote to an admirer that 'lamentation has frequently preponderated; yet I know that one is only justified in making such full use of the strings of lamentation if one has resolved to play on them, by means of them, later, the whole of that triumphant jubilation that swells up behind everything hard and painful and endured, and without which voices are incomplete'.

In the great tenth Elegy he did so triumphantly play on the strings of lamentation, as can be felt in its exultant opening lines:

> Some day, emerging at last from this terrifying vision,
> may I burst into jubilant praise to assenting Angels!
> May not even one of the clear-struck keys of the heart
> fail to respond through alighting on slack or doubtful
> or rending strings! May a new-found splendour appear
> in my streaming face! May inconspicuous Weeping
> flower! How dear you will be to me then, you Nights
> of Affliction! Oh, why did I not, inconsolable sisters
> more bendingly kneel to receive you, more loosely surrender
> myself to your loosened hair? We wasters of sorrows!

How we stare away into sad endurance beyond them,
trying to foresee their end! Whereas they are
nothing else
than our winter foliage, our sombre evergreen, *one*
of the seasons of our interior year, — not only
season — they're also place, settlement, camp, soil,
dwelling.[1]

Rilke drew in this Elegy a contrast between the 'City of Pain', the false distracted city of the modern world, in which what passes for joy is indeed pain, and pain itself, a mere grin of agonized features, and the spacious landscape of the 'Land of Pain' with its fields of flowering sadness and its pasturing herds of Grief, where to mourn is to be blessed and through which the pilgrim may come to those true lost depths upon which happiness falls like the rain on the dark earth in the early spring.

This contrast corresponds to that which he drew, in other Elegies and elsewhere, between the death that has dwindled and shrunk into a feared antagonist of life and the true Death which is Life's loved otherself, the great night from which the Day is eternally reborn. He himself wrote that in the Elegies 'affirmation of life AND affirmation of death reveal themselves as one. To concede the one without the other is a restriction that finally excludes all infinity. Death is our reverted, our unilluminated, side of life: we must try to achieve the greatest possible consciousness of our existence, which is at home in both of these unlimited provinces, which is inexhaustibly nourished out of both'. In the consciousness in which death and life were reconciled there was also 'neither a here nor a beyond but only the great unity, in which the "Angels", those beings that surpass us, are at home'.

There is not space here to consider at length what the 'Angels' or the 'Angel' meant to Rilke. But of what Death meant to him something more may be said.

[1] For this and other renderings I am indebted to Mr. J. B. Leishman's invaluable translation. The quotations from the letters I owe mostly to Mr. R. F. C. Hull's *Selected Letters of Rainer Maria Rilke*.

2

The conflict of life and death, which it was the supreme task of his genius to try to resolve, determined the pattern of his personal life as it did the quality of his poetry. In his personal life it appeared as an acute struggle between the more elementary human demands and the deeper spiritual ones. In living out this conflict as creatively as he could, Rilke, judged by ordinary standards, may seem to have evaded the more intimate stress of human relationships and even sacrificed people now and then to the needs of his genius.

His English biographer, Miss E. M. Butler, has too often so judged him, partly in an understandable reaction against the idolatry of some of his German admirers, partly, it would seem, because there are traits in his character for which she feels a strong antipathy.

Admittedly Rilke lived by and through feeling to a greater degree even than Keats, whose masculine vigour of heart and mind he lacked. But his was an aestheticism of the spirit and the heart as well as of the senses. His nature reached out to the infinite Beyond into which, he felt, death opened, and what he deplored in human existence was the closing of this open way.

He had not, as he confessed, always recognized how intimately the affirmation of death and life should be one, and in himself he never fully realized his poetic ideal of reconciling them. For although aesthetically he loved existence, it also aesthetically appalled him. His delicate spirit recoiled before the ugly and insensate and even before the vulgarly natural in it. He could worship the young girl as a flower of unawakened womanhood, but he felt unequal to the demands of Mother Eve and shrank from her coarse and insatiable appetite for life, as Blake's 'Thel' from 'the Matron Clay'.

In perception he could affirm again and again the reality of the visible world and its necessity as the form of the invisible. And his hostility to Christianity sprang, rightly or wrongly, from a conviction that it had devalued and even despised the world known to the senses. For he believed that 'aversion from any kind of existence is as little permitted to the creator as selection: a single withdrawal at any time thrusts him from the state of grace, makes him wholly and entirely sinful'.

Yet in the depths of him and in the human sphere this ideal of total acceptance, of profound self-giving, was hard to realize. In the fine agonies of *Malte Laurids Brigge*, that 'heavy, heavy book', as he called it, because it had drained his spirit so heavily, he distilled the morbid element in his sensibility of which he was conscious and which he hoped, by thus crystallizing, to cast out. But the immediate effect of his labour on it was to heighten the torments of self-centred sensibility which he impotently endured.

'Can you understand', he wrote, 'that this book has left me stranded like a survivor, my soul in a maze, with no occupation, never to be occupied again? The nearer I approached the end the more strongly did I feel that it would mean an indescribable cleavage, a high watershed, as I always told myself; but now it is clear that all the water has flowed towards the old side and that I am going down into a parched land that grows no different.'

Yet his resolution did not falter then or at any time. The task of awareness to which he had dedicated himself may well seem inhuman in the sacrifices it demanded. Yet it was based on a belief that for an artist art and life were an inseparable whole and that every object which came to him, whether it was a flower, a picture, a book, a bird, a person or a letter, belonged to the same task. The task was one of recognition, of lifting the object out of the stream of the transitory into the realm of meaning, of, as it were, discovering it to itself.

That, he most passionately believed, was what the artist existed to do, what, indeed, humanity, placed between the angelic and the insensate worlds, was ultimately meant to effect. It was to qualify himself for this task that he sought solitude, and if his introspection was at times morbid and his sense of impotence unbearable, it was the price he paid in his long, long labour to open himself to a realm of reality beyond the distorting veil of self-love and preference.

His torments of incapacity and spiritual drought often, indeed, suggest the desolations of the religious contemplative. His very language was that of the mystics, as when he wrote, 'how well I know the essence of the matter: "To leave all this behind without desire . . .", I who do nothing else but desire', or when he spoke of still clinging too much to his possessions and failing to achieve that boundless poverty which was his accepted task.

But in this vocation he laboured under a great bodily disability. His physical hypersensitiveness was almost pathological and he believed that he had become prematurely exhausted in spirit and body through his sufferings at the Military Academy to which he was sent as a boy; so much so that he could describe his subsequent life as a 'long convalescence'. But the frailness of his physique only makes the spiritual victory that he won out of weakness the more impressive.

The path which he pursued with heroic constancy from the age of twenty-seven, when he went to Paris to be Rodin's secretary, was in his own words, 'to stop being an outsider . . . to bind myself firmly to the reality which so often eludes me — to be there, not only in feeling, but also in knowledge, always, always'. This task called for infinite patience and humility or, as he put it, for 'responsibility for the deepest and innermost essence of a loved reality to which I am inseparably bound'. It demanded, as we have said, that he should reject nothing, least of all the small things.

It is hardly surprising that one so sensitive should have found this gospel of utter acceptance painful to live in the world as it is or that at times his sensibility should have overpowered him. For although his poetry and his letters are like a lyre, exquisitely responsive to the music and meaning of life as it flowed over and through him, there is always the danger in aestheticism, even when it is as imaginatively informed as it was in Rilke, of a self-centred refinement eating into the solid sanities of body and mind.

He knew this himself. 'Tell me,' he wrote to a friend, 'why it is that I spoil everything,—sometimes it seems to me that I apply too much force to my impressions (which, in fact, is what I do do on so many occasions), I stay too long in front of them, I press them into my face, and yet they are after all impressions of Nature, are they not; but even if you let them lie for a while quite quietly — *au lieu de me pénétrer, les impressions me percent?*'

If this was so with the passive images of Nature, his recoil from the more piercing and demanding intimacies of human relationship is understandable enough.

'How hard', he wrote, 'everything human hits me, what labour, what weariness wherever I enter: instead of helping me, making me a little new and harmless, it sets me to the galleys, I ply the oars, caulk the seams, scrub the decks, and (God forgive) have learnt nothing.'

That human relationships were peculiarly costly to him was as much due to the exactingly high ideal of integrity he set himself as to his abnormal sensitiveness. Experiences which never pierce the armour of the thick-skinned are for the tender what the rain of arrows was for Saint Anthony. But Anthony was a saint, while Rilke, as he more than once protested, was not and had no desire to be one. In this perhaps he was wrong, if it is possible for a saint to be also a poet. And it should be possible. There are passages in his letters which suggest that only in this way could he have found both the fulfilment of his sensibility and release from its disabilities. He could write, for example:

'I am no lover at all, it touches me only from the outside, perhaps because no one has ever really shaken me to the depths, perhaps because I do not love my Mother. Poor as poor I stand before this rich little creature [a woman friend, Marthe, he knew in Paris] in whom a person with a nature less cautious and imperilled than mine has been of recent years could have blossomed forth and found boundless delight. All love is an effort for me, an outlay, *surmenage*, only for God have I any facility, for to love God means to enter, to walk, to stand, to rest and everywhere be in the love of God.'

But to love God so and rest in His love continually it is necessary to love Him not only in the sensible world of images that reflect Him, but first and foremost in Himself, beyond all sense-perception and all self-love, in the transcendent emptiness which is His essential ground.

This the artist in Rilke refused and so in his human relationships his spirit tended to be overwhelmed by the countertides of uncentred feeling. It was not only that he felt his incapacity as a lover, to whom passion could only be a moment of ecstasy followed by disenchantment, revulsion and flight. Even his relationship with people seemed to involve him in falsehood because, in his own words, they galvanized his lifelessness without curing it.

He strove to resolve his dilemma by direct human approaches, but his sensitiveness continued to thwart him, throwing him back upon himself or, if it released him into communion with the being of another, causing him more of anguish than of joy. And so he concluded that his lot was 'to pass all humankind by, as it were, to reach some uttermost extreme'.

If he could have really reached the uttermost extreme, the infinite of Being, he might have found himself wholly at one with man. But this reconciliation of artist and saint was not his destiny. Tenderly human as he was in his sympathies (and few poets have gone to such pains to help those, often unknown correspondents, who brought their work or their troubles to his notice), he continued to feel his link with mankind to be frail, and to be really intimate only with the realm of Nature and that super-Nature which he called the realm of the Angels. In his own words: 'When I, coming deep down from things and beasts, longed to be instructed in mankind, behold the next stage, the Angelic was infused into me, and that is why I have overleapt people and now look back at them with compassion.'

This compassion differed only from that of a Buddha or a Bodhisattva in being still in some degree in bondage to the things of sense. Yet his aim as an artist was essentially the same as that of the true mystic, to spiritualize the senses and the affections so that they became pure channels of communion with life on all its levels.

He expressed his ideal well in a tribute he paid to a dead friend of whom he wrote that in his last years he 'had powerfully, fearlessly and with the modest pride peculiar to him, pored over Life and Death equally. He probed into the one as into the other, his experiences turned nowhere back, did not grow afraid, listened at no doors, everywhere went forward gentle and erect like ministering sisters accustomed to action where others only complain. When I saw him a year ago, so rich, so simple, as ready for joy as for the most painful knowledge, he gave me the impression of a hero, a hero such as men can be to-day, absorbed in the most steadfast action, serene, accomplishing his triumphs in the deepest and most hidden part of him . . . In his work and life he has raised himself to true permanence, to the most incontestable Being'.

In the human realm Rilke may never have fully realized this ideal, but as an Orpheus whose task it was to reunite by the genius of poetry what had become divided, men and things, the visible and the invisible, life and death, his fidelity to what he called the 'inexpressible bond between the quietly creating spirit and the holy, deep self-absorption of Nature', was richly rewarded; and not only in that crowning moment of poetic possession, of dying to live, in which the *Duino Elegies* were completed and of which he wrote that it was 'a tornado of the spirit, an unspeakable storm, the very fibres and tissues cracked in me — there was never a thought of eating, God knows what nourished me. But now it is done. Done. Amen'.

There was, indeed, something overstrained about the mystery, as Miss Butler has called it, 'played out between the poet and the angels in the *Elegies*', and to a less degree in the *Sonnets to Orpheus*, though in these poems he bridged, however tenuously, the gulf which had come to yawn between the human and the celestial worlds. But in the best of his other poetry it was the gulf, equally disastrous, between man and nature that he so tenderly and revealingly closed.

He was the more sensitive to this gulf because, as he said, a silent unison and attunement with natural things was an essential condition of his own productivity, indeed of his daily life itself. And he went on to deplore (he was writing a week after the first world war had broken out) the way in which Man invoked the cruelty of Nature to excuse his own. 'He forgets [he said] how innocently even the most terrible things happen in Nature, she does not treat them as a spectacle, does not hold aloof from them; in the Terrible she is entire, also her fruitfulness is in it, her magnanimity; it is, if one may say so, nothing but the expression of her plenitude. Her consciousness consists in her totality—because she contains *everything*, she contains horror also—but Man, who will never be capable of comprehending everything, is never certain when he chooses the Terrible — murder, shall we say — of containing the opposite of this abyss, and so in the same instant his choice condemns him (since it makes of him an exception) to be an isolated, one-sided being who is no longer subjoined to the Whole.'

In his longing to be subjoined to the Whole, to mediate between the supernatural realm of the Angels and the hidden plenitude of Nature, Rilke chose the path of the solitary, the lonely quest in which a sacrificial self-absorption is the narrow gate through which the soul may ultimately come to the state of 'incontestable Being' which was his visioned goal. In choosing it he was compelled to refuse the false attachments which human beings demand so generally as their right, like the returned Prodigal Son of the parable, as he retold it with such tragic comedy at the end of *The Notebook of Malte Laurids Brigge*, who threw himself at the feet of his all-too-forgiving relatives 'imploring them not to love him'. For 'what did they know of him? He was now terribly difficult to love, and he felt that One alone was capable of loving him. But He was not yet willing'.

Spinoza had written that he who truly loves God must not require God to love him in return and Rilke would seem to have applied this conception to human love in his suggestion that the highest love in woman or man is independent of any return. But what may be ultimately true of man's relation to God is less than true of the love of men and women for each other. And this peculiar view of Rilke's reflected in some measure his own incapacity to stand the strain of love. If he could have experienced the love of God as true religion has, amid so much convention and corruption, taught and enshrined it, he might have broken through to the divine heart of human love. Then the strain would have been relaxed. But despite all his sensitive and patient heart-work, this final release was not granted him. It seemed that God persisted in being 'not yet willing'.

The infinite might 'pass into him so intimately from every side that he could believe he felt the light reposing of the already appearing stars within his breast', but the light of the stars, however intimately felt, was a remote and impersonal glory compared with the light that can glow in the divine depths of another being. Nor is there any reason to believe that it shone with more than a fitful radiance between him and the girls whom, with what might almost seem a foretaste of dissolution, he loved in the last years of his life.

3

Yet when all has been said of Rilke's aestheticism, we can only admire the more his fidelity to his deepest insights and the unremitting sympathy with which he gave of the spiritual riches of his being. Only the insensitive could fail to appreciate the suffering he endured with such costly but fertile awareness or fail to recognize how wonderfully he transformed the morbid elements in his nature into a vision of human needs, which is of profound significance for the sick world of to-day.

For if he tended to magnify art into a religion, he also invested some of the deepest impulses and issues of religion with an imaginative significance which religious thought has so generally lost. To anyone but a man of the deepest integrity so feminine a sensibility as his, with the talent for enchanting expression that went with it, might well have led to an aesthetic *cul-de-sac*. But with Rilke it unfolded as an ever-deepening capacity for suffering life as a condition of expressing it more truly, of passing beyond the alternations of pain and pleasure into the joy which contains all sorrow.

That is why he speaks so poignantly to the Western Soul to-day, to those who are forced to endure the monstrous spectacle of uncreative suffering. The lovely vividness of the pictures in which his poetry abounds sprang from his genius for dying to things in the act of living them. But consistently he repudiated the suicidal yearning for death which afflicts every diseased civilization. Death for him was not a release from creative effort, but something to be laboured for and won as the crown of life. It was inherent in life from birth, and he believed that each individual contained a death of his own which developed as he did and which might or might not come to maturity, like his life. For him living and dying were as dual a necessity as the inflow and outflow of the breath. And the fact that the modern world tended more and more to impose upon men an alien, a mass-death, was as terrible to Rilke as the meaningless mass-life which was also the lot of so many.

A truly personal life, he insisted, must find its fulfilment in a truly personal death, as his own hard death proved to be; and both were nourished by the openness, the emptiness, the acceptance, by which we enable the creative stream to flow through us and our inwardness to flower, and which in different ways Rilke unceasingly affirmed throughout his poetry; as when in one of the *Sonnets to Orpheus* he praised the strength in weakness of the 'ever-opening' anemone and contrasted it with man:

> We, with our shows of violence, deceive.
> Our lives are longer, but on, O, what plane
> Shall we at last grow open and receive.

In another of them he declared how it was that Orpheus was qualified by his sojourn in Hades to sound his lyre in Heaven.

> Only who ventured to raise
> the lyre below
> may proffer some hint of the praise
> angels bestow.

Only who tasted their own
flower with the dead
shall hold the most fugitive tone
sounded or said.

Perishing image the pond
fleetingly tendered —
make it endure!

Not till both here and beyond
voices are rendered
lasting and pure.

'Defencelessness!' he wrote elsewhere, 'Our last and best resource!' And it was through this resource, this naked receptiveness, that he could write:

Birds quietly flying go
flying through us. O, I that want to grow,
the tree I look outside at's growing in me!

Or ask:

Did you feel fully all last summer's flowers?
The roses? (O, be honest — it repays!)
The re-awakefulness of morning hours?
The light-foot walk down spider-woven ways?
Dive deep into yourself, shake up, amaze
dearest Delight; somewhere in you she cowers.
And, finding anything that missed your heart,
be glad to re-perceive it from the start.

It was because sorrow, which to-day we have almost forgotten how to experience fruitfully, could open the heart to receive that he could hail it as 'so often source of blessedest progress'. The task of his life as poet and man was, in fact, to learn so to experience the world that, in the act of experiencing it, he transformed and re-created it, thus rescuing it from the fleeting.

This task he was, perhaps, by temperament too painfully sensitive wholly to fulfil. But of him as a poet it could be said, as of the woman friend of one of his tenderest and most searching poems,

> you passed through life
> open to everything, like a day breaking.

I have only been able to touch here on the nature of his experience and I have said nothing of the quality of his expression, so unassumingly profound, so tender and free from artifice in its symbolism. On his conception of the 'Angel', of the great lovers and those who die young, of the hero and the child, whole chapters could be written. But perhaps I have said enough to suggest that in this Austrian poet the wisdom of the East has come to birth in the West, that he reaffirmed the Unity in which the dual is no longer at strife, that he sensed, as Indian poets and sages had before him,

> that pure,
> unsuperintended element one breathes,
> endlessly knows, and never craves,

and that when he wrote of man, reminding us incidentally of Hopkins's 'Windhover', that 'there is one thing he must again grow capable of: falling, patiently resting in heaviness — he who presumed to surpass all the birds in flying', he spoke to his distracted Western brothers the same truth which Lao Tzü taught so many centuries ago — a truth to which suffering may perhaps open their ears.

X

A NOTE ON RILKE AND THE FIRST WORLD WAR

DURING the first world war, of which he suffered the anguish in his soul, no one saw more clearly than Rilke that, as he wrote in 1917, 'only through one of the greatest and innermost renovations it has ever gone through will the world be able to save and maintain itself'. His whole life was, in essence, as his poetry and his letters reveal, a submission to that necessity in his own being. The renovation which the world refused, he accepted. He opened his heart to those 'gentle, mysterious, trembling transformations, from which alone', he had written, 'the understandings and harmonies of a serener future will proceed'. Rilke's feet were already well set on this path before August 1914. But the war was for him a dark night through which, after a ten years' silence of devoted waiting, he found the light.

And it may, perhaps, be helpful when our task, too, is to discover 'the valid and where possible the somehow fruitful attitude towards the monstrous generality' to recall by a few quotations how this gentle and courageous spirit experienced the disaster which has returned upon us because we refused the challenge it offered to change our way of life.

Rilke, who was born at Prague, was an Austrian by birth. But his innate impulse to belong to no nation, but to all humanity, and through the depths of his humanity to reconcile the natural and the angelic worlds, was greatly strengthened by his visits to Russia in 1899 and 1900, the land where, he wrote, 'one re-learns all dimensions, the land where the people were lonely people and which borders on God'.

If in Russia he found solitude and God, in Paris, where he went next, he experienced not only the horrors and poverty of a great city, but its achievements in art, and above all in the works of Rodin, whose sculpture he described as a revelation and a necessity. Through Rodin he learnt how nature, without ceasing to be nature in the richest objective sense, might be taken up into the human spirit and re-expressed with a weight of human meaning.

It was this task of accepting the realm of nature and by the inward power of spirit, or of 'heart-work' as he called it, transforming it until the fact flowered in the symbol, that he recognized as peculiarly his own. In a letter to his wife in 1908 he described himself as sent forth to dwell among men in order to see the whole of life and to avoid or reject nothing. It was this which dictated his journeys to many parts of Europe in the following years, journeys that relieved the strain of the intense inward concentration through which he was labouring to deepen his incomparable sensibility until at last it might truly 'grow open and receive'.

To such a man, with such a history, the outbreak of the European war was, to a degree that few can have known it, a denial of all that he was. For three days only, as the 'Five Songs' written in early August 1914 show, was he carried away by the elemental tide of feeling which war released, not blindly indeed, but with a certain exultancy. He saw men 'in the grip of something. Already', he wrote,

> our drama had grown unreal,
> the invented image no longer answered our hearts.
> But now the time talks like a prophet, blindly,
> full of primeval soul.

The words recall, with a difference, the mood of Rupert Brooke and others. But two days were enough to convince Rilke that the modern War God, if he seemed at first to fuse men glowingly

> to a new creation he's animating with death,

was an insensate God.

'Is he a knower?' he asked. 'Can he possibly be a knower, this ravaging god, destroying all that is known?' Yet he could believe that the war came as a necessary destroyer of a civilization and a whole attitude to life which had become deathly, and which in its unexampled denial of human values had broken with the tradition of the past. In the war he divined, at first, the terrible process by which man might regain the true line of his development, 'the older heart of an incompletely achieved earlier age' be re-forged, and 'the furthest past and the furthest future come to an understanding'. So it was to be both mourned and praised:

> Don't be ashamed of mourning. Mourn! For, O, not till then
> will our unrecognizable, incomprehensible fate
> be fully fulfilled: till mourned beyond measure, and yet,
> in all its immeasurable mournfulness, longed for and kept like a feast.

But as the war went on, he had to recognize that it bred more falseness than it purged and that its mechanical violence killed man's capacity for that tragic experiencing in which the soul of truth can grow. Already in August 1915, he could write to a friend that sad and terrible as the war was, 'one could almost lament that it is not sufficiently so'. And two and a half years later he wrote:

'Frightful as the war is in itself, what seems to me still more horrible is the fact that its pressure has never helped to make man more recognizable, to thrust him, the individual or the mass, face to face with God, as was in former times the power of great distresses. On the level which has been formed since then, the level on which the newspapers have learnt how to give a conscienceless verbal cross-section of all events (a mob in which the second-hand and the conjectural stand side by side with the actual, the most mercantile side by side with the most incalculable): on this level a perpetual equalization of all tensions is produced, and humanity is trained to go on accepting a world of news in place of realities which no one any longer has the time and composure to let grow great and heavy in himself.'

How even truer this was to be during the second war — with the radio supplementing the newspapers and the Ministry of Information supplying the clergy with sermons — hardly needs stressing. The world, indeed, had 'fallen into the hands of men', as Rilke put it in his memorable phrase. And because man had forgotten

God, he had lost the capacity for suffering fruitfully, for finding in pain and anguish a meaning through which joy and thankfulness and a new life might be born. Modern war had become meaningless. It had deprived even death of meaning.

It was this that Rilke came to realize during the war-years which he spent waiting in Munich, 'always thinking it must come to an end, not understanding, not understanding, not understanding! Not to understand: yes, that was my whole occupation during those years — I can assure you, it was not an easy one!'

For in 'not understanding' he learnt to suffer the truth of the war at a deeper level than intelligence. Only in that kind of suffering, in which the imagination may redeem the evil which it has not resisted but has taken in pity and anguish to its heart, did he come to see any hope for humanity. And in a letter 'On God' he expressed with an insight which few have equalled what the pacifist of to-day is struggling to live. 'One should force oneself', he wrote,

'to see forthwith, in any power that claims a right over us, all power, the whole of power, power in itself, the power of God. One should say to oneself, there is only *one* power, and regard the slight, the false, the faulty as though it were the one that has a right to seize us. Would it not thus become harmless? If in every power, even in wicked and malignant power, one always saw power itself, I mean, that *something* which has an ultimate right to be powerful, would not one then survive, as it were, unhurt, even the unjustified and capricious? Is not our attitude to all the great unknown forces precisely this? We experience none of them in their purity. We accept each as it comes, together with its defects, which are perhaps adapted to our defects. — Nay, with all scholars, discoverers, and inventors, has not the assumption that they were dealing with great forces suddenly led to the greatest? I am young, and there's a lot of remonstrance in me; I can't assert that I act according to my insight in every case where impatience and disgust take hold of me, — but, deep down, I know that submission leads further than rebellion; it puts mere domineering to shame, and contributes indescribably to the glorification of the true power. The rebel forces his way out of the attraction of one centre of power, and perhaps succeeds in leaving that field of force; but above and beyond it he stands in emptiness, and has to look round for another gravitation to include him. And this is usually one of still less legitimacy than the first. Why, then, not see right away, in the one we happen to find ourselves in, the greatest power, without being disconcerted by its weaknesses and fluctuations? Of itself caprice will somewhere strike against law, and we shall save our strength if we leave it to effect its own conversion. To be sure, that is one of those long and slow processes which are in such complete contradiction to the notable precipitancy of our time. But, side by side with the swiftest movements, there will always be slow ones, some, indeed, of such extreme slowness that we simply can't experience their progress. But that's what humanity's for, isn't it? — to wait for what extends beyond the individual. From its point of view, what's slow is often what's quickest, i.e., it turns out that we only called it slow because it was something we couldn't measure.'

There is another passage in one of the series of 'Letters to a Young Woman', which is worth quoting for its relevance to-day both to Germany in the far greater prostration of her collapse and to ourselves in the delusion and demoralization of a victory of the machines.

The failure of the Revolution in Germany had confirmed Rilke's fears that humanity would not learn through the kind of suffering which modern war imposes. The sense of obligation towards a great, better-willed common future, of which he had dreamed, was still-born. The war had not destroyed the inhuman system of which it was the naked expression.

He left Germany for Switzerland, and there, in the continuous solitude of the little Château de Muzot sur Sierre, he realized at last that depth of reality, in which the war in his own heart was assuaged, and in an astonishing flow of creation he completed the *Duino Elegies* and the *Sonnets to Orpheus*. And from there, just a year later in February 1923, he wrote thus of what Germany might have done and been:

'Germany, in 1918, in the moment of collapse, could have put to shame and deeply impressed all the world through an act of deeper realization and conversion. By a clear, resolute denial of her wrongly-developed prosperity — in one word through that humility which would always have been her very life, and an element of her proper dignity, and would have surpassed all foreign humiliations that could be dictated to her. Then (so I hoped for a moment), in the German face which has become strangely one-sided, and one-willed, the lost, vanished trait of that humility which speaks so constructively in Dürer's drawings, would be put in again, added. Perhaps there were a few people who felt that, whose desires were directed towards such a correction, who put their trust in it. Now it is becoming apparent that this did not happen and already there is a nemesis. Something has been left out, which would have thrown everything into proportion; Germany has failed to be her purest and best, to give a re-established proportion to her oldest foundation. She has not built herself anew from the ground, and changed her mind, she has not created for herself that dignity which the most inward humility has for its roots, — she was only mindful of recovery in a superficial, quick, suspicious and acquisitive sense; she wanted to act so as to be off and away instead of, according to her deepest nature, enduring, overcoming, and being ready for her upgrade. She wanted to stay where she was instead of altering. And so one feels now . . . something has been left out. A date is missing that would have been an anchorage, a rung is missing in the ladder; hence the inexpressible anxiety, the fear, the "presentiment of a sudden violent collapse . . ."'[1]

How true it is, not merely of Germany, but in different degrees of us all! Perhaps, only when we have all been brought low in one way or another, shall we as nations recover the humility which has been left out, and be in a condition to build anew from the ground. Meanwhile there are still little Islands-of-life, as Rilke called them, which we must keep, 'doing what we can on them, suffering and feeling what we can'.

[1] I owe this rendering to Miss Angela Petter.

XI

POST-RENAISSANCE MAN

A 'BURNING ORACLE' does not promise to be comfortable to consult. And Professor Knight's style certainly agrees with the title he has given to his book[1] in being volubly ardent. Yet if the heat is often excessive and the order of composition tends to dissolve in a stream of fervid utterance, there is little smoke, and the light that is generated can be brilliant in its penetration. Above all, his criticism springs from that 'golden human centre' which, as we shall see, he regards as the fount of all virtue.

Readers of his previous books, and particularly of *The Christian Renaissance*, will know that in his literary studies Professor Knight has been developing a view of the nature of creative activity which involves the union of two forces. These forces he has described as 'clustering about the dual conceptions of Christianity and Eros'.

Suggestive as his terms are, they are not easy to define. But by Eros he implies not merely the sexual impulse, although that is prominently included in it, but the basic instincts from which all natural life flowers and by fidelity to which the sap of physical being is preserved. What he means by 'Christianity' is less clearly indicated. It is not the tradition of orthodox Christianity, which, in his view, has denied the erotic essence that it should have included and sanctified. He describes it in one place as 'the parental-filial impulse' and perhaps it would be fair to regard it as the power of human imagination, with all that that contains both of idealizing thought and sympathetic feeling. Or, in a word, it might be called the *agape* in which *eros* is completed.

In this union of dual impulses Professor Knight sees 'the very dynamic of life from which all thought, religion, art and action originate'. And it is by the degree to which they harmonized them that he values the achievement of the poets he here considers.

[1] G. WILSON KNIGHT: *The Burning Oracle*. Studies in the Poetry of Action.

His touchstone, as previously, is Shakespeare. And his essay on 'The Shakespearian Integrity' not only condenses very pregnantly the fruits of his earlier exploration in this field, but is the core of his present book.

In both Christianity and Shakespeare, he writes, 'you have a central humility and passivity violently creative, radiating action, a process, as it were, of continual incarnation'. It was, in short, Shakespeare's sympathy that ensured his power.

All creative genius is in some degree bisexual, and Shakespeare was uniquely so. He had, as Professor Knight points out, a feminine capacity for seeing into persons and forces. It is not merely that he could write from the woman's view but that he combined in his art as, perhaps, no other, the feminine genius for love and the masculine for action. His heroines show a maturity of love and are in touch with a wisdom and happy mockery unknown to men, with their showy passions. In love they tap, without conflict, the universal energy.

But it is in conflict and its tragic resolution that his men become great and purposeful. Yet however self-assertive in action they may be, they are protagonists in a sacrifice, martyrs as well as heroes. In Professor Knight's words, 'full of action as Shakespeare's stage is, it yet continually works to transmute action to a peace'.

In contrasting the inner realism of Shakespeare's heroic romance with such a superficial glory-sense as is to be found in *Tamburlaine*, he remarks that 'Shakespeare's mind is married to, while Marlowe has an affair with, valour, honour, kinship; he takes each and all for better or worse with their rooted tentacular relationships, sins and responsibilities . . . Having so felt into the essence, the outside he recreates with full yet never assertive splendour; having recognized the suffering passivity in all things, he can infuse into them the energies of action. The rough English type of a Faulconbridge is as typical as a Richard II. His martial splendours and kingly sceptres, deeds of turmoil and battle, never appear materialistic, since they are fed from something deeper'.

This marriage relationship as the secret of Shakespeare's unique creativeness Professor Knight finds equally implicit in his drawing of a snail, 'a perception of the selfhood's integrity, its inward music'. There is, he remarks, 'a metaphysical depth, a totally non-moralizing yet Christian profundity about it'.

This insistent claim by Professor Knight that Shakespeare's genius was profoundly Christian is at least questionable. It was certainly not Christian in the sense that Dante's was. In Dante, as in other great medieval poets or painters, we are conscious of a realm of experience or, one might say, a world of grace, of which Shakespeare, it would seem, had little, if any, comprehension. Shakespeare was supremely a child of the Renaissance, flushed with its morning pride and too intoxicated with the sense of God in man to humble himself deeply to the mystery of man in God. His was the genius of humanism in its fine flowering, its natural abundance, its nobility and arrogance and pathos, its humour and, in the last resort, its tragic insufficiency. No poet has given us so rich or total an experience of life within the earthly order. But it is doubtful whether the distinctively Christian, or more simply, religious experience, of which Christianity is one expression, was his.

To say this is not to deny that his genius was as creative as Professor Knight argues within its own realm or that the natural order as he expressed it had supernatural overtones and its own visionary splendour and tenderness. But the vision of eternal life peculiar to the religious genius and unique in its power to transform and reveal meaning in temporal life was not his.

Amid all the sensuous and imaginative glories of his world there is, in fact, a lack of that spiritual light beyond creatures and their becoming which shines in the *Divine Comedy* despite inhuman tendencies in Dante of which Shakespeare was innocent. To a less degree the same might be said of Milton. Despite his puritanism could he not evoke, in the opening of the third book of *Paradise Lost*, for example, a world not merely of ideas but of supernal experience which was closed to Shakespeare?

Certainly this is true of the *Paradiso*. And if the resolution of the tragic conflict of earthly life in the *Paradiso* is more convincing than in *The Tempest*, it is because Dante saw this world from the vantage point of another in a way that Shakespeare never did. Shakespeare could not altogether escape the Christian past, but he turned his back upon the medieval heaven. So far as this had become an unreal property of the medieval mind, he was right to do so. Yet in casting off the convention the men of the Renaissance also cast off the reality which the traditional doctrine and cosmology had once enshrined.

In Shakespeare, as in other great Renaissance writers, there was a great release of imaginative energy. What had been pent within a system poured itself into natural life. The dimming of that other-dimensional reality, so carefully cherished in religious tradition to illuminate natural life, was not felt at first as a disability. Men seemed rather to have plunged out of the rigid and partial into a whole universe of inexhaustible becoming. But the wholeness they acclaimed so expansively no longer had holiness as its ultimate goal and sanction. And compared with holiness all other degrees of wholeness are partial. Even the holiness of the heart's affections and the truth of imagination depend ultimately on an ideal of sanctity without which both are subject to the impurities of merely human feeling. The ideal need not, of course, be explicitly affirmed. It need only be inwardly acknowledged, as some would doubtless claim that it is in, for example, the enchanting innocence of the love of Ferdinand and Miranda.

Yet the doubt remains whether Shakespeare ever reconciled poetic and religious insight to a degree that justifies Professor Knight's description of him as an essentially Christian poet. At the most, it would seem, Shakespeare did at his greatest resolve in his imagination and his language the conflict of spirit and flesh in the natural order. To this extent he may be said to have reflected as a poet the redemptive mystery of which Christianity plumbs the depths in its doctrines of incarnation and atonement.

But the conflict raged fiercely in the great tragedies, and beautiful as is the love which, in the last plays, he conceived as redeeming it, we have only to compare it with the sacrificial and supernaturally inspired love of a crucified Christ or an enlightened Buddha to feel its inadequacy. In the scale of religious values the humblest man who daily follows Christ's or Buddha's example has entered a realm of reality closed to the greatest poetic genius whose love, however imaginative, falls short of this.

Yet whether or not we dispute Professor Knight's identification of Shakespeare with Christianity, his interpretation of the quality of Shakespeare's creativeness which he defines as 'a deep marriage-consciousness' is highly suggestive. He errs only in failing with characteristic romantic enthusiasm to qualify sufficiently his claims. The integrity even of a Shakespeare is relative.

What he means by 'a deep marriage-consciousness' is a true integration of the dual impulses in the poet himself and consequently of the world within and without. Shakespeare's sensuousness, for example, is never abstracted, he insists, from the experiencing whole to which it should belong or indulged for its own sake. It has, therefore, an inclusive purity, being 'a love rather than a lust, a vital identification rather than a confined sense-relation'. For Shakespeare, as for Blake, the body was that part of the soul which we can see. Everything was inwardly conceived as well as sensuously known, so that, as Professor Knight well puts it, 'Adonis's blood-life is felt through his physique: he is, as it were, a body lighted from within, and you get more of a real physical existence than in Marlowe's description of Leander's nakedness'.

Similarly a poet capable of such vital identification is not limited to the beautiful and thence by a rebound to the satirically ugly. Everything is trusted, and so opens to him its truth, its deepest selfhood. There is no distorting sense of sin to provoke pleasure in the superficially desirable or disgust at the superficially ugly. Evil, as in Prospero's magic, is at once mastered and forgiven.

2

Such an identity of spiritual understanding and sensuous enjoyment is, for Professor Knight, intrinsic to poetry. A poet is to be valued by the degree to which he redeems some province of human experience from discord, consummating in the act of expression a marriage of heaven and earth, of the inward and the outward, of natural joy and imaginative grace. And it is in the light of this vision of an organic integrity that he considers the work of the other five poets discussed in this book.

If it was merely an abstract vision, it might well prove more of a handicap to sensitive criticism than a help. But perhaps the most fruitful of Professor Knight's qualities as a critic is the closeness of his feeling for a poet's imagery and for the verbal texture of his style. He can, indeed, become excessively absorbed in demonstrating the vital felicities, the rhythms and 'tonings' of his subject's verse. But he is acutely aware of art as the language of nature, of 'the cramming of jerky monosyllables' in Pope's verse, for example, to indicate absurdity, or of the 'remorseless repetition and craggy consonants' which, in another passage by the same poet, 'toll the eternal sameness, rising to the thin tortured vowels' of a subsequent line. His quest, therefore, of the organic in a poet's consciousness is sensitively based in an intimate feeling for the body of poetry and his critical judgments derive from this immediate experience.

Consequently when he turns to Milton, who of all great poets, perhaps, invites critical harshness if weighed in the Shakespearian scale, he can write of the passage describing the approach of night in Book IV of *Paradise Lost*.

> Every word contributes to a close realization. There is an exact wedding of Milton's mind and manner with the mysterious nature of a *living* universe; one does not ask that his manner be changed, only that it shall be fitted, subdued, to his matter; and here it is so fitted. Though the stars are 'sapphires' note that they are 'living' ones; and this blend of the pulsing *with the solid* is all but the supreme excellence, as Keats knew, in any poetry. Life breathes from the description. There is a soft, almost unnoticed movement within the stillness.

This recognition of creative virtue is the more valuable because he considers *Paradise Lost* as a whole artistically fallacious. Not only is it an epic of 'The Fall' but it is an expression of a fallen consciousness which, in the act of creating it, failed to resolve its inward division. Milton, in Professor Knight's words, 'writes of angels, Christ, and God from a consciousness saturated in the knowledge of sin; whereas Shakespeare — or Milton in his own creation of Satan — sanctifies sin by writing of it from a godlike understanding'.

'Sanctifies' is a misleading word, but his meaning is clear enough. Milton, in his view, fell short of that imaginative acceptance of reality by which the war of good and evil is seen in relation to an underlying unity, as it was by Shakespeare. He does not inquire to what degree Shakespeare's acceptance failed to include a kind of evil of which the religious as distinct from the merely humanist consciousness is painfully aware, because its values are pitched higher. But he argues that in Milton sensuousness fought an endless battle with an iron ethical will, and that for him pleasure, however seemingly divine, was for ever shadowed by sinful shame.

It is, of course, the Puritan complex, and few would deny that Milton superbly embodied it. The Puritan is in some degree an egotist and few men have been more sublimely egotistical than Milton. His passion for liberty was rooted in a hatred of anything that would cramp his independence. Expressed alike in the violence of his polemics as a pamphleteer and in the grandeur of his style as a poet, it compelled him to denounce all bonds whether of orthodox dogma, Presbyterianism, the marriage laws, royalism, republicanism, or Cromwellian tyranny. Each in turn was proved wanting because each was in contradiction with his high idea of himself and of human nature.

Indeed his idea of himself was so high that there were no bounds short of divinity itself that could satisfy his demands. When each cause that he had championed failed, he remained blind, solitary, but not disillusioned. He could not conceive of himself as failing. And there was still one reality which he could serve and which would merit and reward his service. He could identify himself with God's party, the few but distinguished elect, and so be the chosen spokesman of Divinity.

Milton's God was, like himself, a supremely independent being, an Absolute, infinitely self-sufficient. In orthodox Christian theology the Father is held to be co-equal with the Son who reconciles in his person the eternal and the temporal. But to Milton the Son could not be eternal because he had a beginning in time. He could not be absolute because, being manifested, he was necessarily relative. Chafing himself at all limitation, Milton could not conceive of a state of being which was both limited and infinitely free, of a God who was timeless in time and an eternally uncreated Creator. Such a mystical conception was beyond the scope of his unmystical mind to which the infinite and the finite must always in the last resort be immeasurably opposed.

And if the Son was for him necessarily relative when regarded as the Creator of the World, Christ whom he conceived to be formed within the Son and as in his turn creating the elect, was even more relative since he was only a part of the Son. Characteristically Milton defined him as intelligence descending into man to dominate passion and so regenerate him.

A man's conception of God inevitably reflects his own nature and in Milton's character, from first to last, pride of intellect co-existed and strove with a powerfully sensual nature. It was this conflict which dictated his morality as it did his theology. Morality consisted for him in the ruling of desire by reason, as of woman by man. In this above all he was a Puritan, though of a majestic cast, loath to admit that reason itself, even when invested with the sanctity of divine intelligence, might be pride and negation or that beyond the conflict of reason and passion there might be a state of creative grace, a Christhood more integral than intelligence, however lofty, an imaginative love in which they served each other as equals.

His morality, however, was as noble within its bounds as his egotism was too serenely exalted ever to be small. And in saying, as Professor Knight does, that Milton 'writes from a deep awareness of *fallen* human — and other — nature; which is poetically fatal,' he goes too far.

For such deep awareness of sin, of tragic division, can be as essential to truth and as poetically necessary as faith in the miracle of creative atonement. Milton could not have expressed the reality of the fallen state, at once self-conscious and self-contradictory, with such imaginative intensity if he had in fact denied, as rigidly as Professor Knight suggests, the dynamic of human life at its source. Yet both the style and substance of his poetry do constantly reveal the ethical will predominating over the imaginative with a consequent substitution of the mechanical, however gorgeously veiled, for the vital.

Professor Knight analyses with unusual subtlety the psychological interplay of repressed instinct and repressive will, but he is at his best when illustrating it in the peculiar excellencies and limitations of Milton's style, in its pictorial rendering of Nature, at once sapless and static, and in a music which is too much that of a private adept, too little that of a created world, and which, with all its richness and glamour, has a too mental and even metallic ring. Yet he does full justice to its 'gong-like effect', its clangours and mysterious reverberations, as he does to the creative reality of Satan as a dramatization of Milton's heroic and tragic self.

3

Of the four other writers whose integrity he assesses, two, Spenser and Swift, are ranged on the Miltonic side; two, Pope and Byron, rather surprisingly, on the Shakespearian. In *The Faerie Queen* he finds no organic heart. 'The poem is always decomposing.' But Spenser's fault was the opposite of Milton's. Instead of being enslaved by the conflict of good and evil, he failed sufficiently to enter it, preferring ideas to reality. His gentle humanism never quite came down into human life to be tested and actualized, and its language was appropriately that of allegory in which spiritual content is to some extent abstracted from realistic form. But here again Professor Knight's appreciation of Spenser's style, its structural weakness and its fluid grace illustrates suggestively, as it underlies, the conclusions he draws.

It is, however, in his long essay on Pope that his unusual powers of 'in-feeling', to borrow his own word, of experiencing poetry as a living organism, are best displayed. His appreciation of *The Rape of the Lock* is particularly fine. He makes us feel the 'softly beating movement' of its life, and while he describes it happily as 'a flirtation with the sublime', he distinguishes clearly Pope's profound treatment of superficiality from a superficial treatment of human profundities.

It is, indeed, refreshing to find a modern romantic vindicating the human warmth and insight of a poet whom earlier romantics dismissed too summarily as artificial and as a neurotic misanthrope. But in his eagerness to demonstrate Pope's virtue in harmonizing reason and poetic faith, he tends to exaggerate his achievement. It is difficult, for example, to accept his estimate of *Eloisa to Abelard* as 'probably the greatest short love poem in our language', and the compact coherence of the *Essay on Criticism* and *Essay on Man* hardly justifies the high claims he makes for Pope as a creative thinker.

His appreciation of Byron also tends to extravagance and, as often in his writing, to loose Shakespearian comparisons. He cannot, indeed, claim Byron as a reconciler of opposites, but he applauds him for asserting the primacy of instinct through an agonized self-conflict. Beneath the proud individualist he discovers, too, an ardent force of social sympathy. At Byron's heart, as at that of the tormented Byronic hero, there was, he insists, 'a love, a softness'. It is in exposing this quality in Byron's work, and particularly in *Marino* and *Sardanapalus*, that he adds most to our understanding of a poet whose feminine depths are not easily divined beneath what Goethe called his 'daring, dash and grandiosity'.

Professor Knight himself tends to overlook the theatrical and the vulgar in Byron in admiration of his puissant personality and verbal power. However immediate Byron's instinctive contact with the living universe was, he was a divided man. And in claiming that 'the powerful sexual thrust of his imagination' was 'conjoined to keenest intellectual awareness of all the issues involved', Professor Knight reverses far too violently Goethe's famous opinion that 'the moment he reflects he is a child'. Yet his essay ends in a really revealing exposition, in relation to *Don Juan*, of the nature of sympathetic as distinct from derisive humour, which brings us back to that 'basic and golden human centre' to which we referred at the beginning of this article.

It is by their fidelity to or denial of this centre that he measures the virtue of these poets. And since poets live out with prophetic intensity the problem that faces us all, he believes that in his study of them 'lies the germ of a new psychological, social and religious reconstruction'. Certainly his book has a more than literary value and importance.

Yet the Shakesperian synthesis, even when so vitally expounded, has its dangers. In commending it Professor Knight writes in one place: 'Properly to act and live an experience the mind must be subdued, dissolved, itself unpossessing. Creative things are often accomplished half aware; while excessive awareness tends to the immoral.'

Excessive awareness is, in fact, insufficient, self-conscious awareness, that cannot relax into the unconscious depths of being. But the mind that can so relax needs, also, to be continually alert to inform and discriminate what in humility it receives.

It is this determining capacity of the human reason which Professor Knight both in his theory and his own practice tends to undervalue. Hence the frequent formlessness, and at times even lush excess, of his writing. But he has explored from within the self-conflict of the post-Renaissance man, even if the solution of conflict he offers is too much of a romantic simplification.

XII

THE HIDDEN TENNYSON

MUCH criticism of Tennyson during the last thirty years has been criticism of Victorianism rather than of the poet. The two can never, of course, be wholly dissociated. For seldom has a poet so choicely represented, in certain aspects of his work, the temper of his age. Yet 'Victorianism' itself is a generalization which cannot survive a close scrutiny. So far as it means or meant all that we of the twentieth century find most antipathetic, the smug, the moralistic, the stufflily over-dressed and over-furnished, the pompous and insincere, it excludes much that was most real in the Victorian age. To do justice to the sixty years during which Tennyson wrote we should need to discriminate almost between every decade and to look beneath the upholstered surface for which we may well have a reasonable distaste.

The second half of the nineteenth century may not have been quite so dark and disastrous a period of English history as Humbert Wolfe claimed that it was, because it was steadily and remorselessly destroying the old civilization without creating a new. But we can see now that beneath its confident and materially prosperous exterior the forces that would destroy it were growing at an alarming speed. The conflict in men's minds between the new claims of natural science and the old assurances of religion was only one aspect of the gathering challenge of a mechanistic to a humanistic civilization.

Nothing less than the disintegration of the whole individualistic culture, which had originated with the Renaissance and the Reformation and signed its own death-warrant in the inhumanities of the Industrial Revolution, had visibly begun, though few could then perceive it. To-day we witness its actual death-agonies and in the presence of them the anti-Victorian distaste of twenty years ago seems too often to have been a reaction against the superficial and unimportant.

In thus coming nearer to the realities of Tennyson's age we should come nearer to the reality of Tennyson himself and reach beyond 'Victorianism' to the fundamental poetic quality of his work. There is a curious parallelism here with Wordsworth. For many years after Wordsworth's death he continued to be regarded as a highly respectable Laureate who might well have worn the gaiters of his brother, the Bishop. It was only gradually that the strangeness, the 'otherness' of his genius, which A. C. Bradley stressed in his famous lecture, came fully to be recognized and that 'strange fits of passion', not calm bouts of platitude, were seen to underlie all that was most original in his utterance.

Tennyson, too, was admired by his own generation chiefly for the moral, theological, sentimental or pseudo-dramatic parts of his work. The dignified bard, personifying poetically the virtues of the Prince-Consort which he had incongruously fathered upon King Arthur, was the figure which bulked largely in the public eye, and the *Confessions of a Second-rate Sensitive Mind* with its cry of anguish,

> O weary life! O weary death!
> O spirit and heart made desolate!
> A damnéd vacillating state!

was forgotten or dismissed as an echo of morbid adolescence.

Yet this view of Tennyson and his poetry had not at one time been that of other sensitive minds, of such men, for example, as Aubrey de Vere who wrote of the startling originality of the early poems: 'about that originality there was for us a wild inexplicable magic and a deep pathos, though hardly as simple as Wordsworth's pathos, and with nothing of its homeliness'.

'There is black blood in all the Tennysons', said Alfred, and to anyone who had wished to see it the dark melancholy that was the background of Tennyson's thought was continuously apparent at least until the publication of *Maud* in 1855, and it haunted many of his later poems, if often, then, in the form of premonitions of social disaster.

The publication, too, during the last decade of his *Unpublished*

Early Poems and of his astonishingly precocious play, *The Devil And The Lady*, written at the age of fourteen, have shown that this secret melancholy and neurotic distress were deep-rooted in his nature, though the play reveals even more clearly a passionate Elizabethan gusto which was to be soon repressed.

To the end of his life there survived, indeed, beneath the recoiling sensibility, fastidiousness and moral dignity which he showed to the world a more primitive and healthy strain. And perhaps the secret of that 'dark undercurrent woe' which kept breaking through the crust of moral earnestness, as in the lines from *The Two Voices*,

> Again the voice spoke unto me:
> 'Thou art so steep'd in misery
> Surely 'twere better not to be.
> Thine anguish will not let thee sleep,
> Nor any train of reason keep:
> Thou canst not think but thou wilt weep',

was that of a passionate nature driven in on itself.

For this the age in which he lived was in some measure responsible. But it was not the only cause. A poet is free to react in different ways to his age and Tennyson reacted as he did because he was made that way. In his private life, too, fate dealt him just the blow which an innate melancholy had, as it were, foreseen. Arthur Hallam's death in 1833 made real to him, as nothing else could have, the desolation which previously had been an objectless emotion inspiring the lonely music of *Mariana* or of *The Lady of Shalott* or the self-torment of the *Confessions*. For fifteen years he withdrew to wrestle in himself with a desolation no longer fanciful, but actual, with a passionate longing, a grieving hunger, which at first, it seemed, nothing could assuage.

The fruit of that struggle was *In Memoriam*. In that great poem he expressed the deepest sorrow of his life, and in reasoning with it translated what had been a floating introspective mood into an interpretation of the everlasting issues of life and death. He also released thereby something of the passion which, through repression, had been a self-consuming fire and which informed all that was rarest and most compelling in *Maud*.

The morbidity of the hero of *Maud* revealed, however, something that Tennyson never outgrew, yet which underlay or was infused in all his greatest poetry. That it was responsible for much that was maudlin is equally true. But the sense of cosmic sorrow, of the infinite pathos of life, of those 'tears from the depth of some divine despair' that,

> Rise in the heart, and gather to the eyes,
> In looking on the happy Autumn-fields,
> And thinking of the days that are no more,

was at the very heart of his loveliest lyrical singing even when he heard the horns of Elfland faintly blowing or summoned his reader to seek with *Ulysses* a newer world, to dare the perilous gulfs, since

> It may be we shall touch the Happy Isles,
> And see the great Achilles, whom we knew.

His nostalgia for those Happy Isles, which in the *Lotos-Eaters* could be as voluptuous as it was keyed to heroic endeavour in *Ulysses*, was conditioned by his age, already dimmed by middle-class commercialism.

Because Tennyson was a poet, sensitive to the inner pulse of things, recoiling from all that violated the beauty and freshness which life intended, he felt, as we to-day can all too clearly see, that humanity had entered on a false path which, if pursued, could only end in appalling disaster. The era of the machine and the merchant had begun and although as a national Laureate he did his best to salute the possibilities of expansion and human betterment, the real poet in him already felt the threat of those 'Satanic mills' to all that was comely and sensitive in the civilization which man had so laboriously built up.

The artist in him as well as the man with his deep hidden roots in something primeval clung to the classical pattern of life as a defence against the chaos of elemental forces and the clash and clang of machines which man no longer controlled. Yet in mood and feeling he was a child of the romantic movement, divining how precariously the traditional classical and humanistic culture survived over an abyss which already seemed to be opening to engulf it.

What has been called his compromise was an attempt to combine the best of the old and the new. He was, in fact, the one great English poet, as Mr. Scaife has pointed out in a suggestive essay, to attempt to express the physical and intellectual rhythms, which were being shaped by railways and scientific theories, in forms modelled in the classical tradition. He was, also, one of the first, despite all his attempts at objective dramatization, to withdraw poetry into the introspective world from which to-day it has not yet succeeded in extricating itself.

I have not attempted here any general appreciation of his work. Much of it can be seen to-day to have reflected the false compromise which was the uneasy reaction of an age that felt its foundations crumbling but could not begin to build anew. But beneath the compromise in Tennyson himself was the stress of a true conflict. Beneath the 'muffled poet of domestic horizons' was a lonely spirit, wild as the eagle of his poem, who watched from his mountain walls and longed at times 'like a thunderbolt to fall'.

His age deprecated thunderbolts and he accepted outwardly its ruling. But all that was untamed and forlorn within him resented the conventions which caution and worldly interest approved. It was from these innermost depths of his nature that the music of his greatest verse flowed, verse that will live as long as English poetry does. For it was modulated by a consummate craftsman. Personal feeling and impersonal craftsmanship met and married in his greatest verse and the subjective was crystallized by a conscious art of which he was an exquisite master. When all that was second-rate in his philosophy, trite in his moralizing or bathos in his sentiment is forgotten, he will be remembered as the supreme lyrical poet of an age whose mortal disease he so deeply sensed and so melodiously assuaged.

XIII

EDMUND BLUNDEN'S LATER POETRY

THE poetry which has gained most attention during the last ten years has reflected with increasing clearness the divorce between the modern writer and a civilization which was very sick. Yeats's often quoted lines

> Things fall apart, the centre cannot hold
> Mere anarchy is loosed upon the world

did crystallize a very general sense that what should bind human beings and human societies together, as it binds the component parts of every true work of art, had collapsed, and that the climax of the disease which had been eating into the body and soul of man ever since the industrial revolution was at hand.

The effect of this upon the sensibility of the poet was inevitable. Denied a fruitful relation with a society that for all its material achievements was drifting into chaos, he was driven back upon himself to seek within a coherence that was so lamentably lacking without.

Some at least of these poets, of whom Mr. Eliot and Mr. Pound were the most notable, strove to gather materials out of the past to shore the ruins which they despairingly depicted in the present. Others of a younger generation abandoned the past and set their minds and hearts upon a revolutionary change in the present, a change alike in the order of society and in the nature and habits of the individual.

As subtle and, at its best, expressive analysis of the contemporary human crisis, much of this poetry, even when it reflects the incoherence which it deplores, has a value in its penetrating diagnosis, can excite the reader to new discoveries by the originality of its idiom, and move him by the struggle implicit in it towards a more integrated sensibility.

Yet the common complaint that it is private and obscure when it is not public and propagandist, that it lacks music and through excess of mental emphasis fails to convey the sense of beauty that springs from 'a more than usual state of emotion with more than usual order' is often justified.

Given the conditions, could it be otherwise? It is hard for a poet to be whole in such a sick world as ours, and though his consciousness of sickness and his struggle to recreate health may be highly significant, and may point forward to the coherence of to-morrow, in which the breach between the past and the future will, we must hope, be healed, his art must suffer so far as it is merely a weapon of offence or defence against disease.

For in true art a man expresses an achieved identity and is so truly himself that he can be unconcerned with himself and wholly given over to the experience which he values. He is free to perceive and to love, and instead of nursing a lacerated sensibility he creates through one that is hale enough to be equally enriched by the dire and the delectable. Only out of the strong can come forth sweetness, and it is because he values intensely, that in realizing truth he communicates beauty.

It is this intensity of value, of self-forgetful and self-realizing love, rather than any external tradition, which forges a living link between the true poetry of any age, however strange or exacting its idiom, and what Mr. Eliot has called the 'living whole of all the poetry that has ever been written'. So far as a poet maintains this intensity he need have no fear, particularly in an age of unexampled betrayal of human values, that he is seeking escape from the harsh demands of the present in the graces of the past. For he will be, in something deeper than the literary sense, in the true tradition.

Mr. Blunden, within the limited province he has chosen, is such a poet. He has not escaped the horrors of warfare,

> Moving through those nights
> Of sad immense unknowingness,
> Led by dodging lights
> Of pale disordered power. . . .

Yet the vision that reconciles has not failed him. And if events have grimly shattered the hope struggling to be faith which he voiced in October 1938, in the poem entitled *Exorcized*, the essential truth of the lines

> The meeting of four men as friends unhorses all the ancient fiends;
> Believing still the best will ever yield the best,

remains, even when it is seen to have been too credulously applied.

Yet that he could so apply it may perhaps be taken as an illustration of the limits within which Mr. Blunden's imagination is sure-footed and to which he owes his characteristic virtues as a poet, above all that primal virtue of the countryman, a loving attention to the objective world.

This is something more than using fragments of the past in a despairing or at least deeply pessimistic attempt to shore the ruins of the present. It is to cherish the timeless quality of poetry, a quality which in our time-wracked days is little felt or can only be evoked with a sort of apocalyptic violence which lacks the deeper vibrations of repose. In one of his sonnets Mr. Blunden confesses:

> The ages of the men whose path met mine
> Seldom aroused my question; what I sought
> And found in them was of a different sign
> Than Time may recognize: the native thought,
> The character, the self, the singular gift,
> Whatever names a man more than his name.
> Gray hair or golden did not change my drift,
> All seemed of youth; their years might be the same.

'Not date, but quality' — the preference is characteristic. All his poems reveal the delicate antennae of his spirit feeling out for the rare and the real in every object of experience.

For such a poet the past is inevitably as living, as discoverable as the present. As he writes in *Cabaret Tune*:

> The flash of the brook and the life of the look
> And the scent of the may and the charm of the book
> Move for ever between Now and Then.

It is this province between Now and Then, a province in which the mellow grace of the past meets the immediacy of the present and blends with it that he rules with such distinction, whether he is rewriting a Latin hymn or making a song of a Jacobean sermon or recalling Lamb as a child listening to the Bible being read at Christ Church, Greyfriars. Even modern war is somehow included in it, somehow framed and forgiven in this perennial peace, whether in the remembrance of a column moving slowly into a land of fear or of a strange group of trees, seared, shamed and mutilated.

The English countryside, of course, still needs but little transfiguration to become poetry's province, when 'the bees of Dalham' are 'in the bramble-flowers' or big-woolled sheep at the 'plain green work of eating', or a village or market town affirm their stubborn antiquity and harmony of detail.

In his rendering of all these experiences there is the same quality. They have been taken up into that immemorial Now which is the realm of the loving imagination; a realm in which the distinctions of past and present are maintained but reconciled in a timeless instant. Often the Then, in Mr. Blunden's verse, may be poignantly contrasted with Now. Yet, if ever he deplores the present, it is for lacking the integrity, not the picturesque trappings, of the past.

Yet it is admittedly in his response to a larger convulsed present that his imagination is least adequate. The charge brought against him that he has failed to come to grips with contemporary reality and is for that reason inevitably only a minor poet has some truth in it. His very virtues are here his defects. His rootedness in the past and the soil make him impervious to the distractions, the mechanized tensions, the life-and-death struggle of the modern world. He does not stand between two worlds, one dead, one struggling to be born, but in a world of his own, secure and at peace, though tempests rage without or its tranquil air quivers now and then at the thud of distant explosions.

Probably Mr. Blunden recognizes clearly enough that civilization is at a major crisis of death or rebirth. But as a poet he does not identify himself with that crisis. If he felt it intimately in himself, he would be compelled to do so. But manifestly he does not. He would seem, to a great extent, to be immune from the conflict which tests and torments so many of his contemporaries. Not so completely as Robert Bridges, but relative to the acuter sickness of his age with something of a like aesthetic detachment, he cultivates the virtues of an unwounded sensibility and a quiet mind. So far as he seeks to heal the wounds of his time, it is by reaffirming the peace which has been the quality of happier times and which survives, both by the good fortune of his birth and upbringing as a countryman and by faithful cherishing, in himself.

In the realm of poetry integrity is the one essential quality. It alone gives creative order and permanence. But its content, its degree of intensity by which the strife of opposites is resolved in a harmony that includes them, varies from the high-strung to the low, from the large to the small. In the great poet there is the greatest intensity and comprehensiveness. He has adventured most, has challenged most discord and conquered it imaginatively. No poet can be great without such spiritual adventure, such suffering of extremes.

Many of Mr. Blunden's younger contemporaries have so ventured and suffered, but they have not conquered, not yet. Their verse at best reflects the stress and anguish of the battle as it sways now this way and now that. Mr. Blunden has not plunged deeply into the fight, though he has passed through it. He has accepted only so much of the discord as he can master and subdue without endangering his poise. And so, much of his verse is bathed in the pastoral or even bookish placidity of a gracious backwater.

In maintaining the continuity of human tradition he has mostly turned a blind eye to what is involved in the shattering of that tradition. His poetry is neither burdened nor intensified by any acute sense of crisis or of crumbling walls. And when momentarily his vision turns, as in the poem *Exorcized*, from the near and known and loved to a large but emptier world in which perverted forces grapple, he can be unrealistically innocent. Yet he is wise in this, that he seldom treads ground which his imagination has not intimately worked, circumscribed as that ground may be. Consequently the tradition which he maintains, he also renews.

2

The more sophisticated writers of verse to-day are impatient of nature poets, and there is some reason for their impatience. But Mr. Blunden is not a nature poet in the merely descriptive sense that some of the Georgian poets were. He is a poet whose imagination struck its roots inevitably and deeply in the English countryside, but which, because it was imagination and not merely sensibility, recreated what it received.

There is little mere description in his verse, though there is a wealth of distinctive detail, and through it all, in different degrees, there is a visionary quality, a sense of unearthly enchantment which only earth can fully disclose. As he writes in *The Recovery* turning from the 'celestial leafage' of the sky:

> The meadow-stream will serve
>   For my refreshment; that high glory yields
> Imaginings that slay; the safe paths curve
>   Through unexalted fields.
>
> Like these, where now no more
>   My early angels walk and call and fly,
> But the mouse stays his nibbling, to explore
>   My eye with his bright eye.

Or again, in some verses in memory of the country round Christ's Hospital:

> Sylvan and human, still it blooms and calls.
> Past Bonfire Hill to Muntham Woods the grace
> Of this kind secret sings with every dove;
> No airy nothing lacking bound and place,
> It likes its own small spires, its ponds, its walls,
> Asking the closest conscience of observant love.

Such 'sylvan wonder' and he have not drifted asunder, as he grieves to think they might, because observance in him, minute and particular as it has been, has never lacked the vision of the whole in the part and of the part in the whole, and of something by which nature is at once homely and transfigured.

Mr. Blunden's perception of nature is not as pure and direct as Clare's nor is it as charged with thought as Wordsworth's. But he blends the human and the natural with an unpretentious fidelity to each as he has known them in his most impressionable years, in a way that no other English poet has done.

How happily authentic his experience of English country life has been and how fruitfully he grew up beneath its cherishing is told in a long poem, entitled *A Summer's Fancy*. It is a poem which tells not only of himself but of a friend who shared his boyhood, and who later passed also through the hell of war to take up again the honest husbandry in which he had been reared. It is an excellent example of Mr. Blunden's capacity to be so truly personal that his characters, including his own, are both human and pictorial. They are at once in life and lifted out of life by an unobtrusive artistry.

It is the same with all the evocative wealth of natural detail. Mr. Blunden's art owes much to that of his predecessors, and the debt is felt in this poem as in many others. But he has gone to literature as he has gone to nature, to make it his own, even if it is at times by mingling in the same poem echoes of diverse notes.

Even, however, when one of his lighter poems recalls both the style and the temper of an earlier poet, as *A Tale Not in Chaucer* recalls Cowper, it is no mere pastiche. Or again, when the influence of Hardy is felt, as it is in a number of his poems, it is with a transmuting difference, as the following stanza from *The Spell of France* will suggest:

> Thus now it comes, and from blest occasion
> Of later date though brief,
> That some deep music from that country
> Shakes me like a leaf,
> And the happy storm of dreams or pictures
> Origined there
> Will occupy my whole existence
> And seem my native air.

An imaginative poet can afford to be hospitable because he gives as much as he receives. And so Mr. Blunden's learning in the English poets is as much part of himself as his knowledge of nature or of country worthies.

So is his craftsmanship. He has always been a conscious craftsman, and there are times even now when his interest in the texture of his verse is stronger than the vision which it should clothe, or when in his play with words he comes near to prettiness, in such lines, for example, as

> The impulses of April, the rain gems, the rose-cloud,
> The frilling of flowers in the westering love-wind.

Or in the opening stanza of *The Subtle Calm*:

> Seas like Roman glass,
> Where their prow advances,
> Spread a tinted shell;
> They in wonder pass
> As a white moth dances
> Over a woodland well.

Indeed the literary scholar in him is apt at times to cultivate verse much as a pastime — or merely to quote his own words, as 'attempts of a mind usually taxed with very different affairs, to avoid estrangement from a way of life beloved since childhood'.

Yet when he distils that way of life his verse is never occasional. And he has no need of the doubts which trouble him at the end of a tender invocation of a 'calm rain', when he asks:

> What worth is his
> Who fashions thus a selfish universe,
> And weaves dead leaves with living tragedies?
> While the strong world goes forth in symphonies
> Of action, passion, science and resource,
> Where shall faint music and far similes
> Befriend it? Has this stealing shower a force?
> And yet I fancy sometimes there is pain
> That still requires this shy and dream-like rain.

It is no fancy, though machines in our day have deadened men's awareness of their deepest needs. And in some of his poems, Mr. Blunden's imagination is fired by an impulse which carries him beyond the industrious delicacy with which he has learnt to 'catch the country's meaning'.

This 'otherness' at the heart of the familiar is felt in the haunting little ballad entitled *The Dreamer*, which is the more itself in sending the mind back to *Lucy Gray*; in the 'ambushed utter thing without a face' of another poem; or more explicitly in such a moment of ecstasy as *The Surprise*:

> Shot from the zenith of desire
> Some faultless beams found where I lay,
> Not much expecting such white fire
> Across a slow close working-day.
>
> What a great song then sang the brook,
> The fallen pillar's grace how new;
> The vast white oaks like cowslips shook —
> And I was winged, and flew to you.

But his imagination is surest, when its reach is less obviously exalted, when it is 'touched with a certain silver light' in retrospection, or when it finds heaven in the 'earth-born joy that's whispering through the tall white grass', in the tiniest hillside spring, or in horses, heads together, under a tree.

In the poems, too, entitled *Echoes from the Great War*, the realist who has suffered with an unflinching pity the outrage of modern battle is reconciled with the visionary who never fails to see through all the horrors the human goodness that he has loved in country inns, and who in a 'denatured gunland' never forgot the 'something primeval and perennial' that waited to erase and forgive.

All Mr. Blunden's best poetry is thus truly rooted in nature. Its ground is narrow, but deeply cultivated. And because his imagination is so fondly at home there, it seldom ventures into realms of modern thought or controversy.

'Agree,' he writes, 'the way to live is not to dissect existence', but to accept with sensitive awareness its living flow. So, too, he disclaims with Hardy any attempt to deliver 'an elaborated philosophy through the separate productions of varying impulse and circumstance'. His philosophy does occasionally become ironically explicit in such poems as *The Scientists* but it is essentially implicit in the integrity with which he maintains, through all he writes, that natural piety in which by quiet and 'simple watching' heaven and earth are reconciled.

In a machine-age this may seem an old-world fashion. But while many of his later poems, notably the series of *Sketches of Trials*, have a literary interest and recall other days, they live by the art of their human understanding. What Mr. Blunden loves in the ancient he loves, when he can find it, in the modern. He is possessed neither by the fever nor the dynamic forces of his time, but his is the music, gentle and composed, which he invokes in one of his later poems as *The Sum of All*:

> So rise, enchanting haunting faithful
> Music of life recalled and now revealing
> Unity; now discerned beyond
> Fear, obscureness, casualty,
> Exhaustion, shame and wreck,
> As what was best,
> As what was deeply well designed.

PART THREE

THE REALM OF SPIRIT

I

KIERKEGAARD AND THE PRESENT AGE

IT will soon be a hundred years since Sören Kierkegaard died in the Frederiks Hospital in Copenhagen. He had been carried there when he collapsed in the street some weeks before. He knew then that his task was over and almost the last words he wrote were these:

> Thou plain man! I do not hide from thee that according to my notion, the thing of being a Christian is endlessly high, that at no time are there more than a few that attain it — as Christ's own life attests when one considers the age in which He lived, and also His preaching indicates if one takes it literally. Yet, nevertheless, it is possible for all. But one thing I adjure thee for the sake of God in heaven and by all that is holy, flee the parsons . . .

With this characteristic fling, Kierkegaard ended the attack on the established Church, to which he devoted the last year of his life. This attack was no splenetic outburst. It was as necessary to him and to the truth for which he had fought as it was painful. And no one, not Tolstoy a quarter of a century later, was better qualified to expose 'the betrayal of Christ by the Churches'.

For the whole of Kierkegaard's life and of his work as an author was related, as he wrote himself, to the problem 'of becoming a Christian'. He never claimed to have become one, but no man saw more clearly what it cost to do so. All he demanded was honesty. So long as organized religion professed to be truly Christian, it made of Christendom a forgery, a conspiracy against the Christianity of the New Testament. But if it would admit that real Christianity was too hard for it, that it did not represent the claims Christ made upon his disciples, however well-intentioned and even laudable its activities were in many ways, then the air would be cleared and the paradox entailed in being a Christian would be recognized anew.

Kierkegaard hoped to wring this admission from the Primate of the Church in Denmark. It was, of course, a fantastic hope. Yet the authorities could not answer his challenge. They could only give a sigh of relief when he was dead. Kierkegaard was glad to die, too. God, as he said, had run him to a standstill. And he was sure he had accomplished his task.

Few, if any, understood then the significance of his life-work. To-day the truth of it stares us in the face, and his writings seem addressed particularly to us. Yet he disclaimed any supernatural gifts and any authority. He regarded himself only as a poet and a thinker, who aspired to be 'a witness for the truth' and even a martyr. At the end he was comforted by the thought that he had almost become one.

But before examining what this witnessing meant to him and means to us it will be well to take a glance at his history. That history began nearly fifty years before he was born, when a little boy, who was to be his father, tending sheep on the lonely Jutland heath, stood on a stone, hungry and cold, and cursed God. This curse his father could never forget, and his sense of sin and of the retribution which hung over his head were deepened many years later by what he regarded as an act of incontinence in marrying a servant in his house before the year of mourning for his first wife was up and in becoming the father of a child by her five months later.

Michael Kierkegaard was fifty-seven when Sören, the second son of this marriage, was born, and the link between the old man, devoutly religious but weighed down by a silent despair, and the small boy was extraordinarily close. Sören came to feel later that he was already an old man when he was born and that he leapt completely over childhood and youth. He inherited and was also infected by his father's melancholy, whose fault, he was to write, did not lie in lack of love, 'but he mistook a child for an old man'. Of the suffering which that involved he wrote poignantly:

> When one is a child — and the other children play and make merry and whatever else they do; oh! and when one is a youth, and the others fall in love and dance, or whatever else they do — then, in spite of the fact that one is a child or a

> youth, to be spirit! Frightful torment! And all the more frightful if one understands the trick of making oneself seem as if one were the most youthful of all.

This trick he practised, also, on his melancholy, the depth of which, in his own words, found its only true expression in the equally prodigious expertness granted him to hide this under an apparent cheerfulness and *joie de vivre*.

Nor was it only melancholy that he inherited from his father. He shared also the burden of his father's guilt, until, as he wrote in his *Journal*, he came to suspect that his father's great age 'was not a divine blessing but rather a curse; that the outstanding intellectual gifts of our family were only given to us in order that we should rend each other to pieces: then I felt the stillness of death grow around me when I saw in my father an unhappy man who was to outlive us all, a cross on the tomb of all his hopes. There must be a guilt upon the whole family, the punishment of God must be on it, it was to disappear, wiped out by the powerful hand of God, obliterated like an unsuccessful attempt, and only at times did I find a little alleviation in the thought that my father had been allotted the heavy task of calming us with the consolation of religion, of ministering to us so that a better world should be open to us even though we lost everything in this world'.

So 'crazy' an upbringing, humanly speaking, threw him back upon himself, and in his solitude, upon the 'God-relationship' which his old father impersonated for him as a child. It developed too, the intellectual side of his nature to an astonishing degree, so that he could write later of himself that he was fanatically in love with thoughts. To quote again from his *Journal*:

> Inwardly torn asunder as I was, without any expectation of leading a happy earthly life, without hope of a happy and comfortable future — as it naturally springs from and lies in the historical continuity of family life — what wonder then that in desperate despair I grasped at nought but the intellectual side in man and clung fast to it, so that the thought of my own considerable powers of mind was my only consolation, ideas my one joy, and mankind indifferent to me.

Thought became his passion, and his self-confidence as a thinker was only equalled by the hidden despair of which it was the counterpoise.

For while his real self wanted to forget all the doubt and anguish which his mind generated, his reflective self clung to it with a morbid appetite. And so the torment of never being like others, of being a wild goose among the tame, was at once the spur to his achievement and the cause of his acute suffering. It dictated the wit and apparent dissipation of his student life which he prolonged for nearly ten years, a masquerade behind which he almost concealed from other men his unlikeness to them. And it explains his desperate attempt in the middle twenties to 'realize the universal human' by marrying Regina Olsen, a girl ten years his junior.

2

The importance of this extraordinary relationship from which he felt inwardly that he must withdraw almost in the moment of being accepted by the girl as her lover cannot be exaggerated. All that was most self-exacting and inhuman in Kierkegaard was epitomized in it with all that was most profound and pathetic.

He told the story himself at length, under pseudonyms, in *Either/Or* and *Stages On Life's Way* and without disguise in his *Journal*. His *Fear and Trembling*, too, was essentially an allegorical expression of it, and to Regina, first and foremost, he addressed all his later writings. Through her and all she cost him in agony of mind and heart he came to accept his lonely destiny as a call to an extraordinary vocation.

During the year before he proposed to Regina, Kierkegaard had been reconciled to his father. He had also had an ecstatic religious experience of which he wrote: ' "I rejoice through my joy, in, at, with, over, by, and with my joy" — a heavenly refrain, as it were, suddenly breaks off our other song; a joy which cools and refreshes us like a breath of wind, a wave of air from the trade wind which blows from the plains of Mamre to the everlasting habitations.'

As a result of this and of his father's death, three months after their reconciliation, the tension of his being seemed to be eased and softened and he began to hope that in marriage with Regina it would be fully resolved. Yet in his *Journal*, after speaking of Regina as 'thou sovereign of my heart' he had turned upon his impulse as a lover with the question:

> Thou blind god of love! Wilt thou reveal to me what thou seest in secret? Shall I find what I am seeking, here in this world, shall I experience the conclusion of all my life's eccentric premises, shall I fold you in my arms — or:
>
> *are the orders* 'FURTHER'?
>
> Hast thou gone before me, thou my *yearning*, dost thou beckon to me, transformed, from another world? Oh, I will cast everything from me in order to be light enough to follow thee.

He had no sooner put the matter to the test by proposing and being accepted than he found the question answered. The orders were 'FURTHER' and he had placed himself and Regina in a most painful situation.

The reason for his recoil was, of course, hidden deep in his nature and his history where the psychologists have enjoyed analysing it in their own limited terms. In Kierkegaard the positive masculine element, that of spirit and mind, had so come to dominate his nature that, like the 'seducer' in *Either/Or* he was sometimes 'so entirely *esprit*' as to feel himself 'annihilated as woman'. He therefore at once desired and dreaded woman who represented the sensuous aspect of life which he could not reconcile with spirit in himself. There was in him, as he admitted 'a discord between body and soul', as there was between his reflective and active self.

This discord was not singular to him, though it can seldom have been so extreme. It is found repeatedly in the biographies of those who have devoted themselves to the spiritual life nor is its spiritual significance to be analysed away in terms of 'schizoid personality', 'Oedipus complex', 'libido' or 'existential psyche'. Kierkegaard understood its profound spiritual significance, yet he could see also with self-mocking and self-lacerating clearness how his action must appear to those who lacked his terrible insight.

Heartless, indeed, it was by ordinary human standards. Yet, being what he was, it might well have been more heartless to marry Regina. 'If I had not been a penitent,' he wrote, 'had not had my *vita ante acta*, had not been melancholy, my union with her would have made me happier than I had ever dreamed of being. But in so far as I was what, alas, I was, I had to say that I could be happier in my unhappiness without her than with her; she had moved me and I would have liked, more than liked, to have done everything. But there was a divine protest, that is how I understood it.'

The man who wrote thus was too self-centred to be wholly honest with himself. Often as he might protest that 'my sin has never been that I did not love her' and that he wished only to spare her the fate of being married to one who loved 'like a dying man', he was tortured inwardly by his incapacity for love. That was why he was inwardly convinced from the moment of being accepted by her 'that it must end badly' and why he had to confess that 'to live with her in the peaceful and trusting sense of the word never occurred to me'.

Even less could he be honest with Regina, and the complex strategy he evolved to escape from the trap into which he had fallen and to deliver Regina from it unhurt would be comic, and indeed was excruciatingly so to the ironist in himself, were it not also so pathetic. The virtuosity, at once cunning and disingenuous, of a diabolically clever man, who cannot do or say the simple thing, who is in terror of injuring both himself and another, and tries to relieve his anxiety by devising one 'shrewd plan' after another, has never been more fantastically displayed.

Yet we cannot doubt that it was, as he wrote, 'a time of terrible suffering to have to be so cruel and at the same time to love as I did. She fought like a tigress. If I had not believed that God had lodged a veto, she would have been victorious'.

When the two sides of a man's nature are so intensely at war as they were in Kierkegaard, a woman in love with him inevitably proves a tigress. She takes sides with that part of his nature which he is denying and fights the denier. Her instinct compels her to play the part which he dreads, that of the would-be annihilator of his ego. And if he loves as much as Kierkegaard clearly did, part of him longs to surrender, to be annihilated.

It was that part which led Kierkegaard to propose to Regina. And even when he was fighting and scheming to disentangle himself, he could still long for the beauty and the devotion which he was rejecting, suffering what he called 'this terrible restlessness — as though at every moment I would persuade myself whether it might not still be possible to turn back to her. O would to God that I might! It is so hard, I had set my last hope in life upon her and I must deprive myself of it. How strange, I had never really thought of being married, but I never thought it would come to pass in this way, and leave so deep a wound behind'.

Fortunately Regina came through the painful experience unscathed and later was happily married. But Kierkegaard never really forgave himself for it and it obsessed him to the end of his days because it epitomized his innermost dilemma and because behind all his explanatory dialectic, his pride continued to be humiliated and his inhumanity self-condemned.

Yet it is from such unhealable wounds that a genius wins his most piercing insight. And Kierkegaard may well have been right in believing that 'God had lodged a veto' against his marrying Regina. To the irreligious materialist this may seem to be a sanctimonious gloss upon a pathological impotence. But few men have been less impotent on the plane of thought and spirit than Kierkegaard.

And this recoil from a girl's love, like his abnormal upbringing which was part cause of it, belonged to his destiny. Through these denials his genius was strung for a particular task which only he could perform and only at an extreme cost in normal human satisfactions, the task of elucidating with a peculiar intensity what he called 'God-relationship'. The religious life, when lived at its most intense, has again and again exacted such a price.

3

Kierkegaard himself recognized the path upon which he was now inescapably set, writing in his *Journal*:

> When the bonds were broken my thoughts were these: either you throw yourself into the wildest kind of life — or else become absolutely religious, but it will be different from the parsons' mixture.

He did not really doubt which alternative it was to be. But it needed the scurrilous attack made on him four years later by *The Corsair*, an organ of the gutter Press, an attack which he had courageously provoked and in which he was held up to ridicule for more than a year and became the butt of urchins in the street, to teach him the uselessness of trying to escape from the singularity to which even his frail and odd body testified.

From that time he accepted his 'difference' as a call to perform for Christianity what only an extraordinary individual could do. And he completed his call, as has been said, by challenging 'the Church's highest dignitary, a man to whom, by the memory of a deceased father I felt myself drawn with almost melancholy affection', to acknowledge publicly that for him and his like the Christian gospel cost too much to live.

But this last round with Bishops Mynster and Martensen was, in fact, of secondary importance compared with the series of works which he had poured out with a sustained intellectual passion during the seven previous years.

Kierkegaard inherited from his father not only melancholy and a powerful imagination, but a brilliant capacity for dialectic. It was no mere logical talent, but a necessity of his nature, the central characteristic of his vision of life. For him Blake's dictum that without contraries there can be no progression was a burning truth. It was his conviction of this that gave such a sharp edge to his criticism alike of established religion and of the doctrines of popular liberalism of which he already saw the demoralizing consequences, particularly in an anonymous Press which reduced individuals to an abstract mass. To him anything which loosened the true tension of life was anathema. Genius, he wrote typically, 'is like a thunderstorm which comes up against the wind', and he admitted that the 'polemical craft' was inseparable from his very being.

A friend once reproached him for being 'frightfully polemical'. That he remembered these words to the end of his life suggests that they found their mark. And there was undeniably an arid and merely combative side to his dialectic. The 'contraries' in him were always in danger of declining into the 'negation', into a passionate exertion of the will to achieve intellectual victory. He was, as has been said, deficient in negative capability, in the sensibility that receives. Hence his dislike of what he considered the softness even of Hans Andersen. Hence, too, the limited understanding he had of what a poet truly is and the partiality of his claim to have been one himself.

One who had pathetically to confess that 'I have possessed no immediacy, have, therefore, in the ordinary human sense, never lived . . . I am sheer reflection from first to last', could not conceive that poetry, at its truest, might be an integral activity. This has to be borne in mind when considering the three stages in which he defined the possibilities of human life and of his own life in particular.

He named them the aesthetic, the ethical and the religious, giving the characteristic of the first as 'pleasure-perdition', of the second as 'action-victory', and of the third, which could only be reached by a leap or a break through, as 'suffering'.

The 'aesthetic' life, to Kierkegaard, had no positive quality, no real centre. It was merely a non-ethical response to the impulse of the senses, in which he included the mind. He stated his view with his usual curt clearness in his *Journal* when he wrote:

> What is it to be a poet? It is to have one's own personal life, one's actuality in quite different categories from those of one's poetic work, it means being related to the ideal in imagination only, so that one's own personal life is more or less a satire on poetry and on oneself. In that sense all

> modern thinkers, even those of standing . . . are poets. And altogether that is the maximum which life shows. The majority of people live entirely without ideas; then there are the few who have a poetic relation to the ideal, but deny it in their personal lives. And so the parsons too are poets, and because they are parsons they are 'deceivers' in a far deeper sense than the sense in which Socrates long ago called the poets.

There is much truth in this, although it is applied far too summarily both to the poets and the parsons. There are poets who strive to live personally the life of imagination, the truly poetic life, and are not content merely to catch the gleam of the ideal momentarily in words or sensations. And there are parsons who practise what they preach.

On the other hand it is true enough that the Devil has a genius for design and that the pursuit of form for its own sake can be satanic and reflect a perverted vision. The modern artist's life, too, is notoriously very often a satire on his work, and even the modern philosopher has evolved a system of thinking, which, unlike real wisdom, is not the fruit of a total life-experience, but often, rather, a web of abstraction spun in a mental attic.

So far as the 'aesthetic' is merely the cultivation of a surface sensibility or even an adroit mentality, Kierkegaard was perfectly right in his strictures, as Tolstoy was half a century later. And undeniably, much modern art and poetry is but a decorative veil draping shallow and disordered lives.

But by no means all art or poetry is only this. There were dedicated artists in Kierkegaard's day as there are in ours: imperfectly dedicated, it may be, compared with the artists of ancient China or of medieval Europe, but devoting themselves to finding utmost reality both in the life of their works and the work of their lives.

Such artists may be few to-day and it is questionable whether by the practice of art alone, with however great an integrity, a man can altogether close the gulf between the poetically conceived and the actually lived. We are here in the realm where art and religion meet, and where, it may be, each needs to complete the other, though religion need not imply acceptance of a creed.

Kierkegaard, however, assumed that they must always be divided, as, indeed, the merely aesthetic must always be from an integral expression of life. There could, as he insisted, be no hope of real integrity until the man who merely cultivated his sensations recognized that he was free to choose between one course and another. By that act of choice, freely made, he entered the ethical stage. And what he chose was essentially himself. Moreover, so to choose himself was the only real way to know himself. Having thus chosen the self, it remained to relate this self to its creative principle through surrendering it in the experience of suffering and guilt, until the purity of heart was attained which consists in 'willing one thing', and that one thing the divine purpose. He who reached this stage of active submission was religious.

One less bound by rigid categories than Kierkegaard might have admitted that the great poet can find in the discipline of his art and imagination as effective an ethical directive as the Church catechism. For every real artist is continually having to choose one course or another and in such choosing his deepest self can be involved. All creating is a costly self-finding and self-losing and is therefore a religious activity in Kierkegaard's sense. Doubtless the saint and the mystic go beyond the poet in re-creating themselves. But those who are not poets are as liable to be irreligious through an ethical predisposition as those who are poets through an aesthetic one.

The aesthetic is, in fact, as necessary a part of the truly religious as the ethical. And Kierkegaard tended to exclude it as dangerous because of the feud between his mind and his senses. 'Unity', wrote the Flemish mystic, John of Ruysbroeck,

> is this: that a man feels himself to be gathered together with all his powers in the unity of his heart. Unity brings inward peace and restfulness of heart. Unity of heart is a bond which draws together body and soul, heart and senses, and all the outward and inward powers and encloses them in the union of love.

That unity Kierkegaard's combative mind never allowed him wholly to know, though in such 'religious' writings as *Consider the Lilies* or *Purify Your Hearts* he subdued its dialectic to the deeper movement of the heart.

In his essay, *The Point of View*, he apportioned his writings to one or other of the 'stages' which he had defined, claiming that the 'aesthetic' and the 'religious' co-existed in all of them, but that his intellectual works belonged primarily to the former, his sequence of 'Edifying Discourses' wholly to the latter, while all his works were his own 'education in Christianity'. There is, in fact, far more of the ethical man than the aesthetic in his intellectual works and he never realized how deeply divining aesthetic sensibility could be.

But such classifications are of minor importance to a modern reader. The essential value of Kierkegaard lies in the paradox which he embodied and expressed with an intensity and intellectual clarity which few have approached, the paradox of faith or passion stretched on the rack of consciousness.

The reflective genius and the man of faith are seldom conjoined to-day. And no one has shown with more penetrating irony what happens to an age choked with thought, an age in which abstract intelligence without inwardness transforms the real into virtuosity. A hundred years ago Kierkegaard wrote, in *The Present Age*, of people who 'in all innocence want the established order to continue, but have the more or less certain reflective knowledge that it no longer exists' — a perfect description of a 'democracy' that wants to be left in peace. Indeed, anyone reading this essay to-day might suppose that it was the work of a contemporary author of genius.

The nineteenth century, as we can now see, alike in its common arts, its religion and its social life, revealed a slackening of the creative pulse which resulted in the multiplication of degenerate forms. But it needed a man of acute insight and fearless honesty to diagnose the disease, now so devastatingly apparent, as Kierkegaard did in the forties of the last century.

He began his diagnosis in *The Present Age* by remarking that 'our age is essentially one of understanding and reflection, without passion, momentarily bursting into enthusiasm, and shrewdly lapsing into repose'. Reflection, he made clear, was not the evil. 'But a reflective condition and the deadlock which it involves, by transforming the qualities which precede action into a means of escape from action, is both corrupt and dangerous and leads in the end to a retrograde movement.'

It was because he himself was such a master of reflection and so fanatically in love with it that he knew so well its disabilities, if it was not counterpoised by a faith as strong as itself. Without that counterbalancing faith, virtue went out of life. Reflection left everything standing but emptied it of significance. A minority of people might be highly intelligent, but at bottom they were indifferent. And because they stood in no vital relation either to God or their fellow-men, all their higher powers were neutralized and all that was low and despicable came to the fore. Yeats was to cry the same in some oft-quoted lines a century later.

But Kierkegaard saw the low and despicable particularly in what he called that 'monstrous abstraction, and all-embracing something which is nothing, a mirage, that *phantom* the public'. This phantom, he considered, was largely produced by the modern Press, itself an abstraction. A public, he wrote, 'is everything and nothing, the most dangerous of all powers and the most insignificant: one can speak to a whole nation in the name of the public and still the public will be less than a single real man however unimportant'.

In these days of the radio as well as the Press we are learning that Kierkegaard did not exaggerate when he described a public so addressed and so manipulated as a 'gruesome abstraction'. The state of the world to-day manifests terribly enough the truth of his words that 'it is only after the individual has acquired an ethical outlook, in face of the whole world, that there can be any suggestion of really joining together. Otherwise the association of individuals, who are in themselves weak, is just as disgusting and as harmful as the marriage of children'.

Kierkegaard disclaimed a public for his own writings and addressed each of his 'Edifying Discourses', the most purely religious of his works, to 'the Individual, whom with joy and gratitude I call my reader'. And he insisted that the abstraction of the false levelling process could only be stopped 'by the individual attaining the religious courage which springs from his individual religious isolation'.

Few had experienced that isolation, combined with a sense of mental superiority, more intensely than he. And he had learnt from it how unfruitful it was for the reflective individual, however clever and knowing he might be, to assume an air of authority and distinction as possessing what most people lacked. The false levelling process was not to be combated in this way.

The individual who had truly found himself or, as he put it, chosen himself by leaping in full consciousness into the arms of God, became a man and nothing else, in the complete and only real equalitarian sense. He ceased altogether to want to dominate others or to appear superior to them or exclusive. He was 'unrecognizable', so much so that he might seem to be completely ordinary. Yet the hidden reality to which he had attained would call out the reality in each person with whom he associated.

Kierkegaard's longing to escape from his own 'extraordinary' nature led him to exaggerate the solid ordinariness of the man who had truly found himself, almost to the point of caricature. Such a man is really as extraordinary in his simplicity as Kierkegaard was in his mental acuteness.[1] And it was this quality of simple, but eternally distinctive, being that he meant to depict as the only power which could successfully combat the false levelling process and foster a real equality. It could not be overcome directly, since that would be to impose an assumed superiority. The individual could only overcome it in suffering and in that way express 'the law of his existence, which is not to dominate, to guide, to lead, but to serve in suffering and help indirectly'.

'Suffering action'—that, Kierkegaard came to see, was the only way by which the mere crowd which was always false could be

[1] Cf. John of Ruysbroeck's picture of those who walk in the way of love:

They affect not singular conduct,
They would be like other men.

disintegrated and gradually changed into a brotherhood of real men. It was the paradox which in all his thinking and living he strove to restore to a world which had lost the secret of it. And it was in true faith that this paradox was most sublimely embodied. Reflection was only a snare when one was caught in it. But once, he wrote, 'the "leap" of enthusiasm has been taken, the relation is a different one and it becomes a noose which drags one into eternity'.

Kierkegaard, as he acknowledged, could never himself wholly compass that leap out of the solitude of self-conscious thought into the arms of God. And so he never completely found or chose himself in the unity of the heart. But his writings are a continual incitement by one of the cleverest, most ironic and calculating men who ever lived, to make that leap with eyes open, seeing the shrewdest plan of action as the cunning mind conceives it, but disdaining it and thereby receiving what he called 'the intensity of an eternal enthusiasm'.

4

It was in his interpretation of the story of Abraham's readiness to sacrifice his son Isaac, entitled *Fear and Trembling*, that he defined most memorably what he meant by 'performing the movement of faith'. He confessed that in Abraham's place he would have been capable only of an 'immense resignation'. But this was not faith, but merely faith's surrogate. 'The Knights of infinite resignation', he wrote,

> are dancers and have elevation. They make the upward movement and fall down again; and this pastime has much to commend itself and is not unpleasing to the eye. But every time they fall down, they cannot immediately take up their positions, they falter for a moment and their faltering shows that they are strangers in the world.

Not so the true 'Knight of faith'. He, too, through utter resignation makes the movements and knows the blessedness of infinity.

But he is also equally true to the finite and at home in it. By no melancholy or ironic look does he betray a sense of the contrast of infinity and the finite or a desire to escape from one into the other. Nor is there in him a trace of 'that exquisite exclusiveness which distinguishes the Knight of the Infinite'.

Such a man, in Kierkegaard's astounded contemplation of him, was Abraham. He loved his son Isaac with his whole heart, and he loved God with his whole heart too. He believed that God would not demand Isaac of him and yet responded unquestioningly to his utmost demand. He believed, in Kierkegaard's words, 'by virtue of the absurd; for there could be no question of human calculation, and the absurdity lay precisely in the fact that God demanded it of him one moment and recalled the demand the next'.

The meaning of pure faith can never be captured by dialectic, however subtle. But Kierkegaard went as far as dialectic can in defining its paradox. He had to admit his failure. 'I can, I think,' he wrote, 'describe the movements of faith perfectly, but I can never perform them . . . To be capable of losing one's reason and with it the whole finite world, of which reason is the stockbroker, and then to recover the finite world by virtue of the absurd, this is something which really terrifies me . . . it is the one and only miracle.'

This miracle, he added, 'occupies my thoughts exclusively'. But thinking about it analytically could never lead to its realization. For that he would have had to tread the path laid down and mapped by the mystics, an inward path which he was too mentally positive ever to pursue to the point where the knowing mind is subdued by the works of love, prayer and contemplation until it becomes the sensitive organ of the divine unknowing and its doubts are transformed into inspired discretion.

But if Kierkegaard was always too self-conscious a reasoner, too fated an 'exception', to become a pure knight of faith, he demonstrated how in real faith extremes must meet and how little reality, therefore, there was in the professed 'faiths' of the modern world. He shocked men's rational self-complacence by declaring that viewed from a merely rational standpoint all faith was and must be 'faith by virtue of the absurd'. If it was less than this, it could not be truly faith, but only a compromise with self-regarding reason. It could only become wholly reasonable by a leap into the unknown, the unproven, into the heart of the creative mystery itself. To calculate where one would land was to destroy the virtue of the leap.

Yet only the man who had become an expert in reflection, who had calculated all the possibilities and then disdained them, was really capable of this pure leap, of a faith which triumphed over its opposite by gathering it into itself. And so true faith was qualitatively different from a mere life instinct. It was 'immediacy after reflection'. It was knowledge reunited with being, consciousness centred again in its divine source.

One who had reached this state was not only reconciled within, in the unity of his passional and his reflective selves. But he was at one, also, with the humblest of his fellows, realizing, as Kierkegaard wrote, that 'between the wise man and the simple man there is just this little insignificant difference, that the simple man knows all that is essential, the wise man little by little is aware that he knows it, or is aware that he doesn't know it, but that which they know is the same'.

So it was natural that Kierkegaard should address his last words to the 'plain man'. For such a man had not become so demoralized by speculation as to forget what it was 'to EXIST and what INWARDNESS means', as most of his masters, religious and political, had. For Kierkegaard, therefore, all the Churches of Christendom, supplicating *officially* the aid of heaven, meant nothing. 'But that a poor man who walked down Cheapside sighed in the sincerity of his heart unto God, *that* concerns Him indescribably, infinitely.'

Every time, he said, such an event occurred it was 'of incomparably greater importance than a European war or a war which involves all the corners of the earth; it is a catastrophic event which moves the universe to its deepest depths'.

The demoralization which he analysed with such pungent insight in the upper and middle ranks of his own small country, the cowardice of uncreative living, has spread far since he wrote and eaten into the whole world. All that he foresaw has come to pass. And the forgery of established Christianity is now so apparent that it needs no 'Knight of Faith' to expose it.

Yet the meaning and the cost of living in real faith are still so 'absurd' in men's eyes that they can see in it only a worse destruction than that in which they are being engulfed. Because the paradox is too hard for them, they doom themselves to endless conflict. For want of faith in that which is greater than reason but never really contrary to it, their reason has become madness. And perhaps it will only be through despair that they will ultimately be driven to take the leap.

II

SANTAYANA'S PHILOSOPHY

It is no accident of literary talent that Mr. Santayana is pre-eminent among modern philosophers as a writer of sensitive prose. For although the philosopher in him is in some ways at odds with the artist, he is far more in sympathy with the artist than with the metaphysician. Indeed he has declared himself to be an 'ignoramus' in metaphysics, and this, of course, not through any inability to explore the world of metaphysical abstractions but through a rooted disbelief in their reality.

'I must think humanly or I could not think at all', he writes at the end of this book,[1] itself the concluding volume of his 'Realms of Being', begun sixteen years ago. And to those of his critics who insist that there are two worlds — a natural and a spiritual, or two criteria of truth, he replies that

> to double the world would unspiritualize the spiritual sphere: to double the truth would make both truths halting and false. There is only one world, the natural world, and only one truth about it; but this world has a spiritual life possible in it, which looks not to another world but to the beauty and perfection that this world suggests, approaches, and misses. On this point, although I am perfectly willing to stand alone, I rather expect that posterity may agree with me; not that mankind will ever accept or remember my philosophy, but that, by fellowship with what is perennial in their hearts, I shall have had a foretaste of their sentiments.

This statement, of course, contains nothing new. Such a view of life is implicit or explicit in all that he has written as a philosopher or literary critic. To it we owe the singular coherence, moral sensitiveness and perceptive charm of those writings. Mr. Santayana has planted spiritual things, in his own words, 'unequivocally on natural ground', but in showing how they spring out of it

[1] George Santayana: *The Realm of Spirit.*

he has also dismissed as no more than poetic fable, as a mythology in the air, all suggestions of supernatural origin.

The fact that the natural world misses and must always miss the perfection of the spiritual life which, in his view, it generates, has never led him to assume an ideal realm from which spirit descends. He admits that everything, including our best inspirations, comes to us from beyond ourselves, but it is, he insists, from the primeval fountains of matter itself.

To many such a philosophy, in reducing the ideal to a mere function of the actual, must always seem biased and insufficient. But as a corrective to idealists who have divorced the ideal from the material it has a saving humility and an abounding human virtue.

For if Mr. Santayana is, as he proclaims, intellectually a convinced materialist, he is aesthetically a humanist, with, to quote his own words, 'a certain affinity to poets and mystics'. He rejects the infinite passion of the mystic on the false assumption that such passion cannot be subdued to the facts of the finite world, but must egotistically override them. But the mystic's acceptance of this world as a realm of discord to be redeemed by insight is his in full measure. And however critical posterity may be of what is one-sided in his theory, it will approve the integrity of his practice and his consistent endeavour to recall the Promethean mind of man to its roots in matter and to its human heart.

For the materialism from which we are suffering to-day reflects not an undue respect for matter so much as a disrespect of it. Such disrespect is a spiritual blindness, and it leads us to exploit matter instead of humanizing it. It also, as Mr. Santayana truly declares, kills the belief in God at its roots, though we may not agree with him that its earthly roots are its only roots.

The Realm of Spirit, then, reveals as richly as ever its author's characteristic virtues, and, while completing a larger work, is itself a self-contained interpretation of human experience. In originally undertaking his task Mr. Santayana disclaimed any attempt to produce 'a system of the universe'. And although he may be held, in effect, to have produced such a system, since the realm of matter is claimed to form the groundwork of all existence, the value of his philosophy is not as a system, where it is most open to criticism.

The idealist produces systems and strives to make them as intellectually watertight as possible. But Mr. Santayana's philosophy neither is, nor does he wish it to be, scientific. He calls it rather a lay religion and, like that of the ancients, a discipline of the mind and heart. It is intellectually consistent, but its consistency does not hamper the free play of sensibility and imagination. Consequently his view of life is expressed quite as much implicitly in the play of intuition and even in the texture of his style as it is explicitly in argument.

The human virtue of his philosophy is, in fact, best proved perhaps in the quality of his expression. This quality derives directly from the limitations which he accepts and which he claims to be those of common sense or the orthodox human tradition. No theme perhaps is less docile to such limits or gains more by them than that of spirit. The very word seems to defy the material categories, to be a wind or a breath or a flame that no temporal prison can hold. And even if clothed in the shimmering veil of ideas, of dreams, of exalted sensations, it tends ever to rise on wings into the thin air of some universal reality or to diffuse itself as the hidden principle of life astir in all things that are.

But for Mr. Santayana, to whom there is nothing less spiritual than the shallows of indistinction and of torpid oneness, all such conceptions of spirit are 'poetic confusions', natural to any imaginative mind attuned to cosmic currents, but merely bemusing to the explorer intent on human truth.

This is the only truth with which he is concerned. Infinity, it would seem, has never allured him, eternity never overawed him. The 'something far more deeply interfused, whose dwelling is the light of setting suns', he deems an irrelevant romantic hypothesis. Spirit for him dwells, not in setting suns, but in human bodies, 'bodies breeding a thousand passions and diseases by which the spirit also is tormented, so that it congenitally longs at first for happiness and at last for salvation'.

And since for him the flesh breeds the spirit as impulses breed ideals, he need not go beyond it to establish a relation with any cosmic centre. He can concentrate on the working of spirit in animal man and limit it to 'that inner light of actuality or attention which floods all life as men actually live it on earth'. In other words, spirit is 'a moral stress of varying scope and intensity, arising in animal bodies and raising their private vicissitudes into a moral experience'.

Spirit, so regarded, being itself born out of natural life, can never disclaim its source. It is never hostile to matter, but requires only that matter shall have order and harmony. It is sympathetic to all forms of life, but its love 'is not physical and procreative, multiplying commitments; rather reflective and spiritual, understanding those commitments, absolving them from their mutual guiltiness, and consoling them for their vanity and ultimate dissolution. In so doing it simply fulfils its own commitment to see things as they are'.

It will be seen, therefore, that Mr. Santayana is careful not to attribute power or active will to Spirit. He regards it rather as the witness of the cosmic dance which it suffers and blesses, if it is allowed to, with awareness and understanding. It is not, in his view, positively creative, but is itself created or evolved by the psyche, which he defines as the organic life of the body, the substance of which is the common matter of the whole universe. As the psyche becomes materially sensitive to remote things, it assumes spirit as its conscious principle.

But while sharing in the vitality and specific impulses of the psyche, spirit cherishes always its own dream of being pure, omniscient, safe and joyful. That dream it can never wholly realize because of its intimate bond with its native psyche and her native world, 'which it cannot bear to feel dragged hither and thither in tragic confusion, but craves to see everywhere well ordered and beautiful, *so that it may be better seen and understood*'.

This, for Mr. Santayana, is the specific function of spirit which it lives by fulfilling, and dies if it cannot somehow fulfil. And having traced to his own satisfaction its origin, he devotes the rest of his book to a study of its internal economy, to the tragic situation in which it is involved through the profound moral gulf between the flux of existence and its own inward perfection, to the faculty of intuition in which momentarily it reconciles perfect actuality and perfect insight, and to its efforts to clarify and discipline itself.

It is in these chapters, which form the bulk of his book, that Mr. Santayana proves best his virtue as a moralist, with the disinterested eye of a philosopher, and as a philosopher sensitive to the conflicts and aberrations of the human will. And although his comment is seldom directed towards the modern world, much of it is implicitly a criticism of the modern spirit which has denied its source and divorced itself from piety.

Mr. Santayana's conception of the spirit's source in the psyche may seem to us insufficient, but he is not for that any less revealing a critic of the pride of mind which is blind to the mystery of earthly incarnation and violates the order of nature. In his view it is not the spirit which so errs, but the psyche with its limitless urge to power and its radical animal will which usurps the prerogatives proper to pure spirit, its innate freedom and omniscience, and claims them as its own.

The Will in spirit is 'precisely *not to will* but to understand the lure and the sorrow in all willing'. But the self-assertive will of the psyche, unchastened by the spirit whose prerogatives it has usurped, becomes a satanic egotism that proclaims itself absolute both in knowledge and power.

> Such is the odious parody and corruption of divinity which we see in all wilful egotism, be it in a man, in a nation, or in a philosophy. Then spirit, instead of being a deity in swaddling clothes, born helpless and despised, to suffer in all who suffer, and rejoice in all who rejoice, becomes the voice of an animality that has taken to praising itself, unnecessarily and wickedly confirming itself, in the name of heaven, in all its partiality, delusion, injustice, and hate.

The Christian reference here is not fortuitous. For later Mr. Santayana returns to and elaborates it, using the terms of Christian theology to describe the sin of Lucifer, of the spirit-drunk psyche that defies its origin and proper bounds, denying matter, despising form and claiming an absolute self-sufficiency.

> Spirit [he writes] proceeds, it is always proceeding, from the Father and from the Son; and, if it would not grow mad and suicidal, it must go about the Father's business, and repeat the eternal Word that it hears spoken in heaven.

Theologians will doubtless question the analogy he draws between the three elements in his system—primordial substance, organic form, and conscious spirit — and the three Persons of the Trinity, and also his claim to be reducing Christian theology and spiritual discipline to their secret interior source.

Yet there are certainly vital and suggestive affinities between them. And no modern philosopher is more faithful to the fact and the mystery of incarnation, whether in regarding man as 'irremediably a human person assuming a human nature', or in insisting that 'consciousness is a gift of nature, happiness is a fruit of piety and order: and spirit, being the final fruition of existence, absolutely needs the other realms to evoke and to feed it'.

Perhaps, indeed, Mr. Santayana's greatest achievement is to have reconciled as a philosopher and despite his system a natural and a religious piety, as when he writes that

> our knowledge is but faith moving in the dark, our joy a gift of grace, our immortality a subtle translation of time into eternity, where all that we have missed is ours and where what we call ours is the least part of ourselves. We are not impatient of injustice. It is not the fate that overtakes us that makes our dignity but the detachment with which we suffer it. All belongs to the necessary passion and death of the spirit, that to-day rides upon an ass into its kingdom, to be crucified to-morrow between two thieves, and on the third day to rise again from the dead.

Yet with his attachment to the homely verities of the Christian faith goes an equal appreciation of the metaphysical intensity of Indian thought.

Just as he rejects any element in Christian morality which

falsely denies nature, so in his chapters on 'Liberation' and 'Union' he distinguishes carefully in the Indian conception of Brahma between the spiritual experience which is a moral victory over existence and that which is only a passive lapse from it. In the true interpretation of Nirvana, as he reads it, it is not existence which is suspended but ignorance, and what is gained is not indifference but equilibrium. The true spiritual sublimation of love is charity, not blind ecstasy, which, 'instead of cleansing the lamp, puts out the light'.

To maintain truly the tension of spirit and yet through spiritual humility to be hospitable to life on all its levels is the equilibrium which Mr. Santayana commends as at once true to nature and to human dignity, and which he analyses in such suggestive detail in this book. And because spirit for him is the child as well as the crown of nature he can value it as truly in laughter as in prayer. For him it has 'its lyric triumphs in childhood and in the simple life: wedding-days and moonlight nights and victories in war and soft music and pious trust. It breaks out momentarily in the shabbiest surroundings, in laughter, understanding and small surrenders of folly to reason'.

But in all this the nature of spirit everywhere is pre-eminently 'by its own intellectual insight to introduce us into the spheres of truth or of essence, detaching us from each thing with humility and humour, and attaching us to all things with justice, charity and pure joy'.

It is this spirit which Mr. Santayana has not only expounded but expressed in the great work which he has now brought to a conclusion.

SOME CRITICAL AFTERTHOUGHTS

In all his writings Mr. Santayana has opposed with delicate determination the claims of absolute idealism or, as he would call it, transcendental egotism. He has consistently sought to vindicate a view of truth in which man as spirit is not high-mindedly divided from man as an animal fragment of the material world.

No one has exposed more sensitively, particularly in his study of 'Egoism in German Philosophy', the 'curious self-degradation' which characterizes transcendental as it does less abstract kinds of egotism.

'You seem to be making yourself and your experience absolute,' he has written, 'yet by that very arrogance you cut yourself off from all intellectual dominion over everything else, and renounce the very thought of natural knowledge or genuine truth.'

He himself, in 'the orthodox human philosophy' which he professes, has, he claims, pursued sincerity instead of omniscience, and has even argued that a system of philosophy is a personal work of art 'which gives a specious unity to some chance vista in the cosmic labyrinth'. But poet though he be in his intuitions and artist in his reasoned exposition of them, he has propounded a philosophy which, in its basis at least, claims to be true, not only for him, but for all who would live as God intended they should.

It is this basis which is most questionable and, in a larger view of human experience and potentiality, manifestly partial. His materialism is not, of course, a new conception of life, and compared with Marxian materialism it is sensitive, enlightened and humane. It is as old as Democritus and the basis upon which much of humanistic culture, with its roots in natural instinct and its mental, moral and aesthetic disciplines, has rested.

But in view of the collapse of that humanism, so tragically evident to-day, we cannot but ask whether even so humane a materialism conforms to the deepest reality or can prove the rallying point which the humane spirit needs in face of a materialism that is not humane, and which threatens to annul the realm of the free spirit altogether.

The cultivated materialist, possessing as he does the graces of the artist, is undeniably a much more agreeable guide than the abstract idealist. But how much does he leave out which is essential to an integral view of things? Is he not, in his own fastidious realism, one-sided?

We may applaud Mr. Santayana's distrust of abstractions and his admiration for the sceptical temperament which keeps the mind in touch with concrete reality. But despite the delicate play of his scepticism, he is at heart a dogmatic naturalist for whom man's 'essence, at best, is animality qualified by reason' and who, although he pays tribute to the spirit in us that worships eternal beauty, insists that 'the very life of spirit springs from animal predicaments', that it is not only earth-born but earth-bound. Elsewhere he has written of mind as 'a wakefulness or attention or moral tension aroused in animals by the stress of life' and as existing only in animal organisms.

Man, then, for him is an animal aroused to some degree of consciousness by temporal and physical circumstances, and not a spiritual being, striving as he awakes to self-knowledge, to establish here on earth his heavenly estate. That man is both a bound animal and a free spirit, and that of the two aspects of his being the spiritual is primary and ultimately determining, has been the belief and experience of the wise in all ages but this.

If, to quote Eckhart, the soul in any man 'prefers the inferior powers of her five senses to her higher ones, whence comes her knowledge of celestial things, then she grows ignoble and base'. But the wisest and best among men have never doubted the reality of these higher powers or inward senses, or that they are original and creative as the bodily senses are not.

There is in fact no convincing evidence that spirit is merely the product of the psyche or the physical organism, intimately as it may be conditioned by it, particularly in the childhood of being, though progressively less so as real consciousness grows. The weight of evidence is all the other way and to affirm that spirit is such a product is a piece of private dogmatism, based on a limited and partial experience.

Mr. Santayana confesses that the only belief which he himself entertains, because he finds it irresistible, is the belief in a realm of matter, the expectation of persistence and order in a natural world. And so truth for him is descriptive of existence and as such wholly contingent, while the presumptions of man's intellect are only true so far as they are based upon, and adjusted to, the actual order of nature.

Within limits this is an acceptable view, but the limits he imposes are arbitrary. They would exclude all that realm of supernature which is the realm of unchanging value, and they confine man's reason to intellect regarded merely as a sixth physical sense. At a certain stage in his development man's mind can seem to be no more than this. But it can evolve into something far greater and other. To borrow Blake's symbolism, it can cease to be *Urizen*, the instrument of a selfhood divided against itself, and become *Urthona*, the organ of creative imagination, of enlightened spirit which is the very reason of being.

Mr. Santayana is a tireless critic of *Urizen* when it flaunts itself as the mechanical mind, too conceited and insensitive to see the wonder of the commonplace. But he is blind, in theory at least, to *Urthona*. He is the enemy of all unrooted speculation, of ideas which intervene between us and things and keep the things from being known. But he will only know things himself on his own terms which are those of a sensitive outsider. Nor will he admit that they can be more intimately known.

He views subject and object as opposite partners in the dance of life, which truly they are. But in his determination to maintain the independent status of object he would arrest the growth of subject, of the experiencing self, whenever he sees signs of it striving to exceed his own discrete dualism and bring the self and the not-self into the fearless identity in difference of a true marriage. In fact, through failing to surrender himself deeply enough to spirit, he fails also to commit himself deeply enough to matter, concerned as he is to cherish it. His love halts at gracious, humorous and tender liking.

We may agree that 'to set up in the place of substance any spontaneous ideas or pert exigencies of our own is contrary to religion'. But true religion has always professed not only a humble reverence before the thing, but the freedom of spirit to re-create the thing in the likeness of its essential being. 'Substance' for it is not material but spiritual. It is divine Being of which matter is only the becoming.

'Being' for religion is not a by-product of existence; it is the power which enters into existence from an eternal realm and redeems it. Human life is or should be the gradual realization of this power, this free creative being. Gradual such realization must be and perhaps never fully attained. For in the life of the spirit some degree of tension between its innate perfection and the stormy flux of existence must always remain.

But in Mr. Santayana's view the spirit as a product of matter must always be distracted and, though it strive endlessly for freedom, can never know it or even achieve any lasting gain. Neither in life nor in death, since death must end everything for a spirit that is a product of a particular animal body, can its striving to realize the purity of its nature be more than a will-o'-the-wisp flickering over the treacherous marsh of matter from which it derives its vitality.

Such is the consequence of limiting human experience to the order of nature known to the physical senses and the sense-bound intellect. To do so is to arrest spiritual growth at a certain stage, one of precarious balance between divided faculties, and to be forced then to defend this partial balance against all tendencies which might upset it, even the tendency to an eventually deeper unity.

But our desire for the truth of Substance, so dear to Mr. Santayana, cannot be thus arbitrarily arrested. The urge to deepen and complete our identity with it and so to realize freedom of spirit within the bounds of matter and liberate matter itself from its chains is irresistible. And for its fulfilment it depends on the degree to which we commit ourselves more purely to life and become true to what is most real in ourselves.

To know the truth of existence in Being and of Being in existence necessitates a radical inner transformation for which Mr. Santayana makes no allowance in his philosophy. He admits, indeed, that in the direct possession of being which constitutes the mystical experience, there is no division of subject and object. But for him this rapt identification, far from illuminating the object, merely casts a 'luminous fog' over it. Even Plato, he suggests, unlike Herbert Spencer, supplies only a refuge from the world of our daily plodding where the sharp facts vanish into a pleasant trance.

And so ignorant is he of a true mysticism or so biased against it that he can describe it as consisting of 'distaste for the world and of childish dreams with which to sweeten a Titanic egotism'. Elsewhere he writes of the mystic that truth oppresses him and that he passes beyond it in a flight from existence. Yet a true mysticism, whether Christian or non-Christian, represents that very reconciliation of the idea and the thing, of existence and being, in a simple acceptance of reality, of which his own sensitive fidelity to the physical basis of life is a partial expression.

His prejudice against a visionary truth which exceeds his own vision cannot, in fact, be reconciled with that 'reverence for the nature of things' which he professes and commends. It betrays only the limited view of reality to which a cultivated Latin mind jealously holds.

But being an artist, he is fortunately not bound, as a pedantic abstract philosopher would be, by what is narrow and untenable in his theory. Like that very different artist and philosopher, Albert Schweitzer, his conscious mind is less enlightened than his innate will and sensibility. His writings abound in the graces and insight of an idealism which disprove his doggedly held materialism.

The eternal values, reduced by him in theory to a play of material atoms, refuse the bondage assigned to them. In his humanism they assert their freedom to transcend the natural world, to which they should, on his theoretical showing, be entirely submissive, and to image through the creative spirit of man another order into which the natural world exists to be changed by that 'Ultimate Religion' of which he writes in an essay so named, that

> To love things spiritually, that is to say, intelligently and disinterestedly, means to love the love in them, to worship the Good which they pursue, and to see them all prophetically in their possible beauty. To love things as they are would be a mockery of things: a true lover must love them as they would wish to be. For nothing is quite happy as it is, and the first act of true sympathy must be to move with the object of love towards its happiness.

III

THOMAS PAINE AND THE BIBLE

THOMAS PAINE'S *The Age of Reason* was published complete on October 25th, 1795. Its first part had been issued a year before and was finished only six hours before its author was arrested in Paris under suspicion of disloyalty to the revolution. He wrote much of the second part during his confinement in the Luxembourg Prison when he was fortunate in escaping the guillotine and from which he issued broken in health, but not in spirit.

Nothing could break the spirit of Thomas Paine, but the world of privilege and prejudice strove its hardest to hound him and his books out of existence, and it continued to do so long after he was dead. He had dealt that world mighty blows in the political and social fields before he turned to assail its tenderest and most sanctified preserve. Twenty years earlier his pamphlet *Common-Sense* and its sequel, *The American Crisis*, had heartened the American colonists to win their independence. And he had fought for them with a musket as well as a pen.

In 1791 he took the field for a second Republic, when, then in England, he published *The Rights of Man*, challenging the reactionary legal arguments of Burke's *Reflections* and expounding the rights in nature and reason of revolution. For this, a year later, he had to flee to the France which he had championed, where he was elected a deputy to the Convention, only to be imprisoned in two years for showing under the Terror that courage of his humanity which to self-seeking men in every camp was treason to their own baseness.

He died, a lonely old man, in 1809. But, as Mr. H. N. Brailsford has written:

> His personal character stands written in his career . . . In a generation of brave men he was the boldest. He could rouse the passions of men, and he could brave them. If the Royalist Burke was eloquent for a queen, Republican Paine

risked his life for a king. No wrong found him indifferent; and he used his pen not only for the democracy which might reward him, but for animals, slaves and women. Poverty never left him, yet he made fortunes with his pen, and gave them to the cause he served.

Such was the man. I am not, however, concerned here with his tempestuous life but only with the book for which he suffered most.

'Paine', wrote William Blake, after reading Bishop Watson's answer to *The Age of Reason*, 'has not attacked Christianity. Watson has defended Antichrist. It appears to me now that Tom Paine is a better Christian than the Bishop.'

But the term Christian, in this general sense, is misleading. Paine, though bred a Quaker, was a Deist and it was as a champion of Deism, as he conceived it, that he assailed the Bible for which Bishop Watson wrote his lame *Apology*. He was convinced that Adam, 'if there ever was such a man, was created a Deist' and for him no second Adam was required to redeem the first, provided he remained true to his innate Deistical principles, which consisted in 'the belief of one God, and an imitation of his moral character, or the practice of what are called moral virtues'. The passages in which he expounds this Deism in *The Age of Reason* possess, indeed, the most lasting value.

Actually he was less qualified for this assault on religious obscurantism than for his championing of human freedom in other fields and for his far-sighted enunciation of social reforms. He himself wrote: 'The natural bent of my mind was to science. I had some turn, and I believe, some talent for poetry; but this I rather repressed than encouraged as leading too much into the field of imagination.'

Certainly any feeling for poetry or for the realm of inner mystery in which poetry has its source had died by the time he came to write *The Age of Reason*. Nor was he by temperament a speculative thinker. It was part of his simplicity and contributed to his unfailing self-assurance that he never felt the want of these faculties. He was perfectly satisfied, to quote his own words, 'with the reason that God has given me; and I gratefully know he has given me a large share of that divine gift'.

Our conception of 'reason' to-day is not so confined or so confident as it was to the pioneers of the rationalistic revolution. We have learned painfully that rationalism can be as partial an expression of reason as the 'revelation' against which it so scornfully strove, and that the reason, which comes at real truth and freedom, needs to be constantly quickened by that imagination which the rationalist is generally at such pains to repress.

Paine, in one place, did admit imagination to be 'the mainspring which puts all in motion', as distinct from the judgment, 'the pendulum or balance, which corrects and regulates that motion'. But imagination was for him a dangerously 'volatile thing', an irresponsible dreaming faculty, for which he had as little respect as his modern rationalist successor, the psychoanalyst, has much.

In commenting, for example, on the Biblical account of the appearance of an angel to Joseph in a dream to inform him that Mary had conceived by the Holy Ghost, he wrote characteristically: 'It is nothing to me what Joseph dreamed of—whether of the fidelity or infidelity of his wife; I pay no regard to my own dreams, and I should be weak indeed to put faith in the dreams of another.'

Imagination, disciplined or undisciplined, was in fact almost entirely lacking in Paine's derisive assault upon the Christian scriptures, and for an adequate appraisal of the truth or falsity of any scripture, as of any poetry, it is essential. 'I have now gone through the Bible', he boasted, 'as a man would go through a wood with an axe on his shoulder, and fell trees. Here they lie; and the priests, if they can, may replant them. They may, perhaps, stick them in the ground, but they will never make them grow.'

His axe in fact had not gone as near to the root of the trees as he supposed, though it lopped off many rotten branches. For his attack on the Bible and on Christian belief was as literal as the dogmatic orthodoxy he assailed. He fought it with its own weapons and had no difficulty in showing that as literal fact much of the Old and New Testaments was historically incredible and rationally grotesque. He did not spare his opponents' susceptibilities or mince his words. And the vilification and persecution which the book provoked, not only against its author, but for decades against anyone who dared to print or sell it, is at least understandable. Moreover he weakened his case by overstating it, often where it was strongest, as, for example, in his repudiation, already referred to, of the asserted fact of a Virgin Birth.

Few believe to-day that Christ was conceived and born without a human father. For to believe that does not make him more, but less divine in our eyes. Instead of redeeming the order of nature and the act of generation, it leaves them eternally unredeemed. The dogma was in fact an interested perversion of ancient mystical teachings which symbolized, truly enough, a spiritual, not a historical or biological, truth.

Paine's arguments against the literal acceptance of the Bible story, which incidentally, as he remarked, is not mentioned in the books ascribed to Mark and John, were forthright and cogent. But he was blinded by rancour when he wrote that 'the story, taking it as it is told, is blasphemously obscene', that 'it gives an account of a young woman engaged to be married, and while under this engagement she is, to speak plain language, debauched by a ghost under an impious pretence' and that 'notwithstanding, Joseph afterwards married her as his wife, and in his turn rivals the ghost'.

Paine here is not merely exposing what he believed to be factually false. In thus putting the story into what he called 'intellegible language', he destroyed the veiled meaning together with the false fact and so did vulgar violence to the beauty as well as the truth of a story that has touched the hearts of countless men.

It may be, as he contended, that 'truth never *envelops* itself in mystery', but it certainly shines in the darkness of mystery, as it exceeds the mere logic of fact and the shallow scrutiny of the rationalizing mind. It is the duty of enlightened reason to disprove the fabrications of wishful thinking, but without prejudice or contempt, particularly when it is dealing with the realm of men's most sacred beliefs.

Paine was not content to be brutally frank. He could, also, be jocose, as when, after discussing the contradictory accounts of those who first came to the sepulchre on the morning of the Resurrection, he remarked,:

'So well do they agree about their first evidence! They all, however, appear to have known most about Mary Magdalene; she was a woman of a large acquaintance, and it was not an ill conjecture that she might be upon the stroll.'

Such scoffing at things held sacred by millions of devout souls, however misguidedly from a rationalist standpoint, was, to say the least, a fault of taste, and it inevitably provoked the very blind resistance to reasoned truth which he was concerned to remove.

Admittedly he wrote not only in times that tried men's souls, as he had declared in a famous manifesto, but of State tyranny and Church corruption. In Blake's forthright words, 'The Beast and the Whore' ruled 'without control'. Nor is there any real answer even to-day, when the Church is at least a reformed organization compared with what it was at the end of the eighteenth century, to his simple assertion that 'the Church has set up a system of religion very contradictory to the character of the person whose name it bears. It has set up a religion of pomp and of revenue in pretended imitation of a person whose life was humility and poverty'.

Although, too, Paine, like other rationalists, may have exaggerated 'the continual persecution carried on by the Church for several hundred years against the sciences', he knew the smart of that persecution himself. Credulity, too, was deep entrenched in sanctified convention. As Paine wrote: 'People have been so long in the habit of reading the books called the Bible and Testament with their eyes shut and their sense locked up, that the most stupid inconsistencies have passed on them for truth, and imposition for prophecy.'

Nevertheless much of Paine's criticism of credulity was negative and partisan because he had no conception of the deeper meaning of faith. Since for him there was no mystery, since in his assured eyes the mechanism of the world and the principles of human conduct were unquestionably clear, obviously no faith was required. Faith was merely an imaginary thing, indistinguishable from credulity, which distorted a rational and human morality and was exploited by a professional priesthood for mercenary ends and by a Government as one of the instruments of its despotism.

It was true enough that much of the so-called Christian faith of his time deserved to be regarded in this way, that the mind of man was consequently, as he said, 'bewildered as in a fog'. For because the true was mixed up with the fabulous an honest man was disposed to reject the one with the other. Or, as Paine bluntly put it,

> A man, by hearing all their nonsense lumped and preached together, confounds the God of the creation with the imagined God of the Christians, and lives as if there were none.

Yet this intermingling of imaginative truth, expressing a reality beyond the reach of mere ethical rationalism, with enslaving superstition was and is characteristic in different degrees of all organized systems of religion. This Paine boldly declared. But of all the systems he considered that none was 'more derogatory to the Almighty, more unedifying to man, more repugnant to reason, and more contradictory in itself, than this thing called Christianity. Too absurd for belief, too impossible to convince, and too inconsistent for practice, it renders the heart torpid, or produces only atheists and fanatics'.

Even allowing for the controversial vigour of the day and the corruption of the official Church, such writing could only reveal to real Christians, of whom there were some in his day as in ours, the ignorance of a pugnacious mind.

Equally revealing a lack of real insight into the Book he was tearing to pieces were the many passages in which he showed a really astonishing insensitiveness to the beauty and meaning not only of the story of Christ's life and death, but, for example, of the book of Ruth, one of the most perfectly-told tales in all literature, which he described as 'an idle, bungling story foolishly told, nobody knows by whom, about a strolling country girl creeping slily to bed to her cousin Boaz'; or of Isaiah, whose 'prophetic' writing he dismissed as 'incoherent, bombastical rant, full of extravagant metaphor, without application, and destitute of meaning; a schoolboy would scarcely have been excusable for writing such stuff'.

This blindness to spiritual truth revealed through myth and image and story was as much due to the limitations of a rationalist outlook as to his restricted aim, which was to show that the Bible, far from being what the priests said it was, the literal 'word of God', was, as fact, a tissue of falsehood and forgery.

It was as fact that he judged it and as fact his judgment was often unassailable. Indeed the 'higher criticism', so called, has largely followed in his footsteps. Nor is his human indictment of the tribal barbarities described in the Old Testament any less valid to-day, when the God of the Old Testament still exercises a malign influence over Western Christendom, than when he wrote, for example: 'Could we permit ourselves to suppose that the Almighty would distinguish any nation or people by the name of his chosen people, we must suppose that people to have been an example to all the rest of the world of the purest piety and humanity, and not such a nation of ruffians and cut-throats as the ancient Jews were.'

More precisely he wrote of one of Moses's commands to slaughter all but the virgins and girl-children of a defeated enemy:

> Among the detestable villains that in any period of the world have disgraced the name of man, it is impossible to find a greater than Moses, if this account is true. Here is an order to butcher the boys, to massacre the mothers, and debauch the daughters.

What shocked Paine, and rightly, in such biblical incidents was that they were said to be done '*by the express command* of God'. Brutal assassination was sanctified as an act of faith, even the assassination of infants, and the commission of such acts was charged upon the Almighty. It followed, therefore, for him that 'to believe the Bible to be true, we must *unbelieve* all our belief in the moral justice of God; for wherein could crying or smiling infants offend? And to read the Bible without horror, we must undo everything that is tender, sympathizing, and benevolent in the heart of man'.

It is, indeed, arguable that many passages in the Old Testament describing the tribal infamies of the 'Chosen People' have tended to make Christians callous and even encouraged them to be brutal as a necessity of their faith, of which their sacred Book provides convincing precedents.

Against this Paine, as an outraged humanist, did well to protest. But his rationalized view of the Almighty as Himself a kindly humanist failed altogether to take account of the darker, destructive forces which manifest in the Universe and in man. Hell as well as heaven need to be included in any authentic scripture and will be found no less in the 'Scripture called the Creation', to which Paine directed his readers, than in the Christian Bible which he bid them throw onto the fire.

The Bible is true so far as it reveals the working of the divine in man and nature at many different levels and through many channels. Some of those channels were choked with deeds of primitive ignorance or benighted cruelty for which their perpetrators claimed divine sanction. Paine himself was right to deny that claim, but wrong to judge human history or the evolving spiritual or moral insight of man by his own limited standards. To justify the ways of God to man or in man, or in the less sensate realm of nature, was not as easy as he thought.

God is something other than a philanthropist, and Paine's philanthropy betrayed its inadequacy, as a measuring-rod of a humanity greater than his own, in his criticism of Christ's teaching about loving your enemies, or of St. Paul's about the resurrection in the spiritual body, which he wilfully distorted. He completely disregarded, too, the Messianic belief held by the Jews for centuries before Christ, when he denounced as legerdemain all the Old Testament sayings cited in the New Testament as prophetic, which were divorced from their actual context.

Here again it was in imaginative vision that he was deficient, as his friend Blake came later to see. This lack affects, too, in some measure his noble presentation of the gospel of Deism. For the Biblical 'Word of God' he substituted: 'the Creation we behold; and it is in *this word*, which no human invention can counterfeit or alter, that God speaketh universally to man . . . We can know God only through his works . . . The principles of Science lead to this knowledge, for the Creator of man is the Creator of science, and it is through that medium that man can see God, as it were, face to face'.

It is difficult for us to-day, who have thrown off so much of the old religious superstitions and are inclined to accept, all too readily, some of the superstitions of modern 'science', to realize how liberating such a gospel was to candid and courageous minds in Paine's day.

Some of the best and most lucid passages in *The Age of Reason* are devoted to it, passages which agree with Madame Blavatsky's more profound statement that 'the silent worship of abstract or *noumenal* Nature, the only divine manifestation, is the one ennobling religion of Humanity'.

> The CREATION [Paine wrote] speaketh an universal language, independently of human speech or language, multiplied and various as they be. It is an ever existing original, which every man can read. It cannot be forged; it cannot be counterfeited; it cannot be lost; it cannot be altered; it cannot be suppressed . . . It preaches to all nations and to all worlds; and this *word of God* reveals to man all that is necessary for man to know of God.

The Psalmist, if Paine could have admitted it, had declared much the same thing in poetic language. But, unlike Paine, he had not believed that the whole of the Book of Creation could be read by the principles of eighteenth-century science. In recalling his readers to the Universe itself and bidding them study it and learn from it, Paine did well. But in limiting knowledge to what could be outwardly seen and measured and in reducing God to a benevolent super-scientist he overlooked the inward depths both of Creation and of man, as a creative as well as a moral and rational being.

For a gospel of Science needs to be comprehensive if it is not to impoverish the soul of man. 'The Almighty lecturer', as Paine characteristically called him, 'by displaying the principles of science in the structure of the universe, has invited man to study and to imitation.' But man himself is also a cosmos and needs to study the universe and the Creator within his own soul as well as through his mind and senses.

Of this Paine had little to say. He was sublimely unconscious of himself. That was his strength and his weakness. Among things to which language gives names there is a whole world of images that reveal the inner life of man as sensitively as the forms of the physical world reveal the inner life of nature. This is the world of myth and symbol, of scripture and fable and poetry. A true gospel of science must embrace that too.

To Paine it was almost a closed book. But in his day it had become so clogged and corrupted with dead forms and the interested literalism of those who were paid to expound that part of it enshrined in the Christian Bible, that to cut away this deadness was as necessary a task as to preach the principles of a new, fearless and reasonable life.

Paine did both. His conviction that 'the world has walked in darkness for eighteen hundred years, both as to religion and government, and it is only since the American revolution began that light has broken in', may seem ingenuous. But in recalling men to belief in 'one God', whose attributes are revealed to us in 'the scripture of creation' and in repudiating any claim by a Book to monopolize God, he struck a blow for truth and honesty, as brave as it was humane.

Much of the destructive argument of *The Age of Reason* is only of historical interest to-day. But its spirit reaches out to that integral science in which man will eventually find his freedom, reading and living Creation as his own eternal nature and the eternal nature of things guarantee.

IV

THE POETICS OF RELIGION

THE intrinsic value of this book[1] is enhanced for us by an element of delighted surprise. We had, a little grudgingly, resigned ourselves to the fact that the ripe harvest of A. C. Bradley's mind was confined to four volumes, of which two only, the *Shakespearean Tragedy*, published in 1904, and the *Oxford Lectures on Poetry*, which followed in 1909, revealed the full scope of his powers. But in 1907 he gave a course of lectures under the Gifford Endowment. He was unable to revise these before his death, and until recently they remained locked up in the difficult manuscript from which his sister, Mrs. de Glehn, with the utmost care, transcribed them, without living herself to see them in print. To her all admirers of Bradley's mind and all seekers after the truth of religion are greatly indebted.

Doubtless so scrupulous a thinker and critic as Bradley would have wished in some ways to rehandle these spoken lectures in transforming them into written chapters, and particularly perhaps to elaborate certain passages in which the implications of a fundamental statement were necessarily curtailed, or elsewhere to reduce certain repetitions in the argument. But against such loss as this there is a positive gain in the directness of approach throughout to a subject which, as it is the profoundest upon which man can ponder, is also one in which his thought may most easily become entangled in side issues.

Bradley was far too sensitive and subtle a thinker falsely to simplify any subject. But he made the most of the limits which the scope of these lectures imposed upon him. He struck home to the centre of his subject and refused to be diverted to the circumference. The impetus and intimacy of his thought, at once detached and personal, are a joy equally in themselves and for the truth which they continually disclose and guarantee.

[1] ANDREW C. BRADLEY: *Ideals of Religion.*

There is another apparent defect which he transformed into a quality. Poetry, not religion, was the subject upon which he concentrated and in which he perfected his powers as a critic. And when, in these lectures, he was approaching the climax of his whole argument, the question whether the idea of God which he had propounded was true or real, he confessed with characteristic humility his inability to attempt a fully reasoned answer to this question. 'I could do nothing', he added, 'but repeat more feebly and with less understanding, in ways that happen to appeal to me, what I have gathered from others in the intervals of years given chiefly to other work.'

Yet both the outline of an answer which he proceeded to give and his whole handling of the problem of the meaning and nature of religion reveal how essentially relevant that other work was to this, and not only in the enlightening comparisons and distinctions which he drew between poetry and religion, but in his essentially poetic approach to and interpretation of experience.

Bradley's outstanding quality, perhaps, as a critic of poetry was his capacity to submit himself to the work he was considering, to feel its inexhaustible mystery, and to retain that sense, as a kind of life-line, through all the subsequent process of analysis. This quality is fundamental to his treatment of religion in these lectures. In the end, as he said in one of them, 'there must be mystery for us'.

The claim to possess the whole truth, to know what God is as God himself knows it, is that blasphemy of the abstract mind against which we have to be constantly on guard. The intellect has its legitimate sphere, where it may and must claim jurisdiction on questions of truth. But to separate this sphere from others, equally vital to reality, from the aesthetic and the moral, for example, is to falsify, instead of clarifying, experience.

Bradley's thinking throughout this book is so valid and illuminating, because from the beginning he took his stand at the centre of religious experience and through all his analysis never erred from it. Yet the truth that 'religious experience is in a sense an ultimate fact and proves itself' did not for him relieve the intellect of its inherent task of deciding the truth of religious ideas. To quote his own words:

> The starting-point is the phenomenon, the psychological fact. It is the experience, on the one side, of my feared or felt separation from something conceived as beyond me, much greater than I am, superior to me in mode of existence and powerful over me; and, on the other side, the experience of the removal of that separation by my submission to, or union with, this something, a removal which gives me freedom and happiness. Or, more briefly, it is the experience of freedom from evil attained by willed union with a being which is free from evil. The existence of this experience is not a matter of reasonable doubt. It is just as certain that people go through it as that they see and hear, hate or love one another, find things beautiful, try to understand things. The intellect then, dealing with this fact, must start from it and must recognize its character truly. And more, its theory of the fact, its attempt to account for it, must in a sense be tested by reference to the fact. I must show that it has accounted for this experience and not for something else.

In short he insisted that the fact of religious experience is equally the starting-point and the test of any theory about it, just as poetic experience is of any theory of poetry.

It is arguable that in places he unduly circumscribed the underlying fact, as when, in his concern to distinguish the ground upon which poetic and religious ideas stand, he remarked that the latter 'spring from an experience in which there is little or no play of imagination, but which is primarily that of the heart and will'. As he later admitted, he stated this distinction too sharply.

For in religion, little less than in poetry, men seek through imagination to satisfy the hunger for reality, both of the mind and heart. But Bradley believed that the aesthetic and intellectual impulses, while playing their part, were secondary in religion to a practical need, the desire 'to escape evil and to obtain good, however these words are understood', and that it was basically a direction of the will towards an object of supreme devotion with which union was desired.

This led him later to the surprising and, as first enunciated, disconcerting view that 'for religion ultimate or absolute truth is not a matter of prime importance. It is so for philosophy, but religion is an attempt at union with the infinite not mainly on the side of thought but mainly on the side of will, and perfectly true ideas are neither essential for that, nor is it essential to religion even to believe that its ideas are perfectly true'.

This, it may reasonably seem, is to carry suspicion of the monopolizing intellect too far. For how could the will be directed aright towards an infinite truth, if it flouted the best guidance the finite intelligence could offer?

But Bradley did not suggest that it should. What he wished to emphasize was that truth and reality, even in the religious sphere, were matters of degree. And in a later passage he denied the assumption of most religious men that religious ideas must be taken to be perfectly true

> because they have in their heads the mistaken notion that, if an idea is not perfectly true, it is false, whereas the majority of religious ideas, as of other ideas, are, in various degrees, inadequate expressions of the meaning they strive to convey.

In this and other passages Bradley may, in his right insistence that the purpose of religion was primarily spiritual experience and not intellectual knowledge, have tended unduly to diminish the importance to religion of the latter. But it was against claims to complete intellectual definition of truth, as distinct from the figurative expression of meaning, at once incomplete and inexhaustible, that he was protesting. And the fact that such a view enabled him to discriminate with the finest justice between the relative truth of different systems of religious ideas, and finally to propound a conception of reality and of man's relation to it, which best accorded in his view with the whole of experience as we know it, is proof enough of the virtue of his intellectual relativity.

For the man who is sure that his religious ideas are absolutely true is ill qualified to estimate the truth of other religious ideas. But Bradley, by basing his study on the psychological fact underlying all religions, whether primitive or advanced, and then inquiring, not into the truth of theology, but into the degree to which the basic needs and nature of the religious impulse were satisfied in one system of religious ideas or another, was able to do the fullest justice to partial or one-sided systems, and also to show how each contained valuable elements, which, if over-emphasized, needed to be taken up into the system which more fully and coherently embodied the original impulse.

Thus after considering inward religion as the state or activity of individual souls, and its ultimate aim of union with God as good in itself and the only good, and then observing with an impartial eye some of the forms of outward religion and their relation to the inward, he went on to consider certain types of natural religion and the degree to which they fulfilled the aim in view.

By natural he meant that which claimed not to go beyond the phenomenal sphere, but which, as he convincingly showed, often unconsciously did so, particularly in 'the religion of ideal humanity', typified in such men as Comte or Mazzini — a religion never to be denied, however much in Bradley's view it required completion.

The 'good will' which such men invoked, or the 'Great Being' of a benevolent collective humanity, was in reality an ideal which transcended the facts of the finite world, including the fact of evil. But a religion which failed to admit this or to relate belief in human goodness to any belief as to the universe as a whole, could not, Bradley concluded, fully perform the office of religion because its object was deficient in both wholeness and power.

The same disability belonged to such religions, as that proposed by Seeley in his *Natural Religion*, which separated nature, mistakenly reduced to the nature known to science, from man, and sought to worship the two apart, or again to such a Theism, as that of Mill, which conceived a God almost as limited and finite as man.

At the other extreme from these religions, which would exclude the infinite, was that of the metaphysical East, which so far as it denied the reality of the finite tended to reduce the phenomenal world to a shadow. In its longing for the infinite, Bradley declared, 'no more genuine religion than this has existed or can exist'. But it gives what religion asks for only on one side.

And here we reach what is the crux of the religious problem and the centre of all Bradley's argument. We have to start, in his own words, 'from the basis that somehow there is to be the infinite, and yet that the finite is not to be evaporated into nothingness', or, more pregnantly: 'What is required is that the infinite should negate the finite in such a way as to include it.' The infinite would not, then, be 'a blank in which all the distinctions of finite existence had run together and vanished, but would be the perfection of the finite which as such it denies'.

This is the creative mystery by which appearance becomes reality or is seen as it truly is. And through failure to comprehend this, any mere worship of ideal humanity, or of a finite God or of an abstract infinite is imperfect and unsatisfying. In such a view of the relation of the infinite and the finite, as Bradley argued, we have a conception in which the dual aspects of experience and its countless parts can be truly reconciled and organically related.

This vision of the finite transformed and redeemed in the infinite fulfils the basic need of religion. And the intellect, as Bradley showed with living logic, approves its truth. Bradley demonstrated this finely in disproving the assumption that the spiritual is the mere opposite of the natural, and so something thin and spectral. Our spirit, he said,

> is the living concentration of all the natural elements and forces that meet in the body . . . It can abstract itself in thought and will from them all and even from its natural aptitudes — and in that sense is free from them. Still it *is* their concentration; and that is obvious in the fact that this spirit, this 'I', which does thus abstract itself, has a definite character, which but for them it would not have: each of us has a distinct natural endowment, and the self or spirit is a mere abstraction or form if you leave this out of account. And again this self or spirit expresses itself in and through these natural elements and forces. It is free not only from

> them but in them; and its full freedom would be that it should find them perfectly subdued to its own element, and so expressive of it and not of their separate natures. It is not a ghost, and it is higher not merely because it is immaterial, but because it is the most intense and far-reaching unity of the natural or material.

Such a passage as this will suggest at once the grandeur and the penetration of his argument, which reaches its climax in his consideration of man as finite infinite, and as capable, therefore, of combining in himself the richest variety and the intensest unity, and which ends with a brief but searching analysis of the relation of good and evil, which at once admits their opposition and sees beyond it.

For in the infinite, as he argued, there cannot be evil as there is in finite experience, where it is the isolation of the part from the whole. It must be changed by the loss of this isolation into something no longer discordant. And we have a faint reflection of the pure creative necessity, into which evil must be transformed in the infinite, in the fact that evil, as we know it, seems in some way to be not only a necessary accompaniment but a condition of good. From which Bradley derived the profound paradox that 'Religion is release from evil, but it is so only because the faith that there *is* no evil is also the will to abolish evil'.

Yet he ended by admitting 'that to understand in detail how evil is essential, and what it would look like from the centre, is beyond us; nor can we tell at all why so much of pain, and again of moral evil, should exist in finite experience'.

And here, as ever, was the characteristic humility of a thinker, whose thought never lost its roots in mystery, but who embodied the infinite-finite integrity which he expounded. We have been able only to touch on his main argument and have done no justice to his felicitous and suggestively human handling of it. Too wise to attempt to pluck the heart out of the mystery, he thought his way into its centre. And this book is in consequence an intellectual experience as rare as it is memorable.

V

'BE NOT ANXIOUS...'

FEAR, it is generally admitted, is at the root of all evil. It strikes deeper than greed, if not than pride, deeper than the lust for power. It dictates the logic by which man rationalizes his cruelty and it lurks unappeased behind all those formidable defences he builds to assure himself he is secure. Man is always building Maginot Lines or negotiating Munich settlements or setting out to conquer the world because fear torments him. Or he is accumulating wealth by exploiting his neighbour or rejecting with violence a truth which might weaken his false assurance or clinging to the old clothes of habit because love would expose his nakedness.

There are a thousand insidious ways in which fear poisons the well of life within us, brutalizing even our courage, transforming virtue into self-righteousness, passion into jealousy, or modesty into a shrinking recoil. So universal an impulse cannot be without warrant in the nature of things and, like all perverted impulses, it must originally have served the needs of life and may do so again in man when he understands his nature better and acts upon his understanding.

Typical of the lack of such understanding is the failure to distinguish between fear as it manifests in the animal and the human worlds. Those, for example, who take a dark view of life and are convinced that high heaven and earth ail from their prime foundation, often cite the unceasing alertness of birds as proof of the internecine terror under which all creation groans.

Yet anyone who has studied the habits of birds or of many animals knows that fear in them seldom affects their capacity for happiness. At times, indeed, it seems to heighten it, if I am to judge by the blackbird which pursues with shrill abuse my cat as he slinks through the shrubbery. Fear helps an animal to preserve its life. It neither torments him into destroying more life than he needs for food nor lays on him a continual burden of anxiety. A bird fears neither life nor death but lives in both and accepts both from moment to moment. And if some animals, such as the bullock driven to the slaughter-house, fear death before it falls on them, it is probably because of their association with man whose conscious purpose at such moment they dimly sense.

It would, of course, be foolish to suggest that wild creatures are not at times paralysed by fear. Victims of the stoat or the snake prove the contrary. In the struggle for life in the animal world fear plays an incessant part and often a grim one. But it is never a disease, as in the human world.

It has become a disease there because man is a self-conscious being capable of isolating himself from life as a whole. The more self-conscious he becomes, the more inwardly and outwardly destructive is his fear. In primitive man, as in children, fear hardly exists as the adult knows it. It is still a mysterious dread, not of some particular thing, but of infinite possibility, of an indefinable something. As such it can, of course, exercise a black tyranny over the undeveloped mind and exact a terrible tribute, as the superstitious practices of savage tribes show. But it can also be a spiritual stimulus, the throb and thrill of life quickening darkly in the womb of the psyche.

As man's ego emerges, however, dread shrinks into concrete fear, which denies its creative source in awe and clings close instead to guilt. Then, indeed, fear poisons the springs of man's being.

Yet awe and dread are so essential to life and so intrinsic to growth that even their perversion in sinful fear must have a meaning and serve a purpose beyond itself. Examined more closely, it may even be found to point the way to a freedom commensurate with the burden which man alone has to carry.

Such an examination Dr. Reinhold Niebuhr has made in the first volume of his Gifford Lectures, entitled *The Nature and Destiny of Man*, basing his argument on the truth that man is the only animal which can make itself its own object. Man alone has a capacity for self-transcendence and from this springs all the trouble. For standing at the juncture of nature and spirit he is involved in both freedom and necessity. As part of nature he is finite. As spirit he is infinite. And this unresolved contradiction provokes in him a continual anxiety.

To ease this anxiety he is driven in two directions. He may seek in his pride to hide his mortality, to overcome his insecurity by his own power and thus to establish his independence. This effort may be mental or physical. If the former, he assumes that he can altogether transcend the limits of finite thought until his mind becomes all-knowing. This is the ideological taint in all human knowledge and it manifests always as an effort to hide ignorance by pretension.

We see it, for example, in the insistent claim of the modern scientist that everything can be ultimately explained. In his view what is at present inexplicable only needs an extension of existing knowledge to be explained. In thus rejecting the concept of an eternally unknowable, of an irreducible mystery, the scientist denies the source from which all real knowing flows. The artist is wiser. For he acts in the conviction that imagination creates truth out of the unknown quite as much as from the facts of observation.

But the rationalist has ceased to trust imagination. And so he strains his eyesight and his mental powers to see as precisely as possible every detail of the surface in the hope that, when he has seen and tabulated them all, the depths will be found to have disclosed themselves. He is, of course, and must always be, disappointed. His misuse of vision leads only to spiritual astigmatism. This is the fruit, on the mental plane, of anxiety or faithlessness.

On the material plane it manifests as anti-social selfishness. Man strives to protect himself against nature's contingencies by building up an unassailable security for himself at the expense of his fellow-men. To this effort there can obviously be no term. For catastrophe or his impoverished victims may always strip him bare.

But he may move in the opposite direction. Instead of seeking to hide his finiteness by asserting the boundless independence of spirit, he may strive to hide his freedom, to escape from it and relax the strain of maintaining it, by abandoning himself to some vital current of the world or of nature.

His sin now is less pride than sensuality. But both spring from the same root, and Dr. Niebuhr rightly insists that sensuality 'is never the mere expression of natural impulse in man. It always betrays some aspect of his abortive effort to solve the problem of finiteness and freedom. Human passions are always characterized by unlimited and daemonic potencies of which animal life is innocent'.

This is what distinguishes the purely natural will-to-live from the human and spiritual will-to-power. And the boundless character of human ambitions or desires is the consequence of man's effort to hide his weakness, deny his dependence and insignificance, and thus to quieten his fears.

Yet mortality and dependence are not of themselves evil. They belong to the order of existence and are necessities of our growth in and through it. They only become the occasion of evil when we refuse to accept them as such. For when accepted they no longer enslave and are found to be not fearful ends, but benignant means.

Dr. Niebuhr, with characteristic dread of being false to the dualistic side of the Christian Faith, will hardly admit that acceptance can ever be profound enough to banish fear altogether, though the mystics of all Faiths disprove his contention. But if not a necessary element in all human creative effort, anxiety is certainly a spur to much of it. What André Gide has called 'gratuitous' or purely disinterested acts are exceptional in human history compared with 'compulsive' acts, though the former have been and are the eternally transforming ones.

But of man in general Dr. Niebuhr writes truly enough that he 'is anxious not only because his life is limited and dependent, but because he does not know the limits of his possibilities. He can do nothing and regard it as perfectly done, because higher possibilities are revealed in each achievement. There is, therefore, no limit of achievement in any sphere of activity in which human history can rest with equanimity'. Anxiety about perfection and anxiety about insecurity are inexorably bound together in human actions, and man's ambition to be something 'is always partly prompted by the fear of meaninglessness which threatens him by reason of the contingent character of his existence. His creativity is therefore always corrupted by some effort to overcome contingency by raising precisely what is contingent to absolute and unlimited dimensions'.

Oh, wretched man, one is inclined to say after reading many pages of Dr. Niebuhr's searching analysis, how pitiable is thy dilemma! Thou, whose heaven-born aspirations are the spur that goads thee to outrage thy humanity in the anguish of thy homelessness.

Yet it is just this apparently insoluble dilemma which gives to man his tragic greatness. And the shallowness of the bourgeois culture and the commercial civilization which are now dying of spiritual emptiness was due to an attempted evasion of it.

The typical modern man tried to live either by reason or by blind instinct. The rationalist depreciated the power and virtue of sub-rational vitalities; the romanticist glorified them. But neither understood that man is free to violate both the necessities of nature and the logical systems of thought and that the human spirit, in its yearning towards the infinite, cannot be held within the bounds of either. 'The very insatiability of human desire', to quote Dr. Niebuhr's words, 'has a positive significance: it means this, that we are attracted by an infinite good.'

In that lies the source of both human creativeness and human sin. And if under the perpetual smile of modernity there is 'a grimace of disillusion and cynicism', it is because man has ceased to measure himself in a dimension high or deep enough to do justice either to his stature or to his capacity for both good and evil. The tragic challenge of human existence has been reasoned away, its vital paradox cut at one end by the mechanical, at the other by the sentimental or sensational. But it is there all the time. And to-day we are being forced to recognize it.

2

But recognizing it, what are we to do? If the contradiction is entwined in human existence, how can it ever be resolved? Can faith ever become stronger than fear in man so that it no longer torments him into pride and sensuality, but inspires him to create?

Never wholly, Dr. Niebuhr believes, because man is a fallen being and however near he may approach to perfection, he must always fall short of it. To claim that he can achieve absolute perfection is to betray the very sin of spiritual pride which for ever, in crude and subtle forms, forbids perfection.

But because it is not man's finiteness, dependence and weakness, but his anxiety about it which tempts him to sin, he is ideally free to reduce (and if to reduce, why not to resolve?) this anxiety in himself and so redeem the conflict in which he is involved by accepting his dependence.

But upon what? If he merely accepts his status as a natural creature, he is denying his freedom as transcendent spirit. But if he asserts his freedom as spirit, he is continually tempted to flout his natural limitations. Unless there is some mystery at the heart of things and of himself in which nature and spirit are reconciled and in which he can find his home, he is at best doomed to oscillate for ever between fearful defiance and miserable abjectness.

The fact of self-transcendence in man leads inevitably, therefore, as Dr. Niebuhr argues, to the search for a God who transcends the world. Or, to quote Augustine's familiar words, 'thou madest us for thyself, and our heart is unquiet till it rest in thee'. Elsewhere, however, Augustine wrote: 'I am of the opinion that the creature will never become equal with God, even when so perfect a holiness is accomplished within us as that it shall be quite incapable of receiving an addition.' And Dr. Niebuhr believes that only in Christian doctrine are the intimacy and distance between the human and the divine truly preserved.

This corresponds with his repeated assertion that all mysticism must lead to a loss of the particular in an ultimate undifferentiated reality and that consequently all mystics view individuality as essentially evil. Such mysticism is in fact to be found in both Christians and non-Christians. But the true mysticism which combines liberation from the transitory with fidelity to the eternal in time and which seeks only to change a divided individual into a whole person is certainly not the monopoly of the Christian religion. At most Christianity, in its doctrine of the incarnation, has laid a special stress on what it claims to be the one perfect expression of the divine in history and in a person.

The error of such thinkers as Dr. Niebuhr would seem, in fact, to lie in a failure to distinguish sufficiently between a justifiable human aspiration to be one with God and a claim to be equal with Him. The claim to equality is the sin of spiritual pride and merits all Dr. Niebuhr's strictures. But the experience of union is that for which man was born, the hidden goal within the dualities with which he has to struggle.

Christian theology has fostered the belief that only Jesus could perfectly realize such union in this world of Time. Yet Jesus himself drew no such arbitrary bounds to man's approach to the divine. To him all men were sons of the one Father, and, if prodigal sons, could through repentance and love be restored wholly to their true estate. He, unlike Dr. Niebuhr, did not stress man's necessary imperfection, but boldly bid him be perfect 'even as your Father in heaven is perfect'.

It is the same with other divinely inspired teachers, whether it be the Buddha declaring:

> Now I, Potthapāda, teach you a way by practising which impure conditions can be put away by you and pure conditions brought to increase, and by which one, *even in this very life*, may attain unto the fulfilment and perfect growth of the wisdom, realizing it by his own abnormal powers, so as to abide therein.

Or Krishna in the *Bhagavad-Gita*:

> He who knows Me to be the unborn, the one without beginning, great lord of worlds, is unbewildered among mortals and released from all sins.

So also say the sages of the *Upanishads* in words, for example, that parallel those of the writer of the first epistle of St. John that 'perfect love casteth out fear; he that feareth is not made perfect in love':

> When a man sees the Atman, the Self of him, God Himself, the Lord of what was and of what shall be, he fears no more.

The evidence of these and of other inspired teachers is that supreme Enlightenment, which implies perfect union, has occurred in certain men and can occur in others.

Man's fear, as Kierkegaard, to whom Dr. Niebuhr obviously owes much, so penetratingly showed in his essay, *The Concept of Dread*, is rooted in the 'anxious longing of creation itself', in the conception and travail and birth of spirit in matter. Spirit is free and eternal. Matter, too, in its essence is eternal, but bound to the temporal flux. As man becomes conscious of his individuality, he becomes conscious, too, of the possibility of spiritual freedom. And this manifests in him as dread, as a kind of dizziness, as Kierkegaard put it.

Gradually this dread, which is innocent and indefinite so long as man is still a dreaming spirit, defines itself in him as fear and so as sin, as a knowledge of good and evil, of the sensuous and the spiritual, and a fear of both. How and why it should so split his being is a mystery which only myth can darkly reveal. But henceforth man is a conscious spirit living in a house, if not violently divided against itself, tensely built of contradictions. And it is through these contradictions, of body and soul, as of sexuality, that the spirit has to labour to create and vindicate its essential freedom.

All human and personal history consists of that task, and so long as spirit fails to resolve the contradictions or, to put it the other way, so long as the dualities fail to conform to the over-seeing unity, fear remains, the fear that springs as much from a freedom misused which proves a bondage as from a freedom undared which is an infinite dread. Dr. Niebuhr declares, as Kierkegaard does, that human history as a whole begins and will for ever continue under the stress of this tension of opposites. Certainly it would seem to have done so hitherto.

Yet as certainly there have lived men, of whom the founder of his Faith is only one, who have transcended these contradictions and, with them, human history, as we sadly know it, men in whom the spirit has found a human home no longer divided against itself. These men have not 'claimed to achieve perfection absolutely', but through their absolute obedience to eternal spirit they have by faith transformed the 'infinite possibility of freedom' into the infinitely realized freedom of love.

It is such creative love which breaks through the fear-stricken dualism which such intellectual moralists as Dr. Niebuhr are so loath to conceive as soluble. In such love the sense of the limitless, of a perfection that can never be complete, does not provoke restlessness and anxiety. For the infinity of love is no longer outside the finite, but eternally redeems it from within.

The creative lover rests in the perfection of which he knows he can never fully compass or exhaust the meaning in any of his acts. There would be no rest for him if he could. Infinite perfection is not a threat to his stability, a challenge to his self-esteem, or a wound to his pride. It is the object and the subject of his adoration. For, in the contemplation of its ineffable beauty and greatness, object and subject become one. Absolute perfection is not something to achieve with strain and anxiety, but to suffer humbly and joyously, and in the union of love to find and to be.[1]

Dr. Niebuhr will have it that such union must always be imperfect or imperfectly sustained, that though man's fear may be infinitely reduced, it can never wholly be resolved. If it were, he argues, man would cease to be an individual confronting God,

[1] 'God is never loved according to His worth by any creatures. And to the enlightened reason this is a great delight and satisfaction: that its God and its Beloved is so high and so rich that He transcends all created powers, and can be loved according to His merits by none save Himself.' – John of Ruysbroeck, *Adornment of the Spiritual Marriage.*

cease to be an actual historical being, and be utterly absorbed in the featureless One.[1]

On the whole, however, any prejudice which Dr. Niebuhr betrays as a moralist does little damage to his interpretation of human nature and its relation to the divine. We can agree with him that the God in whom man's unquiet heart can alone find rest both creates and transcends the world. He is, therefore, in, but not of, the finite world on which man must acknowledge his physical dependence, and He is the eternal source of man's infinite spirit. In Him the contradiction of man's dual being is resolved. For He is both He and She, personal, yet without limitation. The more closely, therefore, man can find this divine, all inclusive, and transcending Being in the depths of his experience, and finding, love, and loving, find, the more is fear swallowed up in faith, its tormenting tensions eased in the inward harmony of the Soul with itself, in a pure willing of that which is divinely willed.

The nearer a man comes to that pure willing, the less has the divine Being, in which he knows and breathes and acts, any outward form, still less any arbitrary gender. The taint of anthropomorphism vanishes and it is through adoration of that which eternally transcends form or man that he values every created form and person, without being falsely bound to them by merely temporal appetite, because he loves them both in time and beyond it, in that fullness of time in which every moment opens into eternity.

In the depth and serenity of that experience, so far as we can attain to it, we cease to fear. The self-concern of fear is resolved in awe, wonder and praise. And, rejoicing in our double birthright as spirit and flesh, we do violence to neither.

[1] But contrast John of Ruysbroeck in *The Book of Supreme Truth*: 'I have said that never creature may be or become so holy that it loses its created being and becomes God; even the soul of our Lord Jesus Christ shall ever remain creature, and other than God. *Yet, none the less, we must all be lifted up above ourselves into God and become one spirit with God in love; and then we shall be blessed.*'

VI

THOUGHTS ON THE DHAMMAPADA

A NEW English translation of the *Dhammapada* by Professor Bhagwat has recently been issued by the Buddha Society of Bombay and is obtainable in England for the small sum of one shilling. It is both a handy edition and a reliable translation, and it includes, for those who can benefit thereby, the Pali text in Devanagari characters.

The Society believes that the *Dhammapada*, which is accepted as a genuine collection of the sayings of the Buddha, deserves to be as widely known as the *Bhagavad-Gita*. And they have brought out this edition to popularize it. Sharing, as I do, their belief that a sympathetic study of it cannot fail to enlighten, I am anxious to commend it as helpfully as I can to the notice of English readers. And perhaps I can do this best by discussing some prejudices which have commonly to be surmounted by Western minds before they can receive the truth of the Buddha's teaching.

Buddha has sometimes been reproached for encouraging his followers to pile up merits for themselves and for regarding women and children as hindrances to perfect living. A recent critic has contrasted his monastic temper with the kindly humanity of Jesus Christ and has contended that Christ's 'is the only religion which says that a man can be at one with God while having a wife, a family, and eating three meals a day — including flesh'.

We may well smile at this easy disregard of such sayings of Jesus as that 'if any man come to me, and hate not his father, and mother, and wife, and children, and brethren and sisters, yea, and his own life also, he cannot be my disciple'. And we may regret the prejudice which allows a writer to suggest that there was no place in Buddha's teaching for the married householder, when actually it provides with great wisdom for the needs of all, whatever their vocation in life.

But no great teacher, in allowing for various stages in the path, has ever reduced his ultimate demands. In those demands both Jesus in his love and Gotama in his wisdom were uncompromising. Neither taught that it was enough to domesticate the physical appetites or to be impulsively warm-hearted. Each, in their different modes, insisted that the Gate was strait and the Way narrow which lead to eternal life. Nor, in their knowledge of the few that really find it, did they ever encourage the many to believe that it could be entered by any wider gate.

After framing his divinely simple and direct moral code for the needs of all, at whatever stage of growth, Buddha addressed himself more particularly to those who were ready to advance towards spiritual maturity. Consequently, despite his rejection of the two extremes of pleasure and mortification, his teaching tends to affront those who are still dominated by a thirst for physical existence. In his five rules, which were sufficient for the immature in years and experience, Buddha sought only to bring this thirst under control, to civilize and humanize it. But ultimately, he insisted, in those who would truly realize Nirvana, the divinely intended state of fruition and freedom, it must be extinguished.

It is the fundamental stress he laid upon the necessity of extinguishing this thirst which offends the instincts of so many Westerners and which they resent as inhuman. They fail to recognize that Jesus expressed the same truth in a different way when he taught that the desires of self must die on the cross of love.

'But what a difference!' many would say, who find it easier to reconcile emotional impulse with Jesus's gospel of love than with Buddha's 'sacred truth of suffering'. And one must admit that there is a real difference, if only of aspect and emphasis, between the 'narrow way' of Christ and the 'middle way' of Buddha.

Dhammapada means the Steps of the Law. Jesus invited men into the Way of Love. Are these but two modes of one Way, each of which, in the expression of imperfect devotees, can reflect characteristic weaknesses, but which, beyond a certain point, merge into each other, love fulfilling the law, the law informing love?

Unless a reader approaches the *Dhammapada* with at least an open mind towards this question, he is likely to allow prejudice to blind him to its truth. But given a readiness to study it in the light of unflinching self-awareness, I think he will find that the law it unfolds is as necessary as the love which he has too easily assumed to be a sufficient inspiration.

Indeed, the distinction which I have suggested between love and law is itself misleading. For the *Dhamma* of which we follow the Foot-falls in the *Dhammapada* is no legal code imposed upon human nature by an austere moralist from without. It is the Creative Order, divined by the Buddha within the living movement of the universe and the evolving Soul of man. He named it 'Truth and Law' and bid each man 'visualize it in himself' and so become '*The Custodian of the Law*'. And it was out of his own experience of the reality of this order that he defined the demand it made upon those who would bring their nature, step by step, into harmony with it, until they entered the freedom at its heart.

Those in the West who have been taught to conceive of redemption exclusively in terms of sacrificial love may well at first find the Buddha's message too cool and collected. But there are different modes of sacrifice, and the heart is not the only altar of purification. The mind must be redeemed too. This is a hard fact for many warm-hearted people to face. They insist that love is enough. Ideally, pure love is pure truth; it opens the doors of vision. It inspires the will; it enlarges and cleanses the mind.

But actually, few are so pure in heart that they can afford to neglect the patient discipline of the mind which brings sustained enlightenment. This discipline does not involve a supreme and sudden act of self-devotion, but rather a persistent reduction of the self to the measure of truth, until at last the illusions of self-will and individual desire are dissipated and the bonds of error are broken.

The sacrificial nature of this patient process of self-effacement is seldom recognized by those who point exclusively to the cross of Calvary without being called themselves to make any such supreme sacrifice. Many, in fact, who shrink from what they consider the inhuman detachment of Buddha betray an unconscious fear lest the quality of their 'human' feeling should be put to a test which it cannot survive.

But for Buddha who knew that a complete self-knowledge was a condition of true self-sacrifice, this test was crucial. Hence the primary emphasis which he laid upon 'right thinking'. Ignorance had begun in the 'awakening of a thought'. In the soil of self-conscious thought had sprung up craving. And this craving, wherein disunited man hungered in all sorts of perverse ways to regain unity, could only cease when his consciousness was reconciled with the original will from which it had lapsed.

The ignorance of partial knowledge must be resolved in the illumination of perfect knowledge. Hence it was that in Buddha's teaching to 'embrace false views' was to be consigned to hell. And the *Dhammapada* continually emphasizes the truth that 'worst of all stains is the stain of ignorance', and that it is the man who is 'full of wrong thoughts' who is at the mercy of his lusts.

Consequently Buddha saw in the resolving of doubt the crux of the spiritual problem. 'Neither nakedness', says the *Dhammapada*, 'nor matted hair, nor dirt, nor fasting . . . nor assuming ascetic postures, can purify a man who has not solved his doubts.'

The primary stress which Buddha laid on the solving of doubt is particularly relevant to the needs and the temper of to-day, when men's minds have turned away from Creeds but are at sea for want of inward enlightenment. Buddha, one might say, distrusted faith as he did love, because he saw how easily the force of both could be exploited by false feeling and interested motive. And human experience proves him right. He saw that the mind had to be perfectly clarified, if the heart's reason was to become truth itself. For let the smallest element of doubt be left imperfectly resolved beneath an affirmation of faith, however enraptured or assured, and it would falsify that faith — it might even infect it with fanaticism (how often it has!) and make the faith a bondage, not only to its professor but to thousands of others.

But the man who had truly thought his last doubt away by correctly understanding the nature of reality and accepting in full consciousness its self-renouncing conditions, was free from both doubt and faith, as he was from yearnings in regard to this world or the next, and from the fetters both of merit and demerit.

If Buddha encouraged his followers to 'accumulate much merit', as Jesus did his to lay up riches for themselves in heaven, it was only that they should attain to a pure worth beyond all self-interested attachment, of which considerations of merit and demerit were a reflection. But in his view the bondage of the false self would persist, if in subtle and deceptive ways, until the unreality of this self was completely realized. Then reason itself would cut the bonds. And so we read: 'Get yourself rid of this vast suffering by becoming possessed of perfect knowledge.'

But if wisdom was in Buddha's teaching the key to disinterestedness, compassion was the oil by which it was to be continually turned in the harsh locks of the world. Yet the two were never to be dissociated and it is hard for many Westerners to believe in the virtue or perceive the value of a dispassionate compassion.

How, for example, they may ask, can a man be really compassionate who accepts and acts on the following? —

> Impermanent are all component things. He who perceives this with insight becomes thereby immediately unmoved by suffering. This is the Path of Purity Supreme.

To be 'unmoved by suffering' may seem to imply a callousness which makes compassion impossible. Yet we know that Buddha who had perceived this truth and been changed by it was at once the serene and the compassionate one. Do we do right then to resent the stress he lays on the necessity of growing through and beyond suffering? Or is our attachment to suffering but another reflection of our attachment to a false self?

If we are to profit by Buddha's teaching, we need above all to get this clear. The escape from sorrow which he preached was not from sharing and helping to lift the burden of the world's suffering nor was it from consciousness into nescience. None knew better than he that, in the words of *The Voice of the Silence*, 'Thou shalt not separate thy being from Being'.

This is the true suffering without which we cannot live and breathe in all, as all breathes in us. Buddha never counselled escape from that. The sorrow to which he insistently drew men's attention and which he bid them eradicate was of another kind. It was the result of being at discord in the self. It was the price men paid for having fallen, in the pursuit of self-awareness, out of reality into appearance.

Buddha did not inquire how or why this fall into unreal individuality, and the false existence such individuality maintains about it, had occurred. He held such metaphysical speculations to distract men's energy and attention from what was really necessary, which was the casting off of the false individuality and with it the chain of hurtful error, the *Karma* or fate, that went on mechanically unwinding, link succeeding link, until the power that reduplicated them was withdrawn.

Once eliminate the false ego, he said, and the chain was broken. The enslavement by fate was ended, the blind interplay of action and reaction, of sin and suffering, pleasure and pain, ceased, and the freed man entered the realm of real being in which he fulfilled his creative destiny, knowing the truth not as a metaphysical theory but as an ineffable experience, an eternal state. It was the way of liberation, therefore, that alone mattered and the liberation was not from real life nor from devoted service to others but from the delusion that went on generating gratuitous suffering.

Buddha knew that most men must come to truth through the fires of such suffering, but in his compassionate wisdom he sought to save them from prolonging the pains of their own blindness.

Not, however, by acquiring a stoic invulnerability. That is a familiar misreading of his teaching. For the stoic has not entered the realm of being; he has merely fortified himself in the realm of existence. Buddha invited men into the realm of being. He bid them to be 'in full accord with all that lives' by shedding the last veil of the exclusive, acquisitive ego. And if his teaching with regard not only to sensual pleasures, but to the affections seems at times in the *Dhammapada* to demand too much of human nature and to deny its dearest and tenderest ties, it is well to remember how subtle and tenacious is the bondage of egoism, just because it is interwoven with tender affections.

The great teacher inevitably shocks men out of their acquiescence in error, and if Buddha seems too severe in his exposure of men's false conceptions of what is dear and pleasurable and painful, it was that he might release them into the truth. And this truth was no such negative emptiness and indifference as his critics, who have not crossed the gulf, suggest. To those who are still bound and blinded by existence, Nirvana seems a state of nonentity. But those who have entered being through non-being, know it to be the only state of real identity and felicity, and also of true relationship.

Far from denying the hope of joy to men, Buddha assured them that they should experience it in all its fullness and purity. 'Let him renounce his little pleasure', we read, 'in view of the abounding bliss.' And it was 'from the profound happiness which results' that one will put an end to suffering. Nor was this happiness to be enjoyed in a sublime isolation. It was the self-bound man who was alone and homeless in spite of all his apparent attachments, and who, even in his affections, bound others to his own bondage. The liberated man had come home to the real, where alone true and free relationships were possible and where, out of a spirit poised and at peace, he could 'bring out the spirit of the events of ordinary life'.

Doubtless the emphasis which Buddha laid upon the necessity of SELF-possession displeases many people. The calm cultivation of the twin virtues of wisdom and compassion may seem at first inferior to the simple organic surrender to love which the Christian has been taught to revere in Jesus. I have already suggested why Buddha, in his clear vision of man's bondage to false feeling, counselled a different method. But he, no less than Jesus, put before men the ideal of a complete response of the soul to its creator.

There are, however, two ways of realizing this ideal. You may lose the self to find it or you may find the self to lose it. The two ways are not of course separable. But Buddha may be said to have stressed the latter, Jesus the former. The impulsive may lament the cool reasonableness of Buddha's spirit, but they have no right to say that he taught men to elevate the self, not to change it, or that his ideal was one of superior self-centredness.

Certainly he did preach that the true Self, the 'Lord very difficult to find', was the necessary heart of the divine life, and that self-sacrifice, far from destroying real SELF-possession, inevitably brought it into being.

But that is true, and it is one of the reasons why the *Dhammapada* should appeal to the many to-day in the West who recoil from doctrines associated with primitive blood-sacrifice and look for emancipation by becoming more mindful instead of less. Its twenty-six Cantos may not possess the poetic suggestiveness which irradiates the *Gita* and the Gospels. But they throw the light of dispassionate reason along the path that every pilgrim must tread.

VII

RABINDRANATH TAGORE

BY the death of Rabindranath Tagore at the age of eighty, not only India but the English speaking world loses a poet of outstanding charm and versatility. Yet only his own countrymen or those who can speak or read his native Bengali can truly appreciate his achievement as a writer. For it is in Bengali that most of his poems, plays and novels were composed. It is in Bengal that his songs have passed into the daily life of the people and that the range and grace and richness of his lyrical impulse are truly known.

Until he was fifty, he hardly ever wrote in English. And although he achieved a singularly delicate mastery of it which served him well in several prose works in his later year, it was, with one exception, far less adequate as a medium for translating his poems. The exception was the volume of lyrics entitled *Gitanjali* which, when published in 1913 with Yeats's enthusiastic introduction, first brought him fame in Europe and America.

In that volume Tagore re-created rather than translated what he had originally conceived in Bengali. But this was far less true of the volumes that followed, in which his translations were often no more than poetical paraphrases, some of them much truncated. Thus the English versions lacked the metrical vigour and melodious subtlety of the originals and their meaning was impoverished. This explains to some extent the monotony of tone and diction, which even his admirers have regretfully admitted, and the decline of his reputation as a poet in England in recent years.

Yet Yeats was right in recognizing in the poetry of *Gitanjali* a native abundance and simplicity, and in describing it as the work of a supreme culture, and yet appearing 'as much the growth of the common soil as the grass and the rushes'. He was wrong, however, in prophesying that 'these verses will not lie in little well-printed books upon ladies' tables, who turn the pages with indolent hands that they may sigh over a life without meaning'.

Tagore, indeed, should not be blamed for that. Yet it cannot be denied that the natural virtue of his mysticism and of his characteristic moods of joy and sorrow, hope and wistful regret was dimmed in many of his English verses or even lost in an 'endless mist of vague sweetness'.

As an Indian poet, however, he is notable above all for his loving fidelity to nature and his refusal of any life-denying creed. He belonged to a family as devoted to culture as to religion and social reform. But he grew up in an atmosphere of freedom and for long was uninfluenced by any religious teaching, finding, like his Vedic ancestors, his chief inspiration in the tropical sky, with its suggestion of an uttermost Beyond, and in all the seasons and moods of nature.

After his initiation into Brahminhood he began to meditate daily upon the infinite being which united in one stream of creation his mind and the outer world. And when he was eighteen, as he has told in one of the Hibbert Lectures, later published as *The Religion of Man*, this union of himself and the world suddenly became a reality to him as he stood watching the sun rise. It was, to quote his own words,

> as if some ancient mist had in a moment lifted from my sight, and the morning light on the face of the world revealed an inner radiance of joy . . . That which was memorable in this experience was its human message, the sudden expansion of my consciousness in the super-personal world of men.

After four days, however, the vision passed away, and the world once again put on its disguise of ordinary fact.

Two or three years later the revelation returned as he was standing on a veranda overlooking a street. The detached facts of life once again came together and were illuminated in the unity of vision. No person or thing in the world seemed trivial. And from that time he lent himself 'to a travail of creation' that ever exceeded his own personal bounds. He felt that he had found his religion at last, 'the religion of Man, in which the infinite became defined in humanity and came close to me so as to need my love and co-operation'. The poem which he wrote in the joy of this release from self-isolated despondency was fittingly named *The Awakening of the Waterfall* — a waterfall which never languished for more than half a century.

Thus was born the 'poet's religion' by which he lived and worked. All the virtues and defects of his writing are implicit in the experience as he described it, in the fluent surrender of his senses to the supersensuous mystery and in the lack of any severe conflict in his nature which cost much to resolve. It was his virtue to prefer a devoted love of this world to all false asceticism, his defect to float with too easy a grace on the stream of life, cultivating mellifluous feeling overmuch in the degree that his imagination had failed to come to close grips with fact and to wring reality out of the struggle.

Not that he ever overlooked the price which living creatively in the actual world of form and of human relationships exacts. His work as an educationist in the school which he founded in 1901 at Santiniketan and later extended to include an international university, his pioneer efforts for the renovation of the Indian village and his life-long concern for the removal of such social iniquities as child-marriage and the untouchables, are proof enough of that.

Nor does the note of hedonism ever sound in his poetry:

> Whom thou givest Thy banner [he wrote in one of his songs] Thou givest the strength to carry it. Thou givest him love that he may be able to bear the strain of Thy service. I therefore desire with all my heart that I may be liberated from suffering by suffering. I do not desire to achieve salvation by avoiding the pain which is the gift of Thy hand.

Yet in the same collection of songs he wrote: 'Liberation does not lie for me in renunciation. I shall enjoy the sweetness of liberation in the innumerable bonds of pleasure.' And 'the Poet' in one of his later plays, *The Cycle of Spring*, proclaims:

> In the open world all is change, all is life, all is movement. And he who ever moves and journeys with this life-movement, dancing and playing on his flute as he goes, he is the true Renouncer . . . We Poets call to every one to carry all their joys and sorrows lightly in a rhythmic measure. Our call is the Renouncer's call.

This conception of life as play or *lila* is deeply rooted in Hinduism, and although in Tagore's mind it was tempered both by Buddhism and by the monotheism of the Brahmo Samaj, the Church with which his family was so closely linked, it accorded deeply with his nature. He was a gifted musician as well as a poet, and in both mediums the spontaneous flow of his impulse was as remarkable for its delicacy as its exuberance.

He knew the dangers of fluency and once confessed humorously that, like a machine, he was apt when once wound up to run on automatically without stopping. But with his love and understanding of country people went a conviction that the common speech should be the foundation and pattern of good writing. And this kept his style sweet even when it was luxuriant. But while he believed, also, that 'only by following the stream of one's mother tongue can one get to the sea of universal human culture', his longing for such a culture was intensified by the extreme narrowness and parochialism of Bengali life. And his desire to educate his own countrymen grew into a desire to break down the barriers of ignorance that divided East and West, so that each might learn of the other, and in doing so combine their virtues and cast off their defects.

The various lectures which, late in his life, Tagore published in such volumes as *Sadhana*, *Personality* and *The Religion of Man* conveyed to a Western audience the wisdom of the East with singular grace and simplicity. And while he saw in the last War the gathering doom of Europe's rapacious civilization, he never went so far as Gandhi in denying the possibility of a compromise with its political and social mechanism, its science and its machines.

But true to his race and its traditions, the emphasis of all his teaching was upon the inner man, through whom alone, by strenuously humble self-knowing, liberation might come. It was that liberation into reality, into the freedom of the universe in which the self and 'Lord of Life' are one, which he continually sought as an artist. And although the boundless lured him to excess, making him thirsty 'for far-away things', he was convinced that 'the finite is the true infinite, and love knows its truth'.

He was thus well qualified to mediate between the East and the West. For he knew the disabling bias of each. As he wrote in *Sadhana*:

> In the great Western continent we see that the soul of man is mainly concerned with extending itself outwards . . . Its partiality is entirely for the world of extension, and it would leave aside — nay, hardly believe in — that field of inner consciousness which is the field of fulfilment . . . It is because of this insistence on the doing and the becoming that we perceive in the West the intoxication of power. These men seem to have determined to despoil and grasp everything by force. They would always obstinately be doing and never be done — they would not allow to death its natural place in the scheme of things — they know not the beauty of completion.
>
> In our country the danger comes from the opposite side. Our partiality is for the internal world. We would cast aside with contumely the field of power and of extension. We would realize Brahma in meditation only in his aspect of completeness, we have determined not to see him in the commerce of the universe in his aspect of evolution. That is why, in our seekers, we so often find the intoxication of the spirit and its consequent degradation . . . But true spirituality, as taught in our sacred lore, is calmly balanced in strength, in the correlation of the within and the without. The truth has its law, it has its joy . . . When the harp is truly strung, when there is not the slightest laxity in the strength of the bond, then only does music result; and the string transcending itself in its melody finds at every chord its true freedom.

But clearly as in theory he conceived the necessity of mediating between these two extremes, he achieved it with difficulty in the practice of his art, the more so, perhaps, because there was no deep-seated conflict in his nature. The harp was seldom tightly strung. And it was in binding the boundless, in maintaining a really significant tension between vision and life, that he failed most frequently as a writer.

This failure was inevitably more pronounced in the English versions of his poetry or of his plays, in many of which there is more of lyrical musing than of drama or of character. Yet his dramatic output was as rich and various as his lyrical, ranging from such care-free diversions as *Autumn Festival*, through brief dramatic dialogues, based on traditional Indian themes, like *Karna* and *Kunti*, to such symbolical plays as *Chitra*, *The King of the Dark Chamber*, or, on a level nearer to the parable or fable, *The Post Office*.

Tagore wrote many novels and short stories, too, the latter among his finest work. In many of these, while expressing poignant human situations, he was concerned with social questions and particularly with the status of women.

This is true of his greatest novel, *Gora*, of which the theme is the struggle between the traditionalists and progressives in educated Calcutta society. Some of the characters are made to serve unduly their author's opinions with a consequent loss of human reality. But the novel is rich in observation as well as discussion and there is a unity behind its somewhat rambling plot. It is certainly the greatest novel which modern India has produced.

Yet first and last Tagore was a lyrical poet. And it is as a poet that he will be valued most. Only his own countrymen, as has been said, can truly appreciate the quality and volume of his lyrics from the early *Evening and Morning Songs* to the collection entitled *The End* of fifty years later. Only they can testify to the abundance of his natural imagery, the vividness of his pictorial realism, the grace and lightness of his diction, the charm and poignancy of his sentiment, particularly in his love poetry, and the originality and variety of his metrical experiments.

The English reader cannot know the passionate freshness of his early verse. But if, as his verse became more reflective, it lost some of its radiant clarity, its lyrical pulse was never deadened by abstract philosophy. There is, significantly, little development in intensity throughout the fifteen hundred and more songs that he wrote, and there is much repetition of characteristic moods and themes. But in all the best of them, even when the tone is nostalgic or the sentiment most flowery, there is a certain spiritual ecstasy, a true divination of the beauty that is changeless within all change.

No poet has had a more constant sense of the wonder of the created world. And there can be no better epitaph for him than his own words in *Gitanjali*:

> When I go from hence let this be my parting word, that what I have seen is unsurpassable.
> I have tasted of the hidden honey of this lotus that expands on the ocean of light, and thus am I blessed — let this be my parting word.

VIII

WHAT IS MAN?

EVENTS of recent years must surely have shattered any complacency about human nature which the scientific developments of the nineteenth century and the accompanying decline of religious belief had encouraged. Indeed the danger may well now be the other way. Mr. Nicholson in his survey of twentieth-century literature[1] quotes an amusing passage from Miss Rose Macaulay's *Told By an Idiot*, in which she tells how—

> one evening shortly before Christmas, in the days when our fore-fathers, being young, possessed the earth—in brief, in the year 1879—Mrs. Garden came briskly into her drawing-room from Mr. Garden's study and said in her crisp, even voice to her six children, 'Well, my dears, I have to tell you something. Poor Papa has lost his faith again'.

It seemed then no more of a family misfortune than if poor Papa had mislaid his hat again. To lose faith was to lose a set of dogmas which put one's mind at rest, much as a hat shielded one's head from the wind. But to have to go bare-headed, if uncomfortable for a time, was not a disaster. It might even let some fresh air in. And of course there was no question of poor Papa going to the dogs. The moral law seemed to him and his family so self-evident that, in Mr. Nicholson's words, 'they had no doubt that it would stand by itself without any dogma as a scaffolding'.

We may be as dubious of traditional dogma to-day as the more 'progressive' Victorians were, but we are beginning to see that human conduct is very closely related to the view of life which men hold and that so far as the dogma of Progress, of man evolving inevitably towards a perfectly reasoned mastery of himself and his world, was substituted for the traditional reading of his nature, it has led to a moral decline, even if in some ways to material betterment.

[1] NORMAN NICHOLSON: *Man and Literature*.

This is the thesis underlying Mr. Nicholson's stimulating book. A thesis is often fatal to criticism. It is certainly so if it is preconceived and literature is used as an illustration. Mr. Nicholson assures us that it is not so with him and that he has not attempted to measure modern literature by a Christian yardstick. At the same time he declares his aim quite honestly. His book, he says, is not, fundamentally, *literary* criticism at all, but an inquiry into the assumptions as to the nature and purpose of Man which underlie much of modern writing.

Yet in poetry, drama and fiction, with which alone he is concerned, it is, as he acknowledges, by style and by choice of medium far more than by explicit professions of faith or opinion that writers reveal their real beliefs. Acting on this he does perforce practise literary criticism of a kind and his method throughout is to let his authors declare themselves either by quotation or through summaries of their poems or novels provided by himself.

The temptation here, of course, is to select what serves his purpose or to reduce a writer's meaning to the dimensions his thesis requires. This he does not always avoid and his continual summaries of the plots of stories by modern novelists, though necessary to his purpose and quite skilfully done, is apt to suggest the extension-lecturer. His style, too, though refreshingly lively and unpedantic, is at times rather casually colloquial as when he writes of Shaw's *Major Barbara* that she indulges 'in a habit common to other Shavian women (Candida, Lady Cicely Waynflete, etc.), the habit of taking men to pieces with a pin. She is doing it, moreover, in such a school-marmish and self-righteous manner that we wouldn't mind if Bill gave her an answer on the jaw with her own tambourine.'

However it is, perhaps, all to the good that so serious a theme as his, a theme in which nothing less than the destiny of man on this earth is involved, should be treated without solemnity. It certainly strengthens our confidence in Mr. Nicholson's own outlook. There is nothing prim in it. It includes more of life, not less, than the views which he criticizes.

These views are personified for him in two doctrines of Man which, if seldom openly acknowledged, have been very common in modern literature and which he names 'Liberal Man' and 'Natural Man'. He sees the first of these dominating the outlook of writers at the end of the nineteenth century and the first decade of the twentieth. And he chooses Hardy and Housman, Shaw, Galsworthy, Bennett and Wells, as in different ways the perplexed or confident assenters to the doctrine of 'Liberal Man'.

At a first glance there might seem to be little enough affinity between Hardy and Wells or Housman and Shaw. The suggestive comparison which Mr. Nicholson draws between Housman and FitzGerald is on the face of it much more convincing. But Housman's nostalgia can be traced back, he suggests, to the same belief in the natural goodness of Man which inspired in Wells a vision of scientific Utopias. The only difference was that both Hardy and Housman were too critical and too sensitive to reconcile the current belief in the natural goodness of Man with what they saw around them. Having no belief in a world of transcendent being, in relation to which Man's life had meaning, Housman could only view Man as the sport of a Nature in some sense malignant,

> And how am I to face the odds
> Of man's bedevilment and God's?

Writers are, of course, primarily what they are because they are made that way. But they are, too, subject to the climate of their age and to the context of its prevailing belief. To this extent Mr. Nicholson's study of these writers in the light of his doctrine of 'Liberal Man' is revealing, the more so when, as with his treatment of Bennett, he keeps it in the background and is content to show it working implicitly in a writer's choice of subject and the quality of his style. Bennett's characters, he says, except for vague misgivings, have purpose only in the social pattern. It is an overstatement but does not prevent him from appreciating him well as what he calls 'the true poet of materialism'.

The protagonist among the writers who subscribed from 1910

onwards to the doctrine of 'Natural Man', in whom 'Liberal Man' was reduced to his physical dimensions and stripped of his hollow humanism, is for him D. H. Lawrence. Lawrence is a dangerous writer to fit into any thesis and Mr. Nicholson recognizes this. He knows the incontrovertible power of Lawrence's writing. 'All sense impressions,' he writes, 'all experiences, things seen and heard or felt and imagined, seemed to react on Lawrence like a jab on a raw nerve. The reader got the sensation direct on his own finger-tips, like a blind man reading Braille.'

The 'Natural Man', too, as Lawrence conceived him, was no mere breathing, eating, lusting, fighting animal as in Ernest Hemingway's earlier work. He was a Man who had recovered his mystical significance but through the blood and sex, the psychic and non-human. Lawrence repudiated a moral scheme which made a character consistent. He found such a scheme dull, old and dead. And he had reason to do so in the modern world of moribund religion and material ends.

Yet he himself sought release only in a mystical materialism. In his disgust with a diseased humanity, however moral its mouthings, he longed for people to become possessed not by a divine, but by an inhuman will, or, as he put it, to *be* 'inhumanly, physiologically, materially, not to feel according to the human conception'. He repudiated Christianity because in striving to spiritualize life on the conscious level it had, he believed, impoverished and even cut Man's unconscious roots. Unlike other devotees of the 'Natural Man', then, Lawrence did not repudiate a world of transcendent being but he reduced it to one of transcendent non-being. It was in this realm of sensational darkness that he longed to resolve the primal conflict between good and evil in which as a Puritan he so painfully believed.

But in his successors the materialism had no mystical pretensions. In the novels of Henri de Montherlant and the early Aldous Huxley the 'Natural Man' is a sophisticated product of Western civilization, cynically intent on self-gratification and attached to others only for sensual pleasure. And inevitably so, since he regards himself as a creature of impulses, appetites, instincts and nothing else. In Hemingway's novels he is a tough, though often sentimental, animal, whose interests are love and war. They are, as Mr. Nicholson points out, incompatible and so he is continually frustrated. He is also essentially in bondage to life, one 'that things are done to'.

This is even more pronounced in the people of William Faulkner's novels. They do not understand, as Mr. Nicholson writes, 'the motives by which they act, they find themselves involved in events which they had not wished to bring about'. Like the girl in his novel, *Sanctuary*, who 'could hear silence in a thick rustling' as the predatory male moved toward her through it, thrusting it aside, 'and she began to say something is going to happen to me', they abandon themselves desperately to fate, to desires which they cannot control and will never to able to satisfy, because the world of values to which they could responsibly surrender has ceased to exist for them.

That is Mr. Nicholson's diagnosis. Obviously the novelists whose work he has chosen to exemplify it are apt to his purpose and an examination of a wider field might reveal a more complex situation. But while he generalizes too easily, he does keep close to the style of the work he is considering as well as to its content. This is especially so in his appreciations of Hemingway and Faulkner, though his admiration of the tough style of the former may well seem excessive unless we admire a blunt technique for reflecting a blunt perception.

2

But having defined, to his own satisfaction, the assumptions as to the nature of Man reflected in some of the outstanding writers of this century, and by implication in many of their readers, he looks round for signs in literature of a more reliable view. And here perhaps it will be best to quote from the introduction to the third part of his book entitled 'Imperfect Man'.

> Liberal Man and Natural Man [he writes] are both simplifications of the real nature of Man. They are attempts to

> explain his being and purpose on one plane — that of progress or that of animal desire. The traditional view, however, is that Man has being on two planes, the material and spiritual; that his purpose is to be seen in relation to some will or plan which exists outside of himself; that his actions are to be judged in the light of transcendent values. This is the view which has persisted through the centuries of western civilization. It is also the Christian point of view. It is not exclusively Christian, of course, as it was to be found before the birth of Christ and is held to-day by many unbelievers and is shared also by some other religions, such as Islam.

This is certainly a fair statement of the traditional or, one might say, the eternal religious view of man, provided that the phrase 'some will or plan which exists outside of himself' is rightly understood. For God is more within us than ourselves. His will or plan is only outside our false ego; it is the inward genius of our true being. If the eternal will were not as infinitely in Man as beyond him, his imperfection could not be redeemed.

It may be, as Coventry Patmore wrote, that 'nothing is so fatal to that "real apprehension" which is the life of truth, as thinking about the "infinite" '. Yet only the thought which is infinite can reveal the truth of the finite. The difficulty of truly conceiving and living in a two dimensional world is obvious. For it is as easy to deny as to accept the finite wrongly.

Accepted for itself and for the selfish satisfaction we can temporarily derive from it, the finite world is an illusion. But we are equally blinded when we deny its limits in a desire for infinite sensation. To experience the true relation we must cease to crave, yet we must not fall into indifference. There is a sense in which Aldous Huxley is right in saying that 'God is completely present only in the complete absence of *what we call* our humanity'. Yet to shed the perversely less than human without growing into the divinely more than human is to become an abstraction, a ghost in some spiritual limbo.

It is as dangerous, therefore, and as necessary to deny what we are as to affirm it. On the temporal level humanity is imperfect and relatively evil, but it also embodies potentially the highest good which we on this earth can conceive and of which we have examples in the noblest of our kind. We have, therefore, to be continually denying what is mortal in us to express the immortal. Yet humbly to accept our mortality is equally a condition of affirming what is eternal in us.

The history of man and particularly of his religions shows how extraordinarily hard it is to be equally true to the finite and the infinite and to love the one as the necessary expression of the other.

Denis de Rougemont, for example, in his *Passion and Society*, has traced with brilliant insight how a failure to do so has underlain the whole theory and practice of romantic love and also of war in Western Europe from the middle ages until to-day. A love of love as an absolute, unrelated to human conditions, is a love of death. It is the supreme egoism which desires not liberation but annihilation. 'To love love more than the object of love', as de Rougemont puts it, 'to love passion for its own sake', is to love suffering as an end instead of a means.

There is a clear-sighted passion, to which the mystics testify, in which suffering is gladly accepted as a means through which the human will may become more deeply expressive of the Divine will. But for such mystics 'the Dark Night' was something to be passed through. For romantic lovers, of whom Tristan and Iseult were prototypes, it was the culmination of the flame in which they sought to be devoured, the final void to which all sensation, pursued as an end, leads.

Such love, in its extreme, was the apotheosis of egotism. It scorned finite relations, save as a pretext for infinite desire. In de Rougemont's words, it 'treated a fellow-creature as but an illusory excuse and occasion for taking fire'. It even devised separations, if life did not provide them, to fan the flame, that it might burn more fiercely to death. Individuals were but so many defects of infinite non-being, and passion was intensified as an escape from, instead of a fulfilment of, human life.

Extremes of passion such as this may be rare in life, but the love which is a consumption because it fails to be a communion is common enough and has been raging in the world. It is because men are foiled of communion that they seek to destroy themselves in a holocaust of mutual suicide.

For the infinite in man's heart cannot be denied. If it is not polarized in the reciprocity of love, the creative counterpoint of one person with another, the art of neighbourliness, it will sweep through mankind with as blind a destructiveness as an unharnessed electric current. Denied expression in a true interplay of human life, it will gather force as a repressed longing for death which will inevitably explode.

How extreme the denial has now become is shown by the kind of explosion which modern war represents. For if the Light is not married to the Darkness in a continual redemptive communion, it becomes a force of darkness, terrible in its perverted power. And Man, deprived of the joy of being which can deliver him from the woe of existence, ignorant of the transcendent Day which glorifies terrestrial Night, can only become, in his longing for self-extinction, an agent of an elemental darkness.

3

It is in the recognition that Man needs this basic redemption that the traditional view of Man differs from a merely rational or humanitarian one. The upholders of the view of 'Liberal' or 'Natural Man' in rejecting transcendent values rejected also the idea of Original Sin, which needed those values, conceived as divine powers in action, for its salvation. They identified progress with material becoming instead of with spiritual growth. 'Becoming', to quote a modern writer, 'is a real element in existence. But the actual world is fallen, for it is a world in which becoming is erected by the sinful spirit to the absolute, unconditioned value of the eternal.'

The fruits of this misconception are all around us. Yet, often quite unconsciously, the traditional view of Man has remained implicit in popular thought. So Mr. Nicholson believes, and he sees signs of its re-emergence in literature. It would, indeed, be surprising if the events of recent years had not enforced the view that Man is an imperfect and sinful creature.

The three writers, however, whom Mr. Nicholson particularly presents as combining the traditional view with a gift for technical experiment, needed no war to instruct them in the nature of Man. They are James Joyce with his Catholic backgound, Franz Kafka and T. S. Eliot.

A critic without Mr. Nicholson's Christian predilections can hardly derive as much comfort from the contemplation of the works of these three writers as he does. He may even feel that the pessimism which Mr. Nicholson attributes to the liberal faithlessness of Hardy and Housman is almost as pronounced in the work of these prodigal sons of the Christian faith. The difference, Mr. Nicholson would doubtless reply, is that in Joyce, Kafka and Eliot it has a meaning. It is related to a comprehensible and ultimately acceptable view of life. And if in all of them there is also felt a certain spiritual frustration, it is attributable rather to the faithless world in which they have lived and suffered than to the basic insufficiency of their belief.

Nevertheless the Christian faith does seem in all of them to have failed to heal a certain sickness of soul. Joyce's conscious repudiation of Catholicism was at least as potent as the life-long influence which it unconsciously exerted over him. And we have only to compare Kafka's phantasmal and intricately self-involved search, in the person of his anonymous hero K., for the meaning of the cosmic dispensation, and for acquittal from a mysterious and unspecified guilt, with the simple imaginative depth of Bunyan's human allegory to recognize the difference between metaphysical and aesthetic ingenuity, and creative faith. In T. S. Eliot on the other hand Christian dogma has been more of a fortress in a waste land than a home glowing with spiritual light.

Nevertheless in these three writers, though each wanders in a no-man's-land between faith and scepticism, there is a gravity, a sense of eternal issues, which modern literature so generally lacks.

Man is conceived in more than one dimension. Kafka's novels, *The Castle* and *The Trial*, tentative and often tediously enigmatic though they be, are allegories of Man's utter dependence on a divine grace, which cannot be demanded or ultimately even deserved, and of a divine purpose beyond human understanding to be accepted with the utmost humility.

Certainly in him the sense of sin, of guilt and self-disparagement, traceable, as in Kierkegaard, to his relations with his father, was excessive. And this led him to regard the divine powers, before which he bowed, as wilful, incalculable and even malevolent. But we have only to compare his hero's patient waiting for the Light, in which through all the obscurity of his baffled searching he ultimately believes, with Faulkner's characters' doomed abandonment to the sensational something which is going to happen to them, to measure the difference between human dignity and human dereliction, between a dedicated and a merely helpless life.

In all who hold the traditional view of Man the balance between the acknowledgment of sin and the belief in redemption is apt to be precarious. This is, indeed, the test of a really integral faith, the proof that the dark and the bright angels have truly met and become as one over the gulf that in self-conscious man has opened between them.

In none of these three writers has that meeting, we feel, been really consummated. For despite Mr. Nicholson's assertion we may doubt whether in the *Waste Land* of any of them the experience of spiritual rebirth is as compellingly realized as the fact of Man's fallen state, though in his later poems T. S. Eliot has certainly been preoccupied with little else.

Mr. Nicholson does not confine himself to these three writers. But his treatment of others, particularly of the younger poets, is rather scrappy, and although it may be true that 'through the work of most of them runs a feeling of guilt and a consciousness of responsibility to the generations of the future', it is doubtful whether many would consciously subscribe to the traditional religious view as he states it.

It was, however, well worth stating. His book is essentially a criticism of life through literature. From a literary angle it is often much too summary. But at a time when more than ever perhaps men need to build up a faith on true foundations it is well to be reminded that Man is heaven-born as well as earth-born and that hell is not his native estate.

IX

THE DREAM OF RAVAN

THE need to become 'whole' is more and more engaging the attention of poets, philosophers, sociologists and teachers in the West. The reason is obvious. The European Wars have exposed with appalling clarity the abyss of division into which we have fallen. The first reaction of the sensitive was one of disillusion and scepticism. But that is passing. For, as Mr. Lawrence Hyde wrote in *The Prospects of Humanism*, 'to doubt sincerely and consistently is to be in Hell. And this is insupportable. If the suspension of belief is honest, the outcome must either be a paralysing despair or a birth into a new mode of consciousness'.

It would be too much, perhaps, to say that such a 'new mode of consciousness' is already born, but there are signs of its emergence, signs too, that we are beginning to realize that the creative harmony which we seek to establish in the world depends ultimately upon each individual's effort to integrate himself.

But if we are increasingly aware of this to-day, we are still, it must be admitted, very far from having a clear conception of what it involves.

The advice offered to us is very various and each teacher tends to stress one aspect of the problem to the exclusion of all others or to proclaim a manifestly partial way of salvation. This is because our teachers are themselves, so often, still inwardly divided men. They forget that all the great spiritual teachers of the world have painfully established their own integrity before offering a gospel to others. They are in fact in the line, not of the true seers, but of Rousseau.

For Rousseau was the first and perhaps the most influential of our modern evangelists. And all his life he was a sick man in search of a cure. His sickness was our sickness, the malady of a divided being in which heart and head, the senses and the intelligence, were at war with one another. And the solution which he preached was also characteristic. It was a return to a 'state of nature'.

There is a sense in which the spiritual man is indeed the natural man. For he is nature redeemed and so fulfilled. The moralists who have insisted upon a final opposition between the natural and the spiritual betray the same self-enslavement as the romanticists who confuse impure sensation with spiritual joy. But because Rousseau was guilty of this confusion, his 'state of nature' has proved a most delusive Eden. Yet his influence has persisted, not only through the seductive charm of his writing, but because no other man has so eloquently expressed the disease which has been sapping the virtue of the Western world, and because his gospel has had all the fatal attractiveness of a half-truth.

For Rousseau was right in his claim that Western civilization had become morbid through rationalizing self-interest. But he failed sufficiently to realize what a deeply rooted and necessary instinct self-interest is. To invite men to abandon thought for feeling was merely to transfer the working of this instinct from one plane to another.

For feeling is not necessarily more truthful or disinterested than thought. It is in fact the elementary organ of thought. The organs of feeling are in intimate touch with primitive life, as the mind, when it consciously awakes, is the instrument of rational life. And the life of reason is as real as the life of feeling, more real, indeed, since less transitory. Both feeling and thought can be perverted by self-love, but there is nothing gained by transferring self-love from one to the other, as Rousseau encouraged men to believe.

Fifty years before Rousseau was born Thomas Traherne had recognized the truth which Rousseau overlooked that the self-love which was as ineradicable in man as it is in God, who cannot but love His own perfection, needed to be transformed, not transferred, when he wrote: 'Thus is God infinitely preferred by Nature above myself, and my Love to myself, being thoroughly satisfied, turns into the Love of God, and dies like a grain of Corn in the Earth to spring up in a new and better form, more glorious and honourable, more great and verdant, more fair and delightful.'

Traherne's *Felicity* was truly a state of second innocence, of Paradise regained, of spiritual maturity in which 'all transients' were known to be 'permanent in God'. The child in him was completed in the seer. But in Rousseau 'the grain of Corn', self-love, had not truly died to spring up in a new and better form. At best it shed only its outer sheath.

Since his day the disease for which he imperfectly prescribed a cure has become a galloping consumption. In learning partially to know himself, Western man has lost the secret of being more than himself. And until he has regained that secret his knowledge will remain external and his methods of self-cure will be at best only ameliorative. For without inspired insight the problems of human nature cannot be truly solved, however expert we may become as analysts of its mechanism. It is this insight, sensitive and divinatory, which the Eastern sages possessed in a measure only equalled by the greatest Western mystics and seldom by them with as much subtlety and refinement.

Both in their teaching and practice they constantly emphasized the truth that the spiritual life, like the physical out of which it necessarily evolves, is one of organic growth through ascending degrees of self-losing and self-finding. It is for the light that Hindu psychology throws on this process of growth into inner freedom that it compares so favourably with contemporary Western psychology or with the formalities of Christian moralists. What it gives us is a spiritual wisdom that has been intimately lived, unprejudiced either by scientific theory or a religious creed. An inviting introduction to it for readers not yet acclimatized to the Eastern scriptures is a book entitled *The Dream of Ravan*.

This book appeared originally in a series of articles in *The Dublin University Magazine* of 1853, 1854. Its anonymous author was therefore presumably a Westerner, but one who was profoundly intimate with Eastern literature, and in particular with the *Ramayana*, out of which *The Dream of Ravan* develops. Much of the dream is told in verse that has qualities of vision and melody which recall at times both Shelley and Poe. Like the religious oratorios of the Haridasas or Ramadasas, it blends 'moral and religious instruction with music, lyric poetry, mythical narrative, and a dash, now and then, of proverbial wisdom, or amusing anecdote'.

For the true spiritual teacher, being self-emancipated and so inwardly at ease, does not feel an innocent gaiety to be incongruous to a setting forth of spiritual wisdom. The heart can laugh without desiring to ridicule. It can laugh without malice because in laughing at another it laughs at itself. Humour is imaginative as wit is not. And being imaginative it reaches always beyond and through the particular to the universal. In a genuine humour, as Coleridge wrote, there is always 'an acknowledgment of the hollowness and the farce of the world, and its disproportion to the Godlike within us'. An acknowledgment, but also an acceptance. The wit hates imperfection and gloats over what he castigates because he is the slave of it himself. The humorist, being an artist, loves reality, flawed though it be, the good and the bad of it, the grotesque and the sublime, the complacent and the incongruous. For him it is all part of a diverse whole to which he humbly and gladly consents as the first condition of redeeming what is ill in it.

The Dream of Ravan, then, breathes throughout a charming temper, that of a poet who is also a mystic and, in the best sense, a humorist, knowing intimately the humours of which men are so differently composed; one, too, who is not only versed in Vedantic psychology but has proved upon his pulses the truths of this ancient Science of Being.

In interpreting the dream he expounds its imaged wisdom. And perhaps the most enlightening of these interpretations is that which defines the three 'States' or modes of consciousness through which the individual grows to completeness, with a luminous clarity which is in striking contrast to the volcanic flashes and dark convulsions of such a disintegrated searcher after life-wisdom as, for example, D. H. Lawrence.

The three radical qualities into which the primordial unity is described as dividing itself, when reflected in time, and of which every soul born into natural life partakes in greater or less degree, will be familiar to all students of the *Bhagavad-Gita*. They are named *Tamas*, *Rajas* and *Satva*, representing respectively Darkness, Fieriness and Pure Light. It is in his interpretation of these three qualities or strands of being that the author of *The Dream of Ravan* reveals his insight.

Tamas, as he shows, is negativity, inertia, indifference:

> It is the absence of all knowledge, feeling, motion, penetrability, transparency. It is, in fact, what may appear a strange expression, the moral basis of matter; or, in other words, that stolid state or form of spirit, which causes it to appear and be what we call matter.

In its highest development, therefore, it does not go beyond the mere animal life and the region of sense.

Rajas, on the other hand,

> is the characteristic of moral life or soul; the dark opacity is penetrated with a fiery and turbid glare, but not yet rendered purely transparent; the cold obstruction and insensibility are awakened into pangs of painful movement.

This is that state of warring passion and moral division, a restless outward activity, which possesses man when self-consciousness shatters his primitive unity.

Finally *Satva* is the characteristic of Spirit, which though bright, luminous and glorious in itself, still partakes of distinction, being bound in the chains of individuality and limitation.

> The feeling soul compelled by suffering into a profounder self-consciousness and reflection, passion has risen into reason and knowledge. Self-knowledge, reasoning outward, progresses into universal sympathy. The life of emotion reaches its consummation, and all other passions expire in giving birth to an eternal sentiment of justice and love, which are ultimately one.

Where this scheme of life and soul-unfoldment commends itself is in including all the vital factors and avoiding those false oppositions between reason and instinct, flesh and spirit which show that the teacher has not himself really outgrown the *Rajas* state.

It is conceived by one who has himself realized the state of *Satva*, 'when the plastic, and the emotional, and the ideal, become absolutely one, and there is, properly speaking, neither matter, nor soul, nor spirit, but something which is all and yet none of these — call it Bramh . . . OR SOLIDARITY OF BEING, THOUGHT AND JOY'.

The man who has thus achieved reunion with the divine no longer cherishes enmity against either his animal or his intellectual being. He knows that even the *Tamas* 'partakes of good: it contains within itself potentially both the *Rajas* and the *Satva*, which only require to be evolved from it'; while 'in proportion to the large basis of the *Tamas* quality is the intensity and power of that *Rajas* fire and *Satva* light, which movement can evolve'. And again, if the Spiritual seeks to stand alone, denying its humbler faculties, 'it becometh in its proud isolation, a deadly venomous yellow, the colour of serpents, and dragons, and irredeemable Bramha-Rakshasas'.

For though these three qualities or states of being represent an ascending scale of consciousness, they are each binding states until the self which grows through them has itself been outgrown. The man who lives most consistently in the *Satvic* state is most advanced towards the goal of humanity, since *Satva* reflects the harmony and poise of the eternal Light. To that state all must aspire to come, through the insatiable fires of *Rajas* and the dense darkness of *Tamas*.

Yet the self-bondage of the *Satvic* man, enlightened and relatively stable though he be, is only less limiting than that of *Rajas* and *Tamas*. As another Western commentator has written of *Satva*: 'Stainless and sorrowless, its light is still reflected light and binds the soul to the happiness and knowledge that are its manifestations. At any time the love of happiness, the sacred thirst for knowledge, may, through the touch of *Rajas*, degenerate into lust for pleasure and mere curiosity.'

Even if this danger is avoided, the *Satvic* man may become immured in his ivory tower of limited enlightenment, of cultured humanism, for example, or indulgent quietism. He will do the world little harm there and may even enrich it with the graces of his learning. But he will cease to grow and that is inevitably to degenerate.

To go forward to completion the man who has attained to the *Satvic* state must labour to transcend altogether the three states through which he has grown. They are all, as the *Gita* says, moods of nature and his task is to be no longer a creature of nature, but a creator of light *through* nature. Instead of merely reflecting the eternal Light, he needs to incarnate it.

Then only his vision becomes eternally his own, and he sees the moods of nature within and without himself for what they are, recognizing each as necessary to the evolving order of the Cosmos, and reconciling them in the harmony of his own being, no longer as conflicting states but as complementary. The darkness of *Tamas* will then shine with the light to which it gives substance; the fire of *Rajas* will energize the tranquil radiance of *Satva*, and the spirit of the emancipated man will wear these states as a pure garment woven of three blended threads.

Such is the body which man and nature wear in the vision of Eastern psychology and which the author of *The Dream of Ravan* traces anew for us with such illuminating charm. Of the soul's growth within this body he writes:

> The problem to be solved in the case of Titanic Ravan — and in greater or less degree of every human soul, in proportion as it partakes of the Titanic nature, as all in their emerging must in some measure — is, how shall the *Tamas* be changed into the *Satva*, or penetrated and ruled by it? — how shall matter reascend and become spirit ? — the gross darkness and stolid stupidity . . . be illumined into self-consciousness, reflection, reason, knowledge? — the brute self-concentration be kindled into universal sympathy and love? — the blind instinct of coarse desires . . . be sublimed into the eternal conscious principles, self-renunciation, and pure ideality of the divine life?

And he answers:

> This can only be accomplished in one way, and that way lies through the *Rajas* — the life of passion — the life of suffering.

> The result of every passion of our nature, even love, nay, of love more than of all others, is suffering and sorrow. The first awakening of unconscious matter into the consciousness of mere animal life is through physical pain; and the process is carried still further by the mental suffering which is the very nature of the soul's emotional life . . . Brute appetite and blind impulse are first superseded by passion; and passion, working through sorrow and the reflection and sympathy which sorrow generates, begets its own extinction, and finally merges in and is swallowed up in love and absolute resignation. This philosophy seems to rest on a basis of unquestionable truth. For, understood in all its depth, it is identical, in ultimate results, with the way of the Cross.

Such suffering, which is not the negative endurance, the self-bound and resentful distress with which the word is commonly associated, is, indeed, essential to all true growth, and the knowledge of our modern rationalists is superficial to the extent that they have not really suffered in this sense.

It is often said with justice that the East has overemphasized feminine self-surrender in its way of life, the West masculine self-assertion. But the author of *The Dream of Ravan* makes it clear that in the purest mystical doctrine of the East activity and passivity were creatively reconciled, that natural life with its faculties of reason and sense was not denied but fulfilled in the unity of the spirit, and that the human was conceived as realizing its essential divinity by a kindred process to that by which the seed dies that it may live, the plant is submissive to the wind and rain, and the flower both lifts its face to the sun and draws its beauty and vitality from roots deep in the soil.

Thus it is only when all separation, however lofty, is renounced that the *Satva* may re-enter predominant into the *Rajas* and *Tamas*, may penetrate them with its influence and 'all three isolated prismatic rays coalesce into pure universal light and a consciousness of divine reunion'.

Later in the book we find the distinction between a perverse and a true spirituality emphasized in the contrasted characters of the two sages Maricha and Ananta. Both have trodden the path of self-renunciation, but while Maricha, as a result of his grotesque penitential austerities, is a skeleton and a scarecrow, Ananta, though advanced in years, has 'a fresh and almost roseate look. His features, naturally handsome, wore the impress of a loving as well as a reverential nature, and the holy calm of a spirit at peace crowned their blended expression of dignity and sweetness'.

Similarly Ananta avoids 'the pursuit of Siddhis, or miraculous faculties' to which Maricha devotes himself, 'pronouncing it a road beset with dangers, and often leading to the profoundest darkness'. Maricha terrifies all who come into contact with him. Ananta draws his fellow-men towards him by the magnetism of his love. By such practices as standing on his head for a series of years Maricha has acquired strange powers and experienced wild visions. But the spiritual pride which dictated such fanatical penances has not been mortified by them. He has not truly suffered as Ananta who has been content 'with the humbler exercise of fixing the contemplations of his spirit on the infinite moral beauty and goodness of the Divine nature, and endeavouring by contemplation, to transform himself to some likeness of the eternal love', and who in consequence feels a glad sympathy with all living creatures and evokes it too.

In these two characters, then, we are shown the difference between the magical and the mystical, the divided self which exploits spiritual forces, and the completed self which expresses the divine.

There is much else in *The Dream of Ravan* which throws light on the nature of the true mystic and the conditions governing his development, much esoteric lore, too, such as the remarkable catalogue of soul-powers. But the whole is written with such simplicity and charm that the reader needs to be no student of Yoga or occult practices to receive the deep life-wisdom which it breathes.

We are beginning to realize in the West that the most practical psychology is also the most spiritual. And we have only to compare the understanding of a true poet or seer with that even of eminen analysts to see how much deeper and more sensitive is their contact with reality.

The Dream of Ravan is the work of both a poet and a seer. There are elements in it of playful fantasy and caprice. But even its fantasy is a veil through which true vision peeps. For here that path to wholeness, that growth from unconsciousness, through self-consciousness, to pure being, which is becoming, as never before, the desperate concern of the West, is revealed by one who was himself whole, whose vision, therefore, was not convulsed and demiurgic but serenely sabbatical, and who by the light that shone in himself and his Eastern Forerunners could reveal how man might throw off the darkness clouding his spirit and resume his native brightness.

X

SCIENCE AND THE SELF[1]

UNTIL recently most people were viewing with some complacence the Scientific Society of the future. Possibly many do still. But I think they are fewer. It is harder now to believe or even hope that the world will eventually be organized as a whole simply through science in the ordinary meaning of the word.

Indeed we are more inclined now to fear that it will be destroyed by science, unless qualities and powers which science has disregarded and undermined regain their control over human life. It is upon these qualities and the relation of science to them that I wish to concentrate.

The questions I am going to ask and try to answer are these: Has natural science, despite all its mental and material conquests, impoverished our real life? And, if so, must it continue to impoverish it? Is its method for acquiring knowledge the only true method? Or is it fatally partial and one-sided?

This last may seem a surprising question. For during the last hundred years the scientist has popularized the view that he alone was exercising his reason aright, and that those who claimed to arrive at knowledge by other methods than his were clinging to false illusions because they were too weak to face the truth.

He is perhaps less certain of this to-day. Nevertheless the assumption is still prevalent. Yet however intelligible such an attitude was in mid-Victorian times, when Natural Science was fighting a necessary battle against religious obscurantism, it represents itself to-day an equally dangerous kind of dogmatism.

For the scientist's method of acquiring knowledge is not the only valid one. His aim is to reduce the human mind to a sensitive machine which sorts the facts given to it by observation, measures them in relation to one another, and arranges them in a correct

[1] Originally given as a talk on the wireless in a series entitled 'Science in the Changing World'.

pattern according to its own inherent logic. When new facts are discovered, the pattern is modified to include them. The aim is to find the simplest pattern into which the facts will fit.

Obviously in such a process the mind can never be a mere machine. An act of will is involved on the part of the searcher and even a sense of form, akin to that of the artist. But this personal element has been generally denied by the scientist. He has insistently claimed that his approach to truth is purely impersonal. He has striven in his researches to exclude every desire or interest of his own, and the better to ensure this he has taken elaborate external precautions against personal prejudice.

A necessary result of this attempt to acquire exact knowledge independent of any personal act of knowing is that the scientist can only deal with what is constant and common to all observers. He is compelled to disregard the unique reality of an object and reduce it to a mere instance in a series of instances. All qualitative values disappear beneath a ruthless classification and all living form perishes in abstract formulas.

This process of abstraction is displayed perhaps most notably to-day in the subtle but tenuous formulas of the mathematical physicists. But while one may well admire the way in which the material world has dissolved beneath their measuring-rods, their attempt to produce a purely intellectual representation of the universe has inevitably resulted in what is at best only a ghostly skeleton of reality. And every one of the physical sciences which attempts an exclusively intellectual approach to Nature suffers under the same disability. Since Ultimate Reality cannot be calculated, since it must be immediately experienced, so far as that is possible, they can never really know life, but only something of the mechanism of life's expression.

But if ultimate reality has escaped and must always escape the physical scientist, he can justly claim that this method has proved remarkably successful in its own relative domain. And although the knowledge which he has thus acquired has not noticeably increased human happiness, it has made it possible for man to master to some extent his physical conditions, to alleviate physical pain, and to exploit for his own material benefit the forces of Nature.

But there is another and older theory of knowledge. According to it, we cannot know the reality of anything unless we enter into it imaginatively, unless we wholly identify ourselves with it and realize it from within. To achieve real knowledge, therefore, we need not merely to observe and co-ordinate facts, but to live the truth. Knowledge, in short, depends upon the quality of being possessed by him who seeks to know. To know better, it is necessary to become different. For the more deeply harmonized are a man's faculties of feeling and thought, the finer and more fundamental are his powers of achieving contact with reality.

This is the science of the poet, the mystic and the seer, and of all who try to know life with their whole being. And we have an elementary example of such integrity of being in the simple, necessary response to life of the child and the peasant.

I am not, however, suggesting that the progressive claims of modern science can be disproved by pointing to the humble virtues of the peasant or the child. For the rational self-consciousness from which the world is suffering is, it would seem, a necessary stage in human development. And all attempts to revert to childhood are inevitably doomed to failure.

Nevertheless simple people do offer us a suggestive example, on the instinctive level, of wholeness. For however undeveloped their powers of conscious intelligence may be, the knowledge which they possess and the thought which they exercise are grounded in their very being. And this is true, on a more advanced level, of all creative thought. Unlike the critical analysis of science, it is an expression of the whole being.

Such spiritual perception or imaginative knowledge is little regarded in the West to-day, because we have been witnessing during the last hundred years the culmination of a process clearly traceable from the Renaissance in Europe and the Reformation in England. It was as inevitable a process as that which occurs in every individual who in passing from childhood to youth is inwardly divided.

Out of this division a richer unity may be ultimately achieved. But meanwhile, so far as the individual is at conflict with himself, he is at cross-purposes with life. He is either stricken with indecision or he asserts his personal will against life, denying it as a whole in the interests of one of its parts. Consequently his soul loses contact with its depths and he becomes mentally expert but superficial.

Western civilization for the last hundred years clearly reflects such a state, a state in which the personal will of the individual has lacked any creative centre, so that he has sought increasingly his own private gain or glorification. And because modern man has become thus uncentred, modern civilization has been full of discord and aimlessness. With immense resources of wealth and power, it has lacked unity of design or purpose.

And the basic weakness of natural science, so far as it claims to cure the disease of civilization, is that it suffers from the disease itself. In its exploitation of one faculty, the calculating intellect, however impartially, at the expense of all the others, it has reflected and aggravated the separation of knowledge from being. It has, indeed, affirmed the unity of physical Nature, but it has denied that higher unity to which man as a creative spirit belongs.

Certainly science is morally neutral. But it is also spiritually blinkered, if not blind. Concerned itself with the processes reflected in physical matter, it has assumed and popularized the view that these are alone real. Because it can only deal with physical organisms, it has tended to reduce man to the same physical level as frogs or rabbits. And so far as modern man has accepted the scientific view that his body is more real than his soul, he has become the slave of external things and secondary conditions instead of finding freedom through obedience to direction received inwardly from a superphysical source.

Our greatest need to-day, therefore, is not to deny the intellect, but to make it more profound. And we can only do this by recognizing that it must be subordinated to something more essential than itself.

The problem of knowledge and of life, and so of civilization, is, in fact, ultimately, as all the great mystics and spiritual teachers have insisted, a moral one. They admit that man at a certain stage of his development falls into division. But they affirm out of their own experience, that by sustained effort, by humbling himself to a will at the heart of being greater than his own and at the same time exercising all his faculties, man can regain unity. In such unity not only, to use Blake's words, are the windows of perception cleansed and the eternal significance of every particular divined, but at the same time a true disinterestedness is achieved.

The claim of the scientist to be disinterested beyond all other men has been, however, so frequently advanced and generally accepted that it may be well to consider it for a moment. In a famous letter to Charles Kingsley, Thomas Henry Huxley wrote: 'Science seems to me to teach in the highest and strongest manner the great truth which is embodied in the Christian conception of entire surrender to the will of God. Sit down before fact as a little child, be prepared to give up every preconceived notion, follow humbly wherever and to whatever abysses Nature leads, or you shall learn nothing.'

It is hardly necessary to say that the manner in which a little child sits down before fact is very different from that of even the most conscientious natural scientist. For the child's relation to fact is not one of mere mental observance, but of such sensitive and whole-hearted absorption that it is not perhaps too much to say that no facts exist for him.

The same distinction may be drawn between the mystic's or the artist's sensitive surrender of his whole self to experience and the precautions which the scientist takes against personal bias. The one is an imaginative and entire, the other only a mental and partial, act. Admittedly this distinction does not apply to the greatest scientists, who, in obeying the rules of research, have always possessed, too, the gifts of divination. They, like the artist, by submitting to a technical discipline, have prepared themselves for the creative moment when a truth is given to them. But such scientists are as rare as men of disciplined and disinterested vision always are.

Outside, indeed, the province of the laboratory, in which impartiality can be technically guaranteed — in Biology, for example, as distinct from Chemistry and Physics, or in such border sciences as Anthropology, Psychology and Sociology, which deal with life where it has ascended from the purely physical to the human plane — we often find that the scientist has projected his personal prejudice into his interpretation of phenomena while claiming to be wholly disinterested.

The blindness of nineteenth-century evolutionists, for instance, to the co-operative principle in Nature was due to an innate combativeness in themselves and in the outlook of their age. Their concentration upon natural selection and the survival of the fittest to the exclusion of creative variation and mutual adaptability reflected their own individual limitations. In the same way the anthropologists of yesterday explained the life and customs of savages in terms of their own self-assertive consciousness, attributing to primitive man the 'tiger qualities' of a predatory civilization. For, as Amiel wrote, 'a man only understands what is akin to something already existing in himself'.

We must remember, therefore, in our respect for scientific method, that the scientist's interpretation and even his recognition of such facts as cannot be measured and tested by retorts and balances, must depend upon the degree of his own real integrity. Scientific method does not enforce such integrity. For the discipline of the laboratory involves no real change of being and no deep culture of the self. It may and does encourage a specialized habit of cautiousness and accuracy. But there is no necessary relation between the sensitiveness of the scientist's instruments and the real sensitiveness of the man himself. Moreover, by delegating sensitiveness to instruments, or exercising it only in a narrow and abstract field, he tends, as even Darwin regretfully admitted, to lose it himself.

It is possible, therefore, to be a brilliant scientist and yet in feeling to be quite uncivilized.

For what is it to be truly civilized? It is surely to draw upon inward resources and at the same time to be finely responsive to one's environment; it is, out of the fullness of a true self, to respect the uniqueness of every living person or creature and to be incapable of exploiting them. It is to co-operate with the spirit of Nature rather than to master her physical processes by intellectual cunning or for selfish ends. It is to live unattached to material things and desires, yet accepting both as means for the expression of a spiritual harmony.

A scientist may well be civilized in this true sense, but only very partially as a scientist. For professionally he is compelled to accept the physical and quantitative aspect of the world as alone real and to deny through all his working hours the validity of anything but a mental and mathematical approach to it.

2

Modern science, then, by its insistence that perception should be as much dehumanized as possible and by its consequent blindness to those living realities which escape its measuring instruments, has tended more and more to empty life of real meaning. Doubtless the material world has dissolved before it into a fine-spun web of abstract formulas, but the practical effect of this triumph of the technical mind over matter has been to subordinate man to the machine.

For a mechanism is as necessary an offspring of such science as an organism is of love and imagination. And although the elaborate and standardized mechanism which applied science has constructed in the modern world is proof enough of its astonishing ingenuity, the spirit that would love and create has been increasingly stifled beneath it. Admittedly the negative side of the modern scientific movement does not affect the disinterested virtue of science at its purest and best. But the effects of such pure science on modern civilization have so far been slight compared to the overwhelming pressure of applied science, and of its offspring, the machine.

Certainly the machine, apart from its productive and labour-saving uses to society, does impose a discipline upon those who serve it. It claims exactness, efficiency and a subordination of self to its technical demands. But because its technical demands, unlike those of any art or craft, are mechanical, because it severely limits when it does not deny its servants the right to disciplined self-expression, it tends to reduce them to ciphers, to mere cogs in its ruthlessly rotating wheels. They are cut off from the deep rhythm of life and condemned to a sterile service.

The evidence of this sterility extends far beyond those who are actually tied through all their working hours to machines. Wisdom has shrunk as scientific knowledge has grown. Mankind is more, not less ignorant of the meaning of life and, despite all the scientific techniques, of how to live well.

This is not surprising since technical skills require only a superficial kind of learning. The quality of the person manipulating them is of quite minor importance. Indeed the more standardized his capacity the better it generally is. Hence it is that we live in a day when the unique is everywhere being submerged in the uniform, and although we may pride ourselves upon a certain intellectual candour and dexterity and to some extent on a concern for physical well-being, these virtues are counterbalanced by the fact that we have little desire to raise ourselves to a higher pitch or, indeed, to conform to anything but average standards.

Yet beneath our physical and intellectual activities our deepest needs remain unsatisfied. And applied science can do nothing to supply them. It can only strive to distract our attention from them. And it does this in a typical way.

For how often are we asked to bow down before the wonders of modern mechanical invention. And at first we cannot but be impressed; nor would I deny that some of these products, which we owe directly to the scientific mind, may be of value as well as utility. But if we consider the matter more carefully, do we not find that many of them supply no really felt need? That by multiplying trivial objects, we have multiplied trivial desires, and that we could live a life more rich in meaning without them?

For the deepest need in man or woman is self-expression in some sort of creative activity, however humble. And although the burdened housewife may well be grateful to modern science for certain labour-saving devices, and congested city life would be impossible without scientific organization, is not the emphasis which science lays upon labour-saving and its eagerness to substitute the machine for the person or reduce the person to the machine a denial of true life values?

If science were merely striving to mitigate conditions which it has helped to create, one would be more willing to approve its endeavours and acclaim its successes. But if we are to believe one of its latest exponents, it is even working to deprive women of one of the few kinds of labour left in the modern world which can afford a deep creative satisfaction by manufacturing human life in a laboratory. The dangers that attend a dehumanized quest of knowledge could hardly be better illustrated. Yet such a suggestion is wholly in accordance with the logic of science. To manufacture human life is just as reasonable to it as to manufacture poison gas or atomic bombs.

But it may be said that the theory of knowledge and of life, which emphasizes the eternal value of the self and the need of wholeness in man's response to experience, has defects of its own, when put to the test of practice, no less obvious than those of physical science. And this cannot be denied. Modern psychologists, the best of them, have done a real service in showing how those who claim to be inspired servants of the truth and insist most forcibly upon the absoluteness of their vision may be indulging their egotism or compensating themselves for some inner weakness or unsatisfied desire.

Critical detachment is, indeed, essential to truth if self-delusion is to be avoided. But such detachment should be practised as a means, not an end, as an essential but subordinate factor in creative activity. In modern science it has been cultivated exclusively. The part has usurped the place of the whole; analysis has eaten not only into the body, but into the spiritual nerve-centres of life. To-day it has culminated in the splitting of the atom. Disintegrated man can bombard and disintegrate matter. But he cannot integrate his own human world.

Yet we have no right to complain of analysis and specializing in themselves. Natural science has brought light into dark places and led to discoveries which can free man from material bondage and may even, if we can find an inner substitute for the discipline of external necessity which it promises to remove, contribute through its precise knowledge of the lower realms of life to that true science of being to which it has hitherto been indifferent.

But it can only do so if it is recognized as a servant, not a master. 'Scientific method', in the words of Jung, the most imaginative of modern psychologists, 'must serve; it errs when it usurps a throne.' For while a true spiritual science, an enlightened knowledge, can include the mental province of physical science within it, an exclusively mental or mechanical science, however rarefied the fruits of its analysis may become, can never in itself regain the unity of perception from which it has broken away. Yet the fact that we have extended and refined our knowledge of physical phenomena to such a degree is not loss but gain, if we can recover the greater knowledge which should include it.

But this can only be achieved by cultivating an inward life and those values which sustain and enrich an inward life to counteract the immense pressure of material life upon us.

Far from helping us to develop that inward being, to liberate and vindicate that essential self from which true action and true knowledge spring, natural science, when it has not positively denied it, has reduced it to a questionable and impotent by-product of external forces and circumstances. And so its mental victories have been won at the cost of our moral defeat. And we shall remain demoralized until we realize that we must re-create ourselves before we can create value and unity in the external world.

For no true civilization can be achieved by working adroitly on the surface. It is ultimately conditioned by the spiritual strivings of countless individuals. It has a soul, so far as they have souls. Natural science has proved an effective weapon against superstition and selfish ignorance. But it has substituted its own obscurantism and consolidated its own vested interests. And these are in many ways inimical to that real understanding which has been called the knowledge of charity. For the disinterestedness of love differs from the 'impartiality' of science as inspired insight does from controlled observation. To come wholly alive the observer must grow into the seer.

Many people still believe in the possibility of curing the disease of civilization from without. Science for them is the doctor, who, as he becomes more skilled in his profession, may eventually cure the patient, if he does not first kill him.

I have tried to suggest that the patient must cure himself, that he can only recover real health by inward effort and obedience to the deepest laws of his being, and that although he may in his sickness need and profit by the specialist's treatment, the increasing tendency to depend on external aids, the ulterior effects of which are hidden even from the specialist himself, is a very dangerous one. For although a scientific society might be efficiently constructed by technical experts, it would be a society in which the individual was not more but less himself than in a tribal community.

A civilized society can only be created by men and women who are experts, not in some particular science, but in the art and understanding of Life. It is a society in which means are always subject to an enlightened end. The basic end of life is to glorify God and in so doing exalt and transform man. Every means, every technical method, which fails to further this end is destructive of life in some measure.

We to-day amid our hectic activities in which we struggle to stem by every inventive resource the ruin which we are as continually causing, have lost sight of this governing purpose. The essential touchstone which reveals whether an action is wholly good or to what degree it is good is gone. So without any directive from a realm of wholeness men pursue even good means badly as well as practise bad means in pursuit of some mythical good.

The desire for knowledge, for plenty, for liberation from physical drudgery, and even for power is essentially good. But undirected from a realm of value beyond selfish and temporal impulse, each of these desires becomes iniquitous. Men seek to know the wrong things because the motive of their seeking is perverse. Hence, for example, the cruelties and futilities of vivisection. They demand freedom and plenty acquisitively and in merely material terms. Hence chaos, enslavement and starvation. And they pursue power not for human betterment but through fear and for evil domination both of nature and man. Separated from the heaven within and beyond, that realm of unchanging and transcendent reality, they inevitably violate earth.

They will continue to do so until the sense of heaven and fidelity to it are restored. Only then will man regain his proper reverence for life. Only then will science become the organ of a whole self which pursues and applies knowledge wisely. To restore that relation, to re-establish that guidance, to reaffirm that clarifying and sanctifying end, is our greatest need, is indeed our only hope.

XI

THE QUEST OF THE TRUE ACT

ONE of the problems which is soon likely to test anyone who has set out to 'mend himself', as Traherne put it, is that of inaction. Like all spiritual problems it is presented from within and arises out of certain inward changes which are a condition of growth. The mystic *lives* his problems in a far more intimate sense than the man of the world, so that the problem of learning to act and not to act in a new way is for him in simple truth a matter of life and death. It is learning to die in the act of living, to die to division in himself that he may live in acts of real virtue.

The antithesis of action and inaction, as we ordinarily know it, is, like all conflicting opposites, ultimately unreal. It is a distortion of the divinely dual rhythm of the Universe. For in Nature the inflow and outflow of energy are but complementary modes of an enwrapped stillness which contains them both.

It is this rhythm which the mystic is striving to recover. If and when he recovers it, the problem of the degree of doing and undoing which his condition demands will no longer vex him. For every act of his will then possess the virtue of passivity, every motion be charged with meaning. Whether his acts are outward or inward, whether they sound in other ears or only in the stillness of the soul, they will be acts of praise and prayer, of love and enlightenment. For they will be truly centred in That which transcends and harmonizes all diversity.

But this is to look forward to journey's end. At its start the mystic is far from possessing such integrity. He can neither act nor refrain from action with that simple fullness of truth in which to act is also not to act, and not to act is to act. He has in some measure to choose from day to day and hour to hour between partial alternatives.

The needs of every soul in this as in other matters must differ. But it is probably safe to say, at least of Westerners, that the first need of the majority who would mend their lives is to be purposively passive, to refrain actively from action. Yet even when the need is most urgently felt, it is very hard to accept. For to do things or to get them done, is everywhere recognized as a merit, often with little regard to the quality of the act. And this is very understandable. It springs, even in the mere moralist or materialist, from an unconscious awareness of the virtue of what the Italian philosopher, Gentile, has called 'the Will as Pure Act'.

The divine life is the eternal expression of this Will, which is subject in the manifested universe to a dual rhythm of its own creation, but which acts as purely in its ebb as its flow. Happiness can only come in agreement with this creative Will, as is testified alike by the pains of indecision and the relief which decisive action of any kind will bring. But the fact that even a vicious act may be deeply gratifying and seem appallingly necessary at the moment proves at once how essential to life is action and how far the unregenerate human will is from the divinely pure act.

Of this discrepancy the mystic has become increasingly conscious. For him, therefore, the problem of action and inaction presents no simple alternative. He has discovered that apparent action may mask a spiritual incapacity and that seeming inaction may be the most real and necessary deed. He knows by distressing experience that he must grow into truth before he can truthfully act, that he can no longer perform with satisfaction the partial acts which previously had a certain effectiveness, because he has become too conscious of what was false in them.

Many people are not unduly pained, if consciously pained at all, by the way in which they exert or relax their will. Some of them may wistfully remember a childhood in which they were much nearer to expressing the 'Will as Pure Act'. But they have long accepted a condition in which action involves strain and inaction is a respite from strain or merely a feverish variation of it.

In some this tension causes an obscure discomfort and even nervous ailments, for which resort is made to the psycho-analyst. But only the mystic suffers it in the depths of his being and knows that only in those depths can it be resolved. So acute, indeed, may be his distress that for a time he may almost cease to be able to act.

This paralysing sense of his own wilfulness and of the inner rhythm which he has violated may come to him in a sudden vision in which reality possesses him and opens for one indescribable moment his spiritual eyes. Or it may be born gradually of the torment which self-willed action inflicts upon a sensitive soul.

In either event it is a direct seeing by the Soul of the self, a sight so humbling in its revelation of the self's falsity, that for a time, short or long, it may almost kill the power to act.

Indeed, the old stress of action must die, if a new grace of doing and being is to be born and life cease to be degenerate. For that is what it is, despite all its apparent vitality, in the self-willed man, as in the power-seeking State.

In the world of sin man lives by the power of primal instincts, which have become perverted. The mystic is exceptionally conscious of that perversion. He is equally conscious that it cannot be cured by any return to instinctive innocence. That way back is closed. If he is ever to receive and give life abundantly again, he must break through the closed circle of selfish necessity into the pure freedom, which is also the divine order, of Creative Being.

For the mystic this is a compelling need. He has not so much broken with the old order as been broken by it. But however deeply he may have dedicated his will to a greater Will, he is not transformed in a moment. He has yet to become that of which he has conceived the saving truth and to grow into it spiritually and physically. The densities of ignorance formed by wilful habits of mind and body that encrust the windows of the soul have to be gradually dissolved by the eternal sun which can only do its perfect work in a truly surrendered being.

Meanwhile the mystic must endure the desert which lies between the world of flawed impulse from which he has turned and the world of regenerated being towards which he toils. He knows that new world by prevision, but he has not yet become a native of it. This inevitably causes him distress and exposes him to misunderstanding or condemnation. For he has lost much of the will to love and act on the level of impure emotion without having yet regained it at all fully in a purer mode.

All the trials of his life, inward and outward, are reflections of this 'half-wayness', through which he can only pass by an ever deeper dedication of his being to the unseen Will, in that dark silence, where, as John of Ruysbroeck wrote, 'all lovers lose themselves' and the way leads through a waylessness. Then in its good time the Creative Spirit will fulfil its perfect work within him and he will be changed.

But premature action of a wrong kind, towards which he is constantly tempted, can only retard such change. Such action betrays rather a want of faith than knowledge. For the mystic knows, even while he is indulging in it, that he is violating the deep rhythm of truth into which he would grow. He knows and he suffers. Indeed he has to suffer to know more deeply. For ingrained habits are not easily thrown off, however desirous a man may be to become what he really is.

That is why some mystics have even taken and kept a vow of complete silence for a lengthy period. Few of us are in a position to do that, and the constant testing of human relationship, the cost of loving others, its joys and its deprivations, is the best school in which to learn the art of being, if in the stillness, through prayer and contemplation, we return continually to the infinite source of our own and others' being.

Each one of us can alone know to what extent we are free to act positively. It depends on where we stand. What is profitable in one is premature in another. The mystic is learning to live a new life and there is no act, however apparently trivial, which may not retard or foster this transformation. Doubtless every act inspired by love is necessarily right. But the statement is not as helpful in practice as it might seem.

For even the most loving of us have to learn to love. That means ultimately ceasing to appropriate anything for ourselves, ceasing to give, for example, however generously, because we are compelled to it by some hidden want in ourselves which we need to satisfy. Instead we have to learn the pure art of giving, which asks nothing in return because love wholly informs it — that love which in its giving receives, and in its receiving gives. This does not mean being inhumanly independent of the love of others, but rather so dependent on a love that is not our own that in our love for others and their love for us we share a divine gift and a divine communion. It means, too, being so inwardly given ourselves that God's willing in us is really God's will and not our own, even in some Godly disguise.

It is not surprising that such a revolutionary translation of yes into no, and of no into yes should require much ploughing of the fallow soil of the heart before 'the green blade riseth from the buried grain', or that, until we can love and contemplate purely, we may need to forgo much of the emotional and sensational satisfaction which seemed previously the very breath and savour of our life.

Not for nothing have all the spiritual teachers insisted that the pearl beyond price costs all that a man has, including what he may consider his legitimate attachments. To surrender these lovingly and with no bitter sense of deprivation is to receive them back cleansed of all possessive taint. But few can make or maintain that surrender in one life-changing act, and to be detached may well, at one stage of growth, be a more necessary attainment than to love sentimentally or with an element of hate lurking in the heart, as in possessive love it always must. Yet all such negative achievements have virtue only as expressions of an ardent surrender of the self to the Love which is its infinite ground.

It is the same with thought. The mystic's thought has to become a pure and total act of being. His head, like his heart, has to be subdued to the rhythm in which both are in accord. And that can only happen if he has the courage to wait for the knowledge which is love to possess his soul and for the love which is knowledge to build it.

To maintain such devoted patience against all the fret and clutch of egotism is hard, however sensitive a mystic may have become to the untruth of his acts. And he can expect little support or understanding from those about him, who at best are likely to regard his condition as a psychological problem, at worst as a culpable form of self-absorption. Nor can he explain its spiritual significance to them. For the mystic soon learns as part of his discipline, that it is impossible to communicate the meaning of any spiritual state save to those who have gone or who are ripe to go the same way.

But if the incomprehension of others intensifies his sense of isolation, it is his own doubts which are his greatest affliction. The voices that question or chide or seek to entangle from without only strengthen the voice of his own uncertainty. And the Western mystic is likely to be far more tried by such uncertainty than the Eastern.

For the strength and weakness of the West is self-interested action. The Westerner will condone the error of a passionate will far more readily than the inertia of a dispassionate mind. He appreciates the warmth of energy so much that he will sacrifice to it the purer rays of truth. He recoils from the teachings and temper of the East because he feels a want in it of this eager, personal warmth. His recoil is justified in so far as Eastern detachment has been merely an inversion of his own false attachment, a loveless withdrawal from the stream of life into mental abstraction.

Desire, as a modern Eastern sage, Aurobindo Ghose, has written, 'is the lever by which the divine Life-principle effects its end of self-affirmation in the universe and the attempt to extinguish it in the interests of inertia is a denial of that principle, a Will-not-to-be which is necessarily ignorance; for one cannot cease to be individually except by being infinitely'. In other words one cannot, under a wise providence, escape from the desirous self, whether one acts or refuses to act, until it becomes a devoted self in union with the divine.

But the noblest saints and sages of the East were not selfishly detached. If they withdrew from the turbid stream of life in which the sense and emotion-bound man fought and floundered, it was only to enter the same stream where it had become a deep river of being, with their wills tempered in full consciousness to its serene creative rhythm.

The Westerner who finds the serenity of such men too cool and impersonal is himself too hot and personal. He does not recognize that his own restless movement is a sign of spiritual emptiness, that there is more fire and smoke than light in the energies which he so prodigally expends even on behalf of others or of causes and creeds in which he believes. He is too much compelled to activity by what is false and partial in himself, by an interested motive which perverts and largely stultifies the force for good he would exert, as it does, for example, in militant Christianity with its claim to a divine monopoly of truth.

For the love in action which is the complete expression of the spiritual life is wholly devoid of the ego's unrest, as of its pride and violence. The secret of this divinely personal-impersonal love may have been possessed in its fullness on earth by only a few Masters. But it awaits to be discovered by all. And the East in its rejection of interested action has understood it at least as truly as the West in its impatience with characterless detachment.

This impatience inevitably intensifies the doubts and difficulties of anyone who would break with the false and fevered habits of contemporary western life. He has to maintain a wise passiveness, not only against his own nervous itch for action, but also against the prevailing emphasis of his environment. For he knows that to reassert his will as others demand would be as foolish as for a sick man to rise from his bed with the fever still upon him. He knows that his will must be changed through not willing, as his mind must learn not to know. And the alert passivity in which alone this can happen is no languid relaxation, though the ordinary active person generally regards that as the only alternative to his own busy exertions.

True inaction demands more real action to sustain it than all the false activities of the world. In the absorbed silence of creative contemplation the world's clamour and much of its galvanic movement are known to be no more than waves on a restless sea or the reverberations of a hollow drum. But to maintain this stillness within, not only in the hours of meditation, but as he moves and labours in the world, demands of the mystic a continuous effort of recollection.

The mystic in the monastery lived withdrawn and under a rule that fortified at every turn the powers and peace of the inner life. The modern mystic who cannot accept the dubious support of institutional religion or find a teacher or a brotherhood with guidance to offer, has no such support. For the most part he has to keep faith with the unseen alone and amid many distractions and temptations.

Very soon, however, if he can maintain the inner stillness against the unredeemed impulses of his nature and all the forces which would suck him back into the whirlpool, he will find that the pull, against which he has to brace himself, is weakening. His new being with its lucid faculties has begun to unfold, his old self with its restless appetites to pass away.

The transformation is, of course, slow and the more entrenched the ego is, the longer it is dying. All who travel along the path of regeneration must in some degree pass through the state which, in its two phases, St. John of the Cross described as the night of sense and the night of the Spirit.

In the first of these the tide of vital zest which the mystic experienced, in however perverted a form, as he strove and grasped and suffered as a self-centred individual, may seem to ebb away. In the second all the tender 'bright shoots of everlastingness' which quickened his being when first the new tide began to flow, the new sun to shine, the consolation, the sense of release, may seem also nipped by an untimely frost. For a period, short or long, he may be desolated by a feeling that there is no meaning and no nourishment in the abysmal emptiness of life.

Then above all must he endure to the end if he is to be saved. And his salvation is sure. The apparent deathliness of his state is a proof of the radiant purpose of life. The darkness he experiences proclaims the dazzling light, those 'beams of love' as Blake called them, which his spiritual eyes are not yet strong enough to bear. The darkness is not really a deprivation, but the merciful veil in which the divine sun drapes its splendour. And more and more, as his powers of integral vision grow, the mystic is given glimpses of this light which reveal so much of ecstatic meaning in the texture of life that all previous vision seems by contrast to have been blindness.

As the light grows with his power to receive it, the rapture of it will no longer overwhelm him, as it did in these first glimpses. For life can be meaningless through being too full of meaning for our faculties to grasp. And akin to the mystic's experience, in the night of sense, of a life that is without form and savour, can be his sense in the dawn of new being, that it is so infinitely charged with meaning that no finite form can contain it. It is as if he had entered a tide 'too full for sound and foam', as Tennyson described the tide of death,

> When that which drew from out the boundless deep
> Turns again home.

And in very truth he has entered the tide of death which is the tide of life, or rather that ocean of which the ebb and flow are eternally one.

We are all prodigals until we set our feet on the path of return to our spiritual home. But as the mystic treads in quietness that path of return, he changes. He has turned his face to the Divine Sun and all that was veiled before by the shadow of self is more and more revealed in the light of truth. All that seemed positive before is seen now to have been negative; all that seemed negative then is known now to have been a condition of growth into the truly positive.

Then he begins truly to understand the words of the *Gita* that 'He who beholds in Work No-Work, and in No-Work Work is the man of understanding among mortals; he is in Union, a doer of perfect work'.

Little by little, as the Divine Sun clothes him with a body of light, kindred to Itself, he begins to see the depths of people and things which before were opaque and into realms that were veiled. No longer is he overwhelmed by the meaning or the meaninglessness of life. No longer need he refrain from action because his acts are impure. Whether in word or in deed, by the direct contacts of touch or glance or the silent voice speaking in love he expresses the inaction which is the divine counterpart of action. He is possessed by the peace which sanctifies power, by the Eternity through which Time is redeemed.